LOST ON **treasure island**

Also by Steve Friedman

The Gentleman's Guide to Life
The Agony of Victory
Driving Lessons

LOST ON treasure island

A Memoir of Longing, Love, and
Lousy Choices in New York City

Steve Friedman

ARCADE PUBLISHING
NEW YORK

For my brother and sister.

Arcade Publishing books may be purchased in bulk at special discounts for
sales promotion, corporate gifts, fund-raising, or educational purposes. Special
editions can also be created to specifications. For details, contact the Special Sales
Department, Arcade Publishing, 307 West 36th Street, 11th Floor, New York, NY
10018 or info@skyhorsepublishing.com.

Arcade Publishing® is a registered trademark of Skyhorse Publishing, Inc.®, a
Delaware corporation.

Visit our website at www.arcadepub.com.

www.skyhorsepublishing.com

10 9 8 7 6 5 4 3 2 1

Library of Congress Cataloging-in-Publication Data available on file.
ISBN: 978-1-61145-020-0

Printed in the United States of America

CONTENTS

Author's Note 7

Chapter 1   The Man in the Lime Green Suit 9

Chapter 2   Midwestern Decency Is for Losers 20

Chapter 3   The Starlet and the Stalker 32

Chapter 4   The Eyedrop People, the Bard, and Me 49

Chapter 5   Journalist of Tungsten....................................63

Chapter 6   Missy's Earth Suit and the Slavering Dogs of Midnight ...84

Chapter 7   Looking for Mrs. Friedman and Other Really Bad Ideas 98

Chapter 8   You Get What You Get....................................111

Chapter 9   "Make It Meaner" 126

Chapter 10 Dear Dirtbag, I Identify with You 150

Chapter 11 Oy, Wilderness...190

Chapter 12 The Blondes in the Basement..........................196

Chapter 13 My Cold Wars...217

Chapter 14 The Fat Man Makes Me Cry 233

Chapter 15 Voyage of the Damned 250

Chapter 16 She Came from Cyberspace 261

Chapter 17 Cheeseburger Whores, Unite............................290

Epilogue..300

Acknowledgements...304

And the Lord said unto Moses, "Behold . . . this people will rise up and go a whoring after the strange gods of the land."

—Deuteronomy 31:16

Somewhere there's music,
How faint the tune . . .

—"How High the Moon"

Author's Note

Everything here is true. Not true as in emotionally true, or true in the sense of serving-a-larger-and-more-meaningful-but-ultimately-unknowable-truth true. Not true in the way that professional liars and lovers of postmodernism proclaim that because there is no absolutely reliable metric for calculating historical veracity, everyone-should-just-relax-about-the-facts true. No. The stuff ahead is *true*. True, as in, it happened. Let me back up. *Almost* all of it is true. Just about everything. There are a few exceptions.

The famous poet/memoirist in chapter 16 is not really named Violet, but she is widely revered, and she is what many people with benign or willfully uncomprehending understatement have called "feisty"; and she told me if I ever even *thought* about including her in anything I wrote, I would be very, very, *very* sorry, and she scares me. Also, I changed the name and a few details about the alluring eyedrop publicist because she's married now and her husband scares me. Frank the angry Belgian says he never said some of the things I remember him saying. He also claims he's not angry. April, the sexy ophthalmologist, is a different type of physician, and her name isn't April. In addition, I altered some other names and what publishers, lawyers, and other nitpickers like to call "the timing of some events" and "certain identifying characteristics of some individuals" because legal action scares me. I gave the man who molested me a different name. The cruel-calved and gazelle-necked editorial assistant at *GQ* for whom I harbored dark, dangerous feelings is actually a combination of two cruel-calved and gazelle-necked *GQ* editorial assistants. But except for those, some reconstructed conversations and a few other things, it's all true. As in, factual. As in, this is what happened. I really did lie down with cockroaches on New York City's Upper West Side and dream of foie gras. I really did imagine five-course lunches at the Four Seasons restaurant in Midtown Manhattan while, a few short and tragic blocks away, I hunched over the diet platter at the greasy counter of Burger Heaven. The Conde Nast executive editor known as the Queen of Mean really did call me pathetic, which excited me in ways that I still don't quite understand.

I really did accidentally wear a lime green suit to my job interview at *GQ* and the actress Mary-Louise Parker really did weep when I told her a story over coffee, and then she really did send me a book of Raymond Carver's poetry along with a handwritten note about sadness and meaning; and then she became very standoffish when I remarked upon the bottomless and eternal love I sensed we shared. I really did befriend the entertainer John Tesh, and I really did write a letter of condolence to him when his mother died, and I really did—when my boss told me, regarding my profile of Tesh, to "make it meaner"—make it meaner. (I really did describe the entertainer as a blond Frankenstein monster in a purple suit, and that really offended him.) The actress Barbara Hershey really kissed me on the mouth, and I was so worked up and alarmed I couldn't move or speak. (I still regret that, and if you're reading this, Barbara, I love you. Bottomlessly.)

The savage street mime who nearly drove me back to drugs and drink? True. The kindhearted cruise ship comedian who allowed me to glimpse the outsized heart of a hardworking mensch while a gaggle of women dressed as giant pineapples rumba'd and screamed, "It's 'Bamboleo' time!"? True. The psychic psychotherapist and the pillow-breasted advertising saleswoman and the mysterious and quite possibly divine Fat Man and my eye-rubbingly wrongheaded plot to find and impregnate the future Mrs. Friedman? True, true, true, true. Sad, perhaps. Appalling, maybe. But true.

Honest.

CHAPTER 1

THE MAN IN THE LIME GREEN SUIT

I am looking good. I am looking better than I have ever looked in my life. New wing tips, freshly shined. Well-scrubbed mug, recently shaved and lightly patted with aftershave. Where I'm going, the men like aftershave. I learned this last night. Where I'm going, men *respect* aftershave. Below my aftershaved mug, a brand-new, spread-collared, French-cuffed Egyptian cotton white shirt, knotted with a creamy silk tie of bloody, carnivorous crimson. The neck that wears this tie is not weak or vulnerable. It is not indecisive or womanly. It is not gulping, though it wants to. No one can look upon this neck and suspect that it awaits the thin blade.

I know, though. I know terrible things. I know, for example, that the humble but plucky moth caterpillar pretends it's a snake when it suspects another animal is about to eat it. I know this because for the past couple years, I have been studying clever insects on television late at night. I identify with the bugs. I relate to all prey, but especially those delicate beasts who masquerade as predators. They are my role models. Because I cannot writhe like a snake, and because I am at the moment in Manhattan, which is lousy with creatures that would like to devour me, I am masquerading as something else. For this I require protective coloration.

It is a simple item of fine worsted wool, exquisitely fitted, loosely draped. It is pearl gray, a shade so clearly masculine that it defies anyone in New York City to make me as a terrified and confused Midwesterner who bumped down at LaGuardia Airport less than twenty-four hours ago and whose life is unraveling so fast he has insomnia every night and stomach cramps every morning.

For the past four hours, I have been looking good in the *GQ* offices in Midtown Manhattan, where I have been summoned from half a continent away for a job interview. I have been looking good, and I have been sounding good.

"Sure, the Big East is tough," I proclaim to three lupine-suited, lightly aftershaved men, "but anyone who isn't looking for at least one team from the Big 12 to make it to the Big Dance this year is going to be very surprised."

I like the way this sounds, so I repeat the last two words. "*Very* surprised."

I learned last night that *GQ* has recently started running long sports stories. I sound good on sports.

"*The Black Dahlia* is a terrific read," I say, referring to James Ellroy's fictionalized account of a notorious murder in Los Angeles, "but if you want some really interesting crime fiction from that area, you should check out T. Jefferson Parker and Robert Ferrigno."

I learned last night that *GQ* likes crime and literature and wants to become more popular on the West Coast. I am sounding very, very good.

I talk about different brands of vodka and the middle infield of the Yankees. I talk about Andre Agassi and Bridget Fonda. I talk about serial killers and Caleb Carr, Mario Cuomo, and Anna Wintour. The moth caterpillar has nothing on me.

"We're glad you could get up here on such short notice," Art, the editor in chief, says. I have never heard such a sound. It is summer thunder and booming surf. It is more a dangerous meteorological event than it is human communication. One of his writers once described Art's voice as "having been soaked in jazz and whiskey." I find the description incomplete. It leaves out the menace.

"Me too, Art," I say. I like the way this sounds—especially the lack of quavering—so I repeat it. "Me too."

Then he asks me a question.

"Is this a downtime in your production cycle?"

GQ staffers, I will learn, refer to Art among themselves as "El Jefe," "the Big Man," and "Himself." He stands six feet tall and has a Samoan chieftain's paunch. Before my audience with Art, I had asked writers what he was like. Descriptions ranged from "a big teddy bear" to "brutal and sadistic." And now he was asking about downtimes and my production cycle. My first test.

With all the sounding good and looking good, I haven't gotten around to mentioning that two days earlier I had been fired from my job as editor in chief of *St. Louis Magazine*. In the midst of all the vodka talk, I haven't told the guys that I had spent a month in a drug and alcohol rehab unit seven years earlier and hadn't drunk since. With all the bonhomie and sports chatter, it didn't seem like the right time to bring up the fact that the notion of living in New York City, of working in the publishing world here, fills me with a terror so black and fathomless that my hands have broken out in blisters and that the outer layer of skin on my fingers has peeled, which has left me with smooth, printless digits and prompted my wisecracking dermatologist back home to suggest that I forget magazines and pursue a career in safecracking.

11

I finger the rich and luxuriant lapels of my pearl gray suit with my whorl-less digits. I put it on this morning in the dim light of the Royalton Hotel, where *GQ* has put me up. It is the smallest, darkest hotel room I've ever set foot in. The velvety worsted wool offers no answers. I'll stick with sounding good.

"*St. Louis Magazine* is always on deadline," I say. Words that wouldn't offend a gentle and house-trained grizzly *or* Genghis Khan. "It's just something magazine editors get used to."

"Heh heh heh," Art says to me and to the other lupine-suited editors. "I like this kid. I want to know more about this kid."

Heh heh heh? Are those the baritone rumblings of a friendly, shaggy pet or the menacing growls of a ravenous beast? Art *seems* like a nice guy. I have heard that if Art likes you, he regularly invites you to his reserved plush leather banquette at the Four Seasons restaurant, where you discuss politics and literature and sports and eat tender, bloody meat. I have heard that if Art likes you, you are in magazine heaven. But if he senses weaknesses or fear, you're as the titmouse to the hungry ferret. I look at Art, and I think of the Man-Thing, the comic book hero whose adventures I followed with monklike devotion before my daily marijuana addiction progressed to cocaine and downers and alcohol, at which point I stopped following anything with monklike devotion. The Man-Thing, like Art, had a nuanced reputation. The Man-Thing possessed a preternaturally developed sense of empathy, and he could feel if you were happy or sad or confused, and he would try—in his giant preverbal slimy green Man-Thingish way—to help you. To know more about you. *Heh heh heh.* The trouble occurred if and when the Man-Thing sensed that you were afraid. Because, as the cover of every Man-Thing comic book promised, "whatever knows fear burns at the Man-Thing's touch!" Because the Man-Thing was nine feet tall, though, oozing brownish green ichors, with three penile-looking proboscises protruding from his/its head, it was kind of hard not to be afraid. Which made for some complicated and unpleasant situations. People who hung out with the Man-Thing tended to get burned.

I stroke my lapels and try to keep the quake out of my voice.

"Heh," I say to Art and the guys, "heh heh."

"Marty, take this kid to lunch," Art booms. Marty is the managing editor, the number 2 man, and as quiet and as steady as Art is bombastic and volcanic. "I want you to get to know this kid."

Marty reports to Art. Art will decide my fate. "Getting to know me" is the last thing I want Marty to do.

Instead, I will encourage him to chat with the eager young fellow who longs to join the ranks of New York publishing, the industrious would-be editor who likes nothing better than finding and nourishing talent.

I actually say this, as we stroll through the cloud-covered canyons of Manhattan toward Marty's favorite Indian restaurant. "Marty," I say, "I like nothing better than finding and nourishing talent." I add a "*heh heh heh.*"

Over chicken vindaloo and naan bread, I let Marty get to know the enthusiastic young man of letters who can riff on the glories of Elmore Leonard's Westerns and Jim Thompson's neglected masterpieces, the sports fan who can reminisce about the '64 series between the Cardinals and the Yankees, who admires the defensive genius of Patrick Ewing, the underrated offensive talent of John Stockton.

I encourage Marty to make the acquaintance of the guy who plays basketball often and whose girlfriend back home is an ophthalmologist. An active lifestyle and a successful sweetheart are necessary accoutrements of the *GQ* man, I learned in my dim hotel room last night—as essential as quirky cuff links (which I'm wearing, naturally; Big Boy, holding a hamburger). I let Marty get to know the guy in the pearl gray suit.

I don't mention that I am so well-versed in *GQ*'s manners and mores because I spent seven hours the night before squinting through the gloom of my dim and glamorous hotel room at the year's worth of magazines I had borrowed from my girlfriend. I had never read the magazine before because most people in Missouri thought *GQ* was only for homosexual men.

I don't mention that I have been cheating on the ophthalmologist with a dermatology nurse, that I could barely look at the ophthalmologist as she helped me pick out the bloodthirsty red tie in St. Louis, that when she drove me to the airport and kissed me good-bye and told me I looked good, my stomach hurt so much that I thought I had come down with the flu and considered postponing my trip until the eye doctor reminded me (with a smile and an unbearably sweet tugging of my collar) that I tended toward hypochondria and to get moving. I don't mention that my stepmother is dying of brain cancer, that my father has been having fainting spells, that my skin-blistering episodes seem to coincide with the weekly brunches I share with my mother.

I don't mention that the writer who told the *GQ* editors about me is the old boyfriend of an editorial assistant I slept with when she was living with a different old boyfriend, or that at approximately the same time I also slept with that woman's boss, an editor, or that when the editorial assistant discovered my love letter to the editor, she accused me of being an "amoral creep," which I found disturbingly accurate even as I was admiring the editorial assistant's way with words. I don't mention that sexual misconduct has been part and parcel of my writing and editing life and has sped my professional trajectory over the years while, I suspect, hastening a descent into whatever hell is reserved for philandering and deceitful and stomachache-plagued, insomniac-suffering would-be writers with no fingerprints. I don't mention that while I have had more girlfriends than most men and am fully aware that some, if not all, of my exes consider me shallow, narcissistic, and a cad, I want true love. I need it. I don't mention that I hope to find it in Manhattan, and with it, a wife.

We emerge from lunch into a sunny Manhattan day, and I'm still looking good. Looking good, having just sounded very good indeed. I am commandeering the sidewalks of Midtown with the managing editor of *GQ*. I am strolling down 45th Street, near Fifth Avenue—I am taking steps into territory I have imagined since I was a child, the land of E. B. White and J. D. Salinger and Joseph Mitchell. I have arrived. The terror, the certainty that I will need to pretend I'm a moth caterpillar in order to survive here? The fathomless dread? They can be dealt with later. Right now, I belong.

I feel my lapels again. Not out of need. From strength. Looking and feeling good, I glance down at my suit. I haven't looked at my suit for hours.

What I see makes me dizzy. Jet lag? Doubtful. It's less than a two-hour flight from St. Louis. Bad chicken vindaloo? No, it's only been fifteen minutes. A trick of the light? I look again. My pearl gray suit isn't pearl gray. What had looked manly and predatory in the St. Louis department store and in the dim smoky mirror of the Royalton and in the fluorescent lights of the *GQ* offices and in the cloudy spring morning is now something else.

My suit is lime green.

Marty is saying something, but I'm not listening.

Midtown Manhattan at lunchtime is filled with suits. Black suits. Charcoal suits. A few brown suits—the effects of the Reagan years still linger. I scan desperately. I can't be the only one wearing a suit of such a hideous, heinous hue. I look, and I look, as Marty continues to prattle on about whatever he's prattling on about. Tina Brown? David Dinkins? Who cares!

Blue, black, gray, black, black, blue, gray. An optimist in khaki. But no lime green. Not a single lime green, not a solitary . . . but wait! There, luminous salvation! Another lime green suit, moving toward us. Is it possible that I'm not a freak, but a trendsetter? Never has a shade made a man more grateful. I want to throw my arms around the other man in the lime green suit, to touch lapels. I want to smell his aftershave. And I will, as soon as I get a better look at the natty peacock.

Then I get a better look. He's fat. He's fat, and he's short, and he's sweating. Flop sweat. He looks like he just got off the Greyhound bus from Des Moines. That's what I'm thinking. A Missourian in Manhattan for less than twenty-four hours and already I despise men from Iowa. He's five foot six, a short, fat, sweaty man from Iowa, and I hate him. I don't want to share the same city block with him. He's Wimpy from Popeye. He's a joke. He's bald too. And he's looking at me. I recognize the look. It's pitiful and beseeching. The fat bald loser is looking to me for reassurance. This can't be true, of course. A stranger in Manhattan—even a short, corpulent, badly dressed stranger visiting from the Corn State—cannot be in need of my reassurance. And I cannot be wild-eyed with panic. But he is. And I am.

"Steve!" Marty cries. And I feel him grab my arm. I can't believe he's touched the lime green suit. Is he color-blind? "Are you okay?"

In my haste to escape the corn-fed village idiot, I have lurched into the street, almost being run down by midtown traffic.

"Oh yeah, sure, Marty, I'm okay. I'm okay."

I think I repeat this a few too many times, because Marty is looking at me with something like concern. Or fear. Or confusion. I think I'm hyperventilating. I am not looking good. I am not sounding good. I need to get hold of myself. Or better yet, of the guy I thought was in the gray suit.

For the next three blocks, I try to focus on what Marty is saying, to pretend my suit isn't the same color as the kind of highlighter favored by eleven-year-old girls who scribble fuzzy hearts on top of their small *i*'s. How could I ever have thought it was gray? Might I have an eye tumor? Shouldn't April have noticed?

"Steve?" Marty says.

"Uh, yeah," I say. I haven't heard anything he's said for the past half block.

"Why don't I take you back to the office now, and you and Art can have a sit-down."

Art? El Jefe? The editor who can smell weakness five miles away? The publishing legend who—like the Man-Thing, "a shambling, mindless mockery of a man," senses fear and can't help himself—is compelled to dispatch mewling cowards like me to their gruesome, fiery deaths?

I can think of a number of reasons to beg off—"My stomach hurts and I have to go to the bathroom really, really bad"; "I have to take this lime green suit off and carry it to one of those landfill sites I've read about on Staten Island, where I will bury it and sprinkle lime on the cursed earth under which it shall stay forever"; "I have to call my eye doctor girlfriend and beg her never to leave me"—but none that would make much sense to Marty.

"Uh, sure," I say. "Heh." I pray the fluorescent lights at *GQ* are as dim as I remember them.

"Great," Marty says and then lapses into a cheerful silence. I say "cheerful" because as he walks, he whistles, and as he whistles, he tilts his face slightly toward the sun I now despise. I suspect that getting to know the guy in the gray suit has been as much of a chore for Marty as it has for me, and he has decided to take a few minutes to enjoy the last few minutes of this pleasant day before facing an afternoon of finding and nourishing talent.

And it is a pleasant day. It is a pleasant day. I silently repeat this phrase to myself. *It is a pleasant day!* I repeat some other phrases too, strings of words the psychiatrist from the rehab center encouraged me to call upon in times of fear or self-loathing or despair. *I am my own worst enemy* being one. *Things aren't so bad* being another. *This, too, shall pass* being a third.

So I walk down the street, thinking these phrases to myself. *It is a pleasant day. I am my own worst enemy. Things aren't so bad. This, too, shall pass.*

And they work. The day is pleasant. Others wish me no harm. The sun is shining. My suit's not so bad. I'm the only one—and maybe the fat guy from Iowa—who knows what a shame-filled, secret-hoarding fraud I really am. I'm a man, not a moth caterpillar or a titmouse. I really need to get over myself.

Then I hear laughter. What could throngs of New Yorkers in the middle of Midtown be laughing at? I don't know a lot about this city, but I know that spontaneous eruptions of glee are most likely to occur in the company of a fellow city dweller's suffering and humiliation. The thought cheers me. I could use a little glee.

I see laughing faces. Laughing faces attached to suits of many dark shades. And some dresses. I look around, and it seems to me that the laughing faces are looking in my direction. They are looking straight at me. This is impossible, of course. But it doesn't feel impossible. It feels more and more possible.

It is a pleasant day. I am my own worst enemy. Things aren't so bad. This, too, shall pass. It is a pleasant day. I am my own worst enemy. Things aren't so bad. This, too, shall pass.

"Don't look now," Marty says. "But I think we've got company."

That's when I see the mime, walking next to us. Let me be more accurate. Walking next to me. Taking long loping strides. Like me. Holding his head a little bit stiffer than is absolutely necessary, like me. (I'm holding my head like that so I won't be able to behold the limeness of myself). Moving his lips nervously as he silently mouths words and knitting his forehead into a knot, like me.

I stop the self-soothing mantras, try to relax my face. The mime's face goes blank. I slow down, try to appear less panicked than I feel. The mime slows down too. So does the crowd that has not only gathered but is also actually following us. I thought New Yorkers were too busy to linger outside their offices! Much hilarity from the crowd, many more peals of laughter. I turn to the mime with pleading in my eyes. He turns to the crowd with the same expression. A baby seal begging Mr. Hunter, Please not to do it, not the club. I have never heard such laughter. Even Marty is laughing now. Why did I ever leave Missouri? I will propose to the eye doctor as soon as I land back in St. Louis. I want a drink. I really, really want a drink.

This, too, shall pass. This, too, shall pass. This, too, shall pass. Peals of laughter. *This, too, shall pass!* Only forty feet till the curb, before we turn the corner outside the mime's territory and away from the laughing New Yorkers. I ignore him. I ignore the laughter. I ignore everything except putting one foot in front of the other. The mime stays with us.

And then we are turning toward safety, and I take one last look at the mime, peer once more into the face of savagery. And then something surreal happens, something that's never supposed to happen.

The mime speaks.

And this is what the mime says. This is what the mime says as I, a man whose uniform has failed him, whose many uniforms will continue to fail him, yet who will wear any disguise—any—to avoid standing naked before the world, listen. This is what the mime says as I step off the curb and toward my future in New York City as a desperate, conniving, poorly camouflaged imposter.

He says it out of the corner of his mouth to me.

The mime says, "Nice suit."

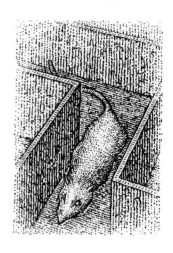

CHAPTER 2

MIDWESTERN DECENCY IS FOR LOSERS

"Are you sure you want to move to New York City?" my father asks. And I say, "Well, I think so," which is what I usually say to my father when I think he is disappointed with me. When I was seven, he asked if I was sure I wanted to read comic books instead of playing catch; when I was nineteen, he asked if I was sure I wanted to study journalism at college and whether I didn't think it prudent to take one or two accounting courses as well; when I was twenty-nine, less than a year out of rehab, he asked if I was sure I wanted to leave a job writing speeches for the officers of Southwestern Bell Telephone Company and take a 30 percent pay cut so I could work for *St. Louis Magazine.* I have been saying, "Well, I think so," for much of my life.

It is Sunday afternoon, and we are watching golf on television in the living room of my father's house in suburban St. Louis as his wife lies dying in the bedroom. I hate the hushed portent of the announcers' voices, how I can't see where the ball is going. How can anyone watch golf and not be utterly lost? I hate the way my mother used to complain to my father about his weekends on the greens. I hate the way he stares at the screen now, even when he's asking me if I'm sure about my life.

I have been back in St. Louis for three days, ever since the mime and the lime green suit. Art had offered me the job that afternoon, and I had told him I'd have to think about it.

"Think about it?" Art had growled, and the chicken vindaloo had growled back. "Think about it?" he had boomed again, and it was midmorning at the Lake of the Ozarks, and I was eight years old, and the big counselor with the blond crew cut was asking why I hadn't baited my hook yet. How could I tell him that I was afraid of worms, that on rainy mornings at home I wept because I was terrified of stepping on those that had crawled onto the sidewalks of St. Louis, and that I begged my mother to please let me stay home from school and read Archie and Richie Rich and Little Lotta comic books in my room and drink hot cocoa? I couldn't tell him that. I said nothing.

"What's wrong with you?" the big blond counselor asked. And when I still didn't speak, he laughed, an ugly metallic sound, and the other kids laughed because they knew that if they didn't, it might be their turn. I still didn't say anything, and the counselor reached into a jar and pulled out a fleshy brownish worm, and then he took my hook and impaled the worm on it, and the worm was still moving. I puked on the counselor's tennis shoes.

Older men and men in power have always frightened me. My mother (who bought me comics and let me skip school more days than she admits) says it's because I'm sensitive. April, my eye doctor girlfriend, says it's because I don't take myself seriously. My shrink says it's because my seventh-grade English teacher, who knew I liked baseball and encouraged me to write stories about my favorite players, stuck his hand down my shirt after school one day and squeezed my nipples, so I am wary of men who seem to have my best interests at heart. Then again, the blond counselor never seemed to have my best interests at heart, and he murdered the worm long before Mr. Haas, the seventh-grade English teacher, locked the classroom door one Wednesday in winter after the afternoon bell rang and felt me up while I was reading aloud for him an essay I had written titled "Stan the Man Musial—the Greatest Cardinal of Them All!"

I listen to all the explanations—now that I might be moving to New York City, a lot of people seem eager to explain my chronic fear—and I nod at everyone and tell them I appreciate their input and I'll certainly have to think about it. All the theories make sense, but none of them help too much. I doubt that if I took myself seriously and tracked down Mr. Haas and engaged him in a dialogue about whether he liked my "Stan Musial" essay or my pudgy seventh-grade flesh, or both, that I'd suddenly become bold and decisive and powerful. The problem is, I know that boldness and decisiveness and power are called for—that they are necessary qualities to exude if I'm to ever make people stop offering help in combatting my wimpiness.

The wily moth caterpillar will help, though. No one at *GQ*—no one in New York City—thinks I'm too sensitive, or tortured. They think I talk sports and detective fiction. They think I look good. I have a job offer—a job offer from a leading men's magazine. So what if I have peeling skin and a delicate stomach? I will buy some real suits, some dark gray and dark blue and black suits, and no one at the hub of American publishing will try to help me understand my fear, because no one will know I'm afraid.

"Do you think you're ready to live in New York City?" my dad asks, a canny variation on his initial query. There's a commercial on. Cadillacs slide from one side of the screen to the other. If I could be honest with my father, which I can't, the obvious answer would be no. I wasn't even ready to have *lunch* in New York City. I wasn't even ready to wear a *suit* in New York City.

But I can't tell him that any more than I can say, "Well, gee, Dad, do you think I was ready for you and Mom to split up?" Or, "I dunno, Dad, do you think I was ready for you to get married again, to a woman who paints her fingernails white to match her knee-high white Beatles boots and white lipstick and her white fur coat and the shag carpet in the house the two of you moved into?"

Am I ready to live in New York City, to leave my father and his dying wife in white, to go work for a man whose voice makes me see seared flesh? Am I ready to put on another disguise and hope no one guesses the truth?

"I don't know, Dad," I say. "I'm not sure. I guess I'll have to think about it."

"I'd like to return this," I tell a salesclerk at Dillard's department store, in suburban St. Louis. "There's a problem with the color."

The clerk looks at the suit.

"This suit's been altered."

The sales clerk speaks the truth. The pants have been shortened, the waist let out, something adjusted with the sleeves. Normally, I would nod my head, slink out the door through which I had entered. Camp counselors, waiters, sales clerks—they all boss me. I have recently decided that this must change if I'm to survive the rest of my life.

"No," I say, "you don't understand. I was sold this suit under false pretenses."

"No. *I* understand. *You* don't understand. Suits that have been altered can't be returned."

I am moving to New York City. I will be working for *GQ*. Still, I'm guessing this guy—bad haircut, bad cologne, certainly didn't go to college, probably rides the bus to work—can sense my weakness like every other sales clerk in the universe can sense my weakness.

Not anymore. It's time for the moth caterpillar to spread his wings.

"I'd like to see a manager, please."

"You'd like to see a manager?"

"Yeah, a manager."

Yvonne, the manager, is polite. Yvonne looks me in the eye when I tell her I'd like to return the suit, and Yvonne tells me the policy regarding alterations. Yvonne is closing in on middle age, has weary lines around her eyes, has probably been at Dillard's for a long time, and if she doesn't screw up, can look forward to a desk job in the corporate office in Arkansas. This is what I'm thinking. I'm also thinking that Yvonne will not thwart me. I will not allow it. I must not allow it.

"But you don't understand, Yvonne. I was sold a gray suit, and this suit is lime green."

She touches it, looks at it, touches it some more, turns it over, and looks at it again.

"Sir," she says, "this is a gray suit."

"Believe me, Yvonne, I'm not delusional. I promise you, you come out in the parking lot with me and take a look at this suit, and you'll see that it's lime green."

And she does, and it is.

"I'll be," Yvonne says, "it is lime green. I never would have guessed. But we still can't take it back. It's been altered."

I am not a moth caterpillar. I am *not* a moth caterpillar.

"Yvonne, I just accepted a job as a senior editor at *GQ* magazine."

Yvonne doesn't seem impressed.

"As in *Gentlemen's Quarterly* in New York City. As in the leading men's fashion magazine in the world."

"Uh-huh."

"We do a lot of stories on suits and retailers and customer service." We do? I don't know. But I guess we might.

"I understand," Yvonne says, "but this suit has been altered. And I'd like to help you, but I can't. It's store policy."

"Fine, Yvonne. You want to refuse to refund someone his money because he altered a suit that you told him was gray and it turns out to be lime green?" (I don't mention that I thought it was gray too. I forgive myself for mistaking gray for lime green. I don't forgive Dillard's.) "Okay, I understand. And I hope a million readers understand, because that's what I will write is the policy of Dillard's department store, in St. Louis, Missouri. That is the policy as articulated by, what is your last name, Yvonne, so I can be sure to get it right in the story, so I can be sure I have it right when I call the corporate communications office in Arkansas?" I nearly shout the words "corporate communications office."

I try to rumble like El Jefe, but what comes out is a screech.

"Because I want to quote you correctly."

I have spent the past fifteen years working for newspapers and magazines, preaching the gospel of rectitude, demanding reportorial behavior worthy of Caesar's wife. To ever use your position for any kind of personal advantage, I have told scores of young and fuzzy cub reporters, was to invite a one-way ticket to the unemployment line.

And now Yvonne is staring at me with contempt while she writes out a refund voucher, and again, I am back at the Lake of the Ozarks on that horrible summer morning, but this time I am not mute and sick and terrified.

I am the counselor, and it feels good.

I wait for my faithful ophthalmologist at her apartment. I sit on her pink couch, surrounded by pink lace pillows, and rest my feet on the stack of *Cosmopolitans* she keeps on her glass coffee table. April lives three floors above me in the Chase Park Plaza apartment building, a grand 1920s art deco hotel that developers fixed up five years earlier and that is listed in the National Register of Historic Places. My grandparents had listened to Benny Goodman in the Crystal Palace nightclub on the top floor. My parents had seen Frank Sinatra there. Ever since the Park Plaza's reopening, the soaring arches and high ceilings and views of Forest Park and the Gateway Arch and the building's swimming pool and proximity to Washington University and that institution's medical center and the offices of downtown and the nightlife of the Central West End had attracted hordes of medical residents and young lawyers.

I was editor in chief of *St. Louis Magazine* at the time, and when I announced that I would be moving from my Southside railroad apartment to the Park Plaza—with its free room service from the Tenderloin Room steak house downstairs and its in-house maid service, and its weekly parties at the swimming pool, and its throngs of attractive and high-earning young professionals—my mother had sighed. "Now, you'll never get married," she had said.

My third night at the Park Plaza, I met April in the elevator. She was wearing blue scrubs and black clogs and no makeup. Thick blond hair pulled back, sad blue eyes, pouty lips.

"Are you a nurse?" I had asked.

"Doctor," she said. She sounded like Betty Boop.

Over dinner the next evening she told me that the local ABC affiliate had been asking her for months to be its on-air medical correspondent, but she had refused. She didn't think people would take her seriously if she were on television. Being taken seriously was important to April, and she'd had problems with it for some time. Since puberty, I guessed. I didn't say that. And I didn't point out that for someone who wanted to be taken seriously, April had an unfortunate weakness for tight clothes, frills, lace, bows, and pastel colors.

After we'd gone out for a few weeks, she gave me a key to her apartment. She worked late, and she liked it when I was at her place when she got home.

For six months April and I have watched college basketball games together and filled out the Are You Compatible quizzes from *Cosmopolitan* and ate Cannelloni from the Tenderloin Room.

April tells me I should write more. "It's your dream," she says, "and you should follow it." April grew up in a small town on the Kentucky–Ohio border. It's there, I guess, where she developed her faith in found dreams as well as her taste for college basketball, frills, and snug blouses, and where she first started subscribing to *Cosmopolitan.* When I tell April about New York, she weeps a little bit and then tells me I'll love the big city. "You'll do great things there." Except for the clothes and the frills and the *Cosmopolitans,* April is the perfect girlfriend. She says she'll come visit me in the city. Sometimes in bed, after sex, I tell April how frightened I am about moving, and she puts one of her cornea-saving hands on my chest and pats it and says, "Shh, shh, you'll be fine, you'll be fine."

My last night in St. Louis, I pick up sandwiches and french fries from a sports bar called Jackie's Place and salads from an Italian restaurant called Rich and Charlie's and ice cream and chocolate sauce from Schnuck's supermarket, because those are my stepmother's favorite places and favorite foods. She has always loved to eat, but now, the steroids she is taking to reduce the swelling in her cancer-ravaged, irradiated brain have made her chronically ravenous.

She is sitting at the kitchen table, which surprises me; it's the first time she's been out of her bed in a week. I tell my father and Elaine that, of course, I'll be back to visit and that when Elaine gets better, they'll come up to visit me. Elaine adores New York City, its neon and shiny hucksterism and endless appetite. It's one of the few places on earth as gaudy and vibrant and swaggering as she is.

"Just send us some lox from Barney Greengrass," she says.

"Don't worry about sending us anything," my father says. "We'll be up there as soon as you're settled."

"Honey, wake up, we're not going anywh—"

"Don't tell me what we're not doing!" my father shouts. He has never been very good at acknowledging reality that he doesn't like, whether it's a comic book–reading son, or a daughter with a taste for unemployed musicians (my sister), or a spouse (my mother) who would rather read Saul Bellow's latest novel, or go to a Fellini film festival than cook. "We are going to New York City, and we're going to visit Steve, and we're going to eat at Barney Greengrass!" he shouts.

"That's fine, honey," Elaine says and raises one eyebrows and smiles at me while my father sticks his head in the freezer to look for ice so we won't see him crying.

I hated her so much at first. I thought it was because of the fur and the lipstick and the thousand shades of white. I hated the gifts she would not stop buying for me. One year, she sent me a plastic wand filled with colored confetti called a "galaxy tube." Another year, a red velour sweater. The next year, an inspirational picture book called *Hope for the Flowers*. My brother and sister got the galaxy tubes and *Hope for the Flowers* too.

Elaine and I eat the chicken sandwiches and french fries and salads, and my dad conducts some critical rearrangement of frozen vegetables or ice trays or God knows what in the freezer. Then he moves to the sink, starts washing dishes.

"You know," he says, "Mel Hirsch's son is a doctor in Atlanta; he makes $2 million a year, and he saw a colleague of his—he had the same thing as you, Elaine, the same disease, and you know what? That doctor is practicing medicine, ten years later."

My brother's wife is also a doctor, and she's told everyone—including my dad and Elaine—that a very optimistic prognosis is another two months.

My father is making a terrific racket with the dishes.

"Do you hear me?" my dad shouts. "Did you hear what I said about the doctor that Mel's son treated?"

"Yes, honey," Elaine says. "We hear you."

"Yeah, Dad," I say, "we hear you."

As my Dad throws dishes around, Elaine leans toward me and says something.

"What?" I say. "What?"

"What color?"

"Huh?"

"What color are the dishes in the sink?"

I crane my neck and look.

"White."

Elaine closes her eyes for a couple seconds and then smiles with tight lips. "China," she says.

He finishes his clattering without breaking anything, joins us, and we finish our sandwiches and fries and salads, and I make sundaes. I give Elaine four scoops and drench them in chocolate sauce. Then Elaine tells my father that his beard needs a trim.

"I'll go tomorrow," he says.

"No, I'll do it now," Elaine says. "Outside, on the deck."

"That's craziness. It's almost dark. And it's cold out."

"Why don't we ask Steve what he thinks?"

She knows how much I hated her. She knows how much we all hated her. She told me just a year after she married my father. "I know you all hate me, and I don't blame you," she had said. "But I love your father, and I am not going to stop loving him, no matter what you do. I love him, and he loves you, and I think we might all be happier if you and your brother and sister would relax a little bit."

So we relaxed a little bit—not a lot, but a little. Everyone relaxed, especially my father. He and Elaine took vacations in California. They soaked in hot tubs. He grew a beard. I think the past ten years have been the happiest of his life.

"It's craziness," my father says. "You are not going outside."

"We'll let your son decide," Elaine says, looking meaningfully at me.

That's another thing I like about Elaine. She never called us her children, and there was never any kind of effort on her part to get us to call her mom or stepmom or anything like that. Just Elaine.

"So, Steve, what do you think? Is it too cold and dark for me to cut your dad's beard?"

If he can pretend that she isn't dying, then she and I can pretend it's a balmy summer afternoon.

"Nah, it's fine. Go ahead, Dad, don't be a baby."

She's been trimming his beard for a decade now. My sister and I watched once, and we had to make an excuse to leave for an imaginary errand. It was that intimate.

"Go set the chair up there. And get the clippies. I mean, clippers," Elaine says. "I'll be out in a second. Steve will help me."

She has difficulty walking now, has lately been slurring her words. She knows this will be the last time she trims his beard. He does too.

"This is craziness," my dad repeats. It's cold. I don't want you—"

"Goddamit," Elaine shouts. "Set up the fucking chair so I can trim your fucking beard. See, now you made me cuss in front of your son."

My dad hurries into the bathroom to get the clippers so we won't see him crying again.

While my dad clatters around on the porch, Elaine puts one of her white-painted fingernails on my forearm.

"Send us a pound of nova when you get up there," she says.

"I will, Elaine."

"And send some sable too and cream cheese and a bagel dozens. I mean dozen bagels. Make six of them garlic. I love garlic bagels. Your father hates them, but that's okay. Here's some money." She fumbles with her purse and then shoves a hundred-dollar bill into my shirt pocket.

"Elaine, don't give me money."

"Take the money."

"Okay, Elaine, and you know, if you—"

"Shhh," she says and then turns toward the patio, where my dad is now sitting in the creeping twilight, looking out at the darkening Midwestern woods. We can both see his shoulders shaking.

"He'll be okay, you know," Elaine says.

"I'm not so sure. And really, are you sure you want to go outside?"

"Listen to me!" Elaine says, and she digs those white-painted fingernails into my flesh. "He loves you, and you love him, and both of you are going to have to figure out a way to start telling each other that."

"He knows."

Elaine has gone limp. Her face is slack; her eyes, unfocused.

"Nova," Elaine says. "And bagel garlic. And nova."

"Are you okay, Elaine? Do you want—"

"Take him to me," she says. No inflection, like she's reciting the alphabet. "I mean, take me to him. Take me to him now."

And I do, and just before I open the sliding glass door, her grip returns. She puts one hand on the side of my face.

"He'll be okay," she says. "You too."

CHAPTER 3

THE STARLET AND THE STALKER

I am waiting to have lunch with a movie starlet. Elaine is dead, and my father has been fainting, and I am living in a Manhattan apartment I'm sure is darker and more cramped and pestilential than anyplace my immigrant great-grandparents were forced to hunker down after they arrived here from Hungary and Lithuania and Poland, nourished only by sunny dreams that their great-grandchildren might be able to afford grander lives than them, with nicer apartments, and I have lately begun to scream at people who make less money than me because that seems to be the only way I can get anyone in New York City to pay attention. None of the grim truths of my life, though, alter the blessed state in which I now find myself. It is a state weird and fantastic and so wonderful and completely outside anything I ever imagined happening that I can't help but think of it in italics—*I am waiting to have lunch with a movie starlet.*

I am waiting for the starlet in a high-priced Italian restaurant on Manhattan's Upper West Side, not too far from my roach-infested one-bedroom apartment of eternal midnight. Over pasta and salad and—I hope—a lot of wine, I will induce the starlet, whose name is Mary-Louise Parker, to reveal things about herself she has never revealed to anyone else, to discuss aspects of her craft she has never discussed before. I will do my reportorial best to determine if, beneath her personally trainered and carefully lip-glossed and dentally perfect starlet exterior, she is temperamentally more akin to the feisty, tomboyish, and sexually smoldering Ruth, from *Fried Green Tomatoes*, or the quiet, thoughtful, and unambiguously carnal nurse from *Mr. Wonderful*. And once I have done that, I will deliver the knowledge to *GQ*'s approximately one million readers in a one-page feature identified on the magazine's table of contents as Emerging Talent and referred to among the men and women at the magazine as Babe of the Month, or simply BOM, as in "Who's the BOM for July?" or "I have to move some copy and write some titles and then crank out that Babe of the Month, what are you working on?"

It is my first writing assignment for the magazine, something I've been angling and pleading and conniving for over the past five months, in between assigning and editing a dispiriting stream of stories on six-pack abs and tantric sex and back hair removal. Art had named me senior editor in charge of the Personal Best section of the magazine, which is devoted to health, fitness, and grooming. Since my arrival in the big city, I have become an expert on exfoliates and adult acne and giving good orgasms. I would do anything to escape Personal Best's clutches and to do some Real Writing. Toward that end, I have been sending Art story pitches a few times a week. I have been arriving early. I have been buying new suits. I have been extending my arms quickly, as if I had an ache in my neck, so that my French cuffs extend (this is a gesture known among the *GQ* staffers as "shooting your cuffs," and it's respected here). Back at my desk, I rub my Big Boy cuff links for luck.

The suit I'm wearing at the moment is navy, of fine linen, with a dark gray shirt, just like what Art wears. My shirt is knotted with a purple-and-green tie, which could not be more bold or decisive and which I persuaded Ursula, the German-born location coordinator, to lift from the fashion closet.

Ursula has blue eyes and long legs, and because she travels to spots where models are photographed in fabulous clothes, she has access to *GQ*'s fashion closet, which is really a room. For all these reasons, I'm fond of Ursula. I think she might be more fond of me. She has told me a number of times how informative and fascinating the Personal Best section is. I'm fairly confident that no one would say that to me unless they had some ulterior motive. She also has a fleshy lower lip, and when she says, "Ach," which she does often, it's very cute.

But my fashion-closet-filching Fräulein will have to wait. I'm more interested, at this moment, in Mary-Louise Parker. I have heard tales of magazine writers bedding the actresses they are profiling, and though I know it's highly unethical, I also know that "ethics" is not a word or concept anyone at *GQ* seems to spend a lot of time discussing. Besides, I am looking good. Good enough, I hope, to persuade the sexually smoldering, undeniably carnal starlet that her starlet life, while filled with wads of cash and flashbulb-popping fame and a groaning smorgasbord of b-level six-pack-ab'd pretty boys, is bleak and barren without a well-read and thoughtful and navy-suited *GQ* editor—who, by the way, has assigned and edited many stories on the intimate pleasures of tantric coupling—as her decent and loving companion. This is my goal.

Because this is my first piece for the magazine, though, I'm aware that if I'm to get another one, I need to keep in mind that there are other goals to consider too. There is the goal of my immediate boss, executive editor Lisa, who made her feelings about the Babe of the Month feature known at an editorial retreat just a few weeks ago.

"Can we for fuck's sake get some women to write these things?" Lisa had asked as the rest of us, Art included, had sat back and waited to hear what latest outrage had made Lisa so contemptuous or dismissive or pissed off. Lisa was contemptuous, dismissive, and pissed off about most things, especially story ideas and writers. This, I had learned in my short time at *GQ*, was the best and safest posture an editor could take when it came to story ideas and writers. It demonstrated that you weren't some lime-green-suited hayseed from Missouri. It showed that you knew what you were doing. It proved that you were decisive and ruthless and not overly concerned with people's feelings. Art adored contemptuous and dismissive editors. The only thing he adored more were loudly profane editors who appreciated good wine and expensive vodka. Lisa was all of these things. I was none.

I had tried to look ruthless. I had tried to nod decisively and contemptuously. Not contemptuously of Lisa. I would never show Lisa anything except my soft, smooth, tender neck; would never proffer anything to her but an occasional fumbling, adoring, invitation to lunch. When people first met Lisa, they invariably commented on her uncanny resemblance to Diane Sawyer. A teacher's daughter from Minnesota, Lisa had smooth skin and an icy allure. Lisa was cold, but she was also hot. Her nickname among the men of *GQ* was Queen of Mean. I wanted Lisa. Lisa terrified me.

"What's the difference who writes these things?" Only a couple people at *GQ* dared to cross Lisa. One was Marty, the phlegmatic managing editor, who could afford to ask reasonable questions free of contempt or overt ruthlessness, given his position at El Jefe's right hand.

"We're all professionals here," Marty had continued. "Do we really need to focus on the sex of the writer?"

Good point, I had thought. Reasonable, well thought out. Weighing both sides, coming to a rational conclusion. I couldn't help myself. I had nodded at Marty. But then I caught Lisa giving me a look, so I tried to stop nodding and to sneer dismissively. Not at Lisa. I didn't have a death wish. I sneered at Marty.

"The difference is," Lisa had said, "I think our readers would like to actually *learn* something about some of these actresses every so often. Like how they feel about their craft. Like what their inner lives are like. When you boys write these pieces, the only thing that comes out is gooey, disgusting, pathetic adolescent longing. Embarrassing teenage crap."

Had Lisa walked into my office when I'd been at lunch and read my journal, which I kept on my computer? How else would she know my feelings about Mary-Louise? Or had the Queen of Mean somehow figured out my longing for *her*? When I had seen her glance at me, I had done my best to appear contemptuous and thoughtful and strong and available. Available for whatever perverted purposes the Queen of Mean cared to use me, separately or all at the same time. Apparently I was attempting too many things with my nodding and sneering and appearing contemptuous and available, because when Lisa saw me, she looked vaguely nauseated, as if she had just gazed upon a squashed frog.

"Give it a rest, Lisa. Give it a fucking rest."

All of us had turned. To pose a reasonable question to Lisa was one thing. To challenge her on intellectual grounds, that was something Marty could get away with. But to issue the Queen of Mean a command, when she was in one of her misanthropic, contempt-slathering soliloquies? What *GQ* editor or writer had the testicles? Even the Big Man kept his booming baritone quiet when Lisa went on one of her rants.

It could only be one man. Only one person would dare curse at Lisa. Only *GQ*'s funny man. Only the food writer with the appetites of a trencherman, the literary stylist with the soul of a Borscht Belt comic. Only Alan, whom Art adores as the king adores his court jester, or pet monkey. "Kid," Alan had told me on my first week on the job, "you cannot suck up too much to Art. When it comes to the Big Man, there is no ceiling on sucking up."

Was it Alan's relentless ass kissing that so endeared him to the Man-Thing, or his undeniable talent and wit? Whatever the answer, it allowed him to defy Lisa in ways the rest of us could only imagine.

"Their craft?" Alan had asked after Lisa had restated her case. "Their inner lives?" I had wanted to snicker but dared not, with Lisa sitting so close. "Do you even *look* at the photos that run next to the BOMs? These pieces aren't about inner lives. These pieces are about one thing. And that thing is, 'Your tits make me hard.'"

And that's how I have ended up watching Mary-Louise Parker enter the restaurant. But watching her is disappointing. This, too, I think in italics. *Watching a movie starlet walk into a restaurant is disappointing.* I was expecting luminous. I was hoping for something nakedly carnal. I was counting on starlet hot. And Mary-Louise is merely good-looking. Slim, clear-eyed, kind of coltish, but honestly, in terms of the Alan reduction, the Queen of Mean does it more for me than Mary-Louise.

Still, she is a starlet, and I am a *GQ* editor, and this is a free lunch; so I shoot my cuffs, tug on my lapels, smile, and offer my hand.

I know that showing some vulnerability often gets others to open up. I mention my blistering skin, how I haven't slept in six months. I mention how I want to write real stuff. I talk about how Art doesn't like me.

And Mary-Louise understands. She understands! She talks about her early days in New York City, how hard it is, how people like us need to make sure we retain our core of sensitivity.

People like us?

She tells me that when she first arrived in New York City from the South, she cried herself to sleep, how the only things that made this big blustering city bearable were the little hidden treasures a sensitive soul might stumble on and hoard. A treasure like H&H Bagels, on Broadway and 80th.

Did she say H&H Bagels? I *love* H&H bagels. I tell her that I spend many late nights there, buying warm hunks of salted dough, which I chew morosely as I trudge back to my cockroach-infested apartment where I lie in bed and don't sleep and wonder if I will ever grow fingerprints again.

"Before I came here," I say, "I lived in a place that had maid service and a swimming pool. I had high ceilings, and I could look at the Arch. You know the Arch? The gateway to the West? Now I live in a place where the tap water is brown."

She stares at me.

Uh-oh. Will she soon be calling her agent to tell him about the neurotic moron from *GQ* who couldn't stop blabbering about the Arch and brown tap water? Will the agent complain to someone at *GQ*? Will word reach the Big Man? Will I never sit in the leather banquette at the Four Seasons? (I haven't been invited yet.) I feel sweat dripping down and soaking the sides of my French-cuffed, spread-collared dark gray sea island weave shirt. I wonder if two-hundred-thread count material stains more easily than oxford cloth.

She continues to stare. What kind of dunce am I? *It is a pleasant day. I am my own worst enemy. It is a pleasant day. I am my own worst enemy.*

She continues to stare. What have I done? *This, too, shall pass. This, too, shall pass.*

Mary-Louise reaches out and touches my hand. What strange starlet magic is this?

"I understand," she says. "I understand completely."

How odd that the only person who seems to grasp my searing dread is a sexually smoldering actress. How reassuring it is to know that beneath our professional shells—she a creamy-skinned starlet with wads of cash and six-pack-ab suitors, me a would-be writer with peeling fingers and chronic stomachaches—we are not so different after all.

We chat. She says that she likes the novelist John L'Heureux. So do I. She says she adores the short stories of Raymond Carver. Me too! She quotes a poem by Raymond Carver. I didn't know he wrote poetry. I want to study his poetry. I will become an expert on the poetry of Raymond Carver. What is the name of that poem? She says she thinks it's called "Beloved," but isn't sure. She says she'll try to dig it up.

I can't believe I ever thought of Mary-Louise as a starlet. Sure, she can act, she's beautiful, she does exude a certain unashamed and proud lust, but she is about so much more than her work.

I suggest wine. Would she like some wine?

"No, none for me, but why don't you have some?"

"Uh, no, but thanks. But really, this is on *GQ*, and you can't possibly have work to do; it's already late afternoon. Let me order a nice bottle for you."

"Steve, you're the one who's been working hard. Let's celebrate. Let's get you a drink."

We are soul mates, Mary-Louise and I. Soul mates understand each other. Soul mates should tell each other their secrets.

"I don't drink."

"Not at all?"

"Uh, no."

"Why not? Would you mind telling me?"

I would not mind telling this slender and gorgeous and sensitive soul anything. So I tell her.

I tell her the story of the cocaine and downers and drinking, my stay in rehab, the twelve-step meetings I briefly attended in St. Louis and from which I drifted away. I tell her about my meetingless twelve-step free recovery, technically dry but awful lonely. I tell it all.

It's slightly embarrassing, so I stare at the table toward the end of it. When I'm finished, I look up. She is crying.

That weekend, I rent every one of her movies I can find.

I would sooner put on the lime green suit than write something shallow or dismissive about Mary-Louise. She is a serious artist, a woman who has known pain, who understands loss. The least I can do is make my story worthy of her. I will not write a typical panting, adolescent Babe of the Month. Mary-Louise deserves better. She demands better. I will use my powers for good. I'm not going to be dishonest, though. Her tits *do* make me hard. But sexual longing does not obviate my true and deep feelings for her, the way we connected over poetry, her tears at my inspirational recovery from addiction. She understands me. I understand her.

I have precisely eight hundred words to express this.

I try an extended dream sequence. Too creepy. I type a long mediation on the sublimity of craft. Too ponderous. What about pure dialogue, letting the human connection and understanding reveal itself in white space and silence? Too pretentious. I make it all physical description from head to foot. I spend three paragraphs on her upper lip. Also creepy.

On Saturday evening, after seven drafts, I call the only *GQ* editor less respected than I am, Eddie "the Ascot", for advice. Eddie writes essays for *GQ* about whether a man should buy pleated pants or not and why the four-button suit is "slightly too fashion forward for all but the most confident." He also carries a paperback copy of *The Old Man and the Sea* in his right hip pocket at all times and often quotes Hemingway. His last piece was on the proper socks to wear with open-toed sandals and summer suits.

I confess my difficulties, my ambitions. I tell him about the poetry and the tears.

"Dude," the Ascot says. "This is a Babe of the Month, not *War and Peace.*"

"Well, yeah, but I want—"

"She's an actress."

"Yeah, but she's much more than—"

"Dude, actresses *act.* That's what she did at lunch. She played you like a violin. No one cares what the words say anyway. It's a friggin' Babe of the Month! Just crank it out."

"But she wasn't acting. I need to find the way into this piece."

"You'd better find your way fast. Because Lisa will cut your balls off if you don't have eight hundred words for her by Monday."

I try third person. I try present tense. I try another dream sequence, one that involves unlikely soul mates reciting poetry to each other through mouths stuffed with bagels. Creepy, ponderous, *and* pretentious.

Sunday morning I emerge from my cramped, cockroached apartment into a New York Indian summer. I grab some coffee, shuffle back toward the bugs, and draft number 19. Walking toward me is an apparition, an answered prayer, an icon of decency and love. She is wearing sweats and a baseball cap, but I'm positive—or almost positive—that it is she. Our eyes lock, I open my mouth, and then she is past me and headed uptown while I remain frozen on the sidewalk, facing downtown and the Statue of Liberty and the uncaring vast sea that delivered my great-grandparents from Eastern Europe, sturdy peasants who landed on Ellis Island with nothing but a few rubles and a lot of hope and who have somehow managed to produce a sniveling great-grandson who wears Big Boy cuff links but who can't even summon the courage to say "hey" to the woman he plans to impregnate.

I consider my options. I can continue south a block, to my apartment, where I will dwell on my cowardice and the nagging feeling that Mary-Louise saw me and averted her eyes, that I had perhaps detected an instance of fear and distaste on her part, that Eddie was right. No, I tell myself, that can't be. *I am my own worst enemy!*

Option 2 would be to continue walking south, into the ocean, to jump.

Option 3: Buy a bottle of vodka. Drink. Call Mary-Louise. Tell her I love her. Make next move a function of her reply.

Option 4: Continue walking downtown, but only for a block. Turn right. Turn right again. Walk nine blocks north and turn right again, until I am at the doorway of the place I suspect Mary-Louise might be headed. It is Sunday morning. Where else would she be going?

Fifteen minutes later, I walk through the doors of H&H Bagel.

"*Steve?!*" she says. Such outsized delight, such sheer happiness in the way she says this. How could I have suspected that she was looking at me with fear just a quarter of an hour and ten blocks ago? How could I have suspected that she looked into my soul and saw what I knew was there, the charcoal chunked heart of a crazed stalker? No, she had not seen that at all. She is truly overjoyed to meet me again, so soon and so unexpectedly. Or is she just pretending? Is she acting?

"Oh, hi, Mary-Louise," I say. Professional. Calm. Not drooling. "I guess we had the same idea this morning."

She extends her hands toward my face. What kind of diabolical female voodoo is she working?

"I was just trying to buy some massage oil at the drugstore, and I spilled it all over my hands," she says.

"Uh," I say. Or maybe it's more like "yerp."

"Here," she says, thrusting her long and tapered fingers toward my eyes. "Smell." I gaze at her cheerful long wrists. Kind wrists. Wise wrists. I close my eyes and inhale.

An hour later, there's a package waiting in my apartment building lobby for me. It's a collection of Raymond Carver's poetry. Inside is a note, tenderly inserted next to the page where "Beloved" is printed. "I'm not crazy," the note says. "I found it. Here it is, in all its sad wisdom."

That's when I realize my story isn't a piece about a starlet at all, or about craft or inner lives, or about tits and dicks. It's about *all* that. And it's about more too. It's about the desire and suspicion that corrodes communication between star and stargazer. It's about the complicated and complicating currents that pass between subject and writer, woman and man. It's about poetry and understanding. It's about love.

I decide I will write about the bagel meeting and the poetry book. I will write about my paranoia and cockroach-filled apartment. I will show that

Mary-Louise's anatomy has an undeniable effect on my anatomy—I can't back away from difficult truths anymore; that's no longer who I am—but what I will stress is how her soul makes my *soul* tumescent. I will deliver to Lisa and Art *GQ*'s first-ever first-person postmodern Babe of the Month.

Sunday, high noon, I start typing again.

> Watch Mary-Louise Parker walk into a restaurant for lunch and
> be underwhelmed by her presence. Pretty, yes, but certainly not
> glamorous. Notice her shyness. Think of the word "coltish," and
> realize that it doesn't do her justice.

That's okay, but kind of flat. It doesn't capture her sexiness. It doesn't show my great expectations or hint at the long journey toward wisdom and love I will be taking the readers on.

I start again.

> Invite an ingenue to lunch. Think of the luminous Ruth in *Fried
> Green Tomatoes*. Ponder the minxlike nurse in Mr. Wonderful.
> Especially ponder the tight nurse uniforms she wore.

Better. "Minxlike" is nice, and it will satisfy the Old-School Babe o' the Month contingent at the magazine. This version will also make Lisa and the other celebrity-conscious editors happy, because I mention Mary-Louise's previous films. And the tight-nurse-uniform reference offers a peek into the dark but harmless mind of the obsessive and vaguely creepy but well-intentioned narrator. By showing him picturing his subject in a tight nurse uniform, it expresses the sad limitations of objectification. And it makes his journey toward true love and enlightenment all that more satisfying. Then again, maybe it's a little too creepy.

I start again.

Invite a starlet to lunch. Remember the luminous Southern belle in *Fried Green Tomatoes*, the winsomely carnal nurse in *Mr. Wonderful*. Expect radiant. Hope for like-like. Watch Mary-Louise Parker walk into the room. Settle for kind of cute.

I sit back from my computer. I smile radiantly. Luminously. It's pure postmodern gold.

I turn in the piece to Lisa on Monday morning. She sticks her head in my office at noon. "Hey, boss," I chirp. She looks at me. Is it my always-raging-out-of-control paranoia, or is she regarding me as a nun might regard a Satan worshipper?

"This isn't about Mary-Louise Parker," she says more contemptuously than usual. More contemptuously than I deserve is actually what I'm thinking. *You are your own worst enemy.* Then again, maybe this is Lisa's way of recognizing the bold nature, the amazing ambition of my achievement.

"Exactly," I say. I say it as decisively and manfully as I can. I think that what comes out is a shriek. "It's about so much more. It's about celebrity and how when we fail to see beneath the superfic—"

"It's about a teenage crush and another boy's pathetic, disgust—"

"No no no. It's really about the nature of love and—"

Lisa flings the copy on my desk.

"Do you actually believe this crap?"

"I was just trying to be postmodern, and to—"

"Rewrite it," she says, then spins, and stalks out of my office. No one at *GQ* can spin and stalk like Lisa. I hate Lisa. I hate her and fear her while still wanting her. Especially I fear the possibility that she's right, that I have deluded myself into inflating my teenaged crush or, worse, a canny actress's poetic and tearful manipulations into something greater. I watch Lisa spin and stalk, hating and fearing and wanting her. And I wonder how I will save my postmodern masterpiece.

I know that playing politics at *GQ* is a game for which I have neither the skill nor the stomach. I know that trying to outmaneuver Lisa is like matching black dress shoes with a brown belt (bold, doomed). I know that Art doesn't seem to particularly like or respect me, and that ever since the mime and the lime green suit, Marty has kept his distance. That leaves David, the editor who ranks just below Marty and Lisa but who seems to be Art's favorite at the moment.

When David likes a piece of writing, he hollers and curses. "This is fucking great," he'll holler. Or, "This is fucking beautiful." At a magazine where cool contempt is the always-safe editorial default option, David's enthusiasm is risky, if not downright foolhardy. Luckily for David, the stories he has recently loved, Art has loved too.

Plus, David *gets* postmodern. And he's proudly ambitious and openly competitive; I think he would like nothing better than to achieve something great at Lisa's expense. Finally, he is slightly obsessed with sex stories. He has told me that he wants to send me to Los Angeles, where I will locate the highest-priced call girl in that city, then pay her to have sex with me, and write about the experience. When he brought up that idea, I had developed a rash on my neck.

I'm optimistic about David's reaction to the Mary-Louise story. I think he'll especially go for the "minxlike."

"This is fucking genius," David says to me, after he reads it.

"Gee, thanks, David, I was hoping you might see—"

"But Lisa's your editor, so I can't help you."

I spend the next five days rewriting. The Ascot suggests that two weeks of my time spent on an eight-hundred-word Babe of the Month represents an unwise allocation of resources. Actually he says, "Dude, do you have a death wish?" Marty demands to know why the research department hasn't yet seen a copy on the nose hairpiece or the essay on the hour-long (female) orgasm, both of which are slotted for the upcoming Personal Best section. I tell him I've demanded revisions from the writers. That's a lie. I don't admit that the stories have been sitting on my desk for two weeks and not only can I not bear to read them, but that I also don't want to take time from my Mary-Louise Parker piece. Art? He ignores me. He doesn't invite me in for the 5:00 PM vodka and story idea sessions in his office. He doesn't ask me to join him for lunch at the Four Seasons. He doesn't stick his head into my office to gossip about the Yankees and Tina Brown. He does all these things with the other editors (except the Ascot), especially with Lisa, David, and Marty.

Hanukkah, Christmas, and New Year's Eve are approaching, so I buy two new suits, a couple more gray shirts, just like Art's. I borrow three more decisive and bold ties from Ursula, who says, "Ach," when I tell her how pretty she looks. Still, nothing from the Big Man.

My Babe of the Month will force Art to take notice. It will make him realize that wanting to get to know the Kid was the right idea, that the Kid can write. Yes, it's only eight hundred words, but it redefines the genre. After Art ponders my take on poetry and understanding and love, he will never think of Babe of the Month in the same way again.

A week later, I turn in my thirty-eighth draft to Lisa.

"What have you been doing for a week?" she hisses after spending about twenty seconds reading.

"What do you mean? I changed—"

"It's eight hundred fucking words. In a week?"

"I took out the dream sequence and—"

"This is not about you," Lisa hisses. "This is about an actress. There is going to be a full-page sexy picture of the actress next to the words, and chances are a lot of people aren't even going to read what you write anyway.

So tell me what movies she has coming up and . . . for fuck's sake, Steve, what are you doing with your hands? That's weird!"

"Nothing, nothing."

I have been rubbing my Big Boy cuff links together for good luck. I've been doing it more and more lately.

Lisa stares at me.

"I just had an itch."

"Well, scratch it outside my office. And give me a rewrite—a *real* rewrite—by tomorrow."

I dial down the lust. I punch up the upcoming movies. I say good-bye to the upper lip paragraph. (I keep "minxlike," though.) Lisa isn't happy, but she isn't miserable enough to justify killing the piece. David isn't happy; he tells me it's a shame Lisa made me take out all the good parts—but he's not frustrated enough to intercede on my behalf with the Big Man. I'm not happy—my genre-redefining, postmodern masterpiece has been turned into just another Babe of the Month—but I'm not stupid enough to complain to anyone but Ursula, who says, "Ach," and gives me some more ties.

A couple weeks after the magazine hits the stands, I see Mary-Louise at H&H. I have been spending an hour there every morning, waiting.

I nod at her, two comrades in a long, fierce battle for postmodernism and understanding, an actress who is more than an actress and a journalist who is more than a journalist. I nod at her some more. I await her return nod.

And I wait. And after she gets her bagel and walks past me and looks at me with slit eyes, I wait some more.

Finally, as she walks out, I can wait no more.

"Hey, Mary-Louise," I bleat.

Nothing. Flat eyes. Where did those shiny, luminous orbs go?

"Steve," I say, "the guy from *GQ*. You know, the one you had lunch with?" My neck itches.

"Oh yeah," Mary-Louise says. "Well, nice to see you, Steve. Catch you later."

No fragrant fingers. No wise wrists. No poetry.

Had she read the story? Had she hated it? Did she hate me? Had I violated some unspoken rule of celebrity journalism?

I walk home, and I call Ursula.

I tell her I haven't talked to her in a long time, that I miss her.

"Ach," she says.

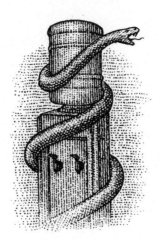

CHAPTER 4

THE EYEDROP PEOPLE, THE BARD, AND ME

Lisa warns me to stay away from actresses. David suggests I commission more sex pieces for Personal Best. He promises that when the moment is right, he will bring up the California hooker piece with Art but that the moment has to be right, and that means I have to work harder at ingratiating myself with Himself. April, to whom I have been complaining every few weeks on the telephone about Art's failure to invite me to sit with him in the plush leather banquette, assures me that if I keep working hard, everything will work out. (She also mentions after reading my piece on Mary-Louise that I "really seemed to like that actress," and I explain to her that actresses tend to be shallow and silly and that it was difficult and even a little bit demeaning to fake affection in my story, but that's what professional writers for national publications are forced to do.) Even Marty—quiet, efficient, don't-rock-the-boat Marty—gives me advice. He tells me I should be nicer to public relations people, that the flak from a local gym had called him to complain about a piece in Personal Best mocking the gym's Mastering the

Run program. It was a three-hundred-word screed I had cranked out after learning the sad and unfair fate of my genre-busting Babe of the Month efforts. I had needed to share my suffering.

"But, Marty, the gym was charging people money so they could learn how to jog. No one needs to learn how to jog. That gym *deserves* our scorn! Aren't we supposed to be . . . ?"

"Just be nice, Steve," Marty says. "That's all I'm saying. Just be nice to the public relations people. Take their calls. Talk to them. Have lunch with them."

"But what about my work? What about my—"

"Your work?"

The Mary-Louise Parker piece is open on Marty's desk. Has he been staring at the sexy photo? Or might there be another explanation? Might Marty be playing mind games with *GQ*'s newest and most heartsick, homesick senior editor? Might the open magazine on his desk be a signal that Marty—his polite suggestions and gentle manners notwithstanding—knows I have screwed up once (twice if you include the lime green suit) and that *GQ* is not a welcoming place for screwups?

"Steve, all I'm asking you to do is to be nice to some public relations folks. Okay?"

"Sure. Okay. No problem."

I retreat to my office. I have been at *GQ* for more than a year now, and except for browbeating a department store manager in Missouri into giving me a refund for my lime green suit, I have triumphed over my enemies much less often than I had anticipated. I think of the world in terms of triumphs denied (no lunch, no postmodern gold, no love from Lisa) and enemies massing against me (Art, Mary-Louise, Lisa). Whether that's because the city is too much for me, with its savage mimes and poetry-quoting starlet-minxes and growling bosses, or because I have always tended to mythologize my life, and my life seems these days to be one epic-length tragic quest—I'm not sure. It doesn't matter, because Marty has ordered me to make nice with the PR folks, and I must obey. I leaf through the stack of press releases I keep next to my wastebasket. I pull one from the bottom. It's an invitation to a lunch announcing a new type of eyedrops. That seems about right for a failed genre buster.

The Eyedrop People are polite, well dressed, and good-looking. We meet in a hotel ballroom. No one spins and snarls, like Lisa. No one vibrates, like Art. No one laughs at me or imitates my walk or looks at me funny or says "nice suit" out of the side of his mouth. In fact, the Eyedrop People seem to like me. They cater to me. A woman named Susan does the most catering. Susan tells me she *loves* the Personal Best section. She tells me it's refreshing to read a magazine that doesn't take grooming so seriously, that she appreciates the "subversive humor" in some of the tantric sex pieces. From what I had imagined about public relations folks—French-manicured and fast-talking velociraptors in high heels—I'm startled that one would dare use a word like "subversive," especially within earshot of her corporate masters. I'm startled that Susan would use *any* words with me. Susan is the Eyedrop People's point person. Because she represents corporate power and the sunny, well-groomed way that money can corrupt ostensibly independent journalism, I should resent her. The trouble is, in addition to flattering my subversive sex stories, Susan is five foot ten, with thick jet-black hair and slender ankles and eyes the color of macadamia nuts.

The trouble is, I'm terrified of Susan's beer girl smile—all moist lips and sparkling white choppers. I'm terrified of her model legs. I'm terrified of what gazing at even one of her long and firm calves does to me. Mostly I'm terrified that if we did what I want to do, which is to flee the ballroom together and then striding up the suddenly sparkling and bighearted avenues of New York City hand in hand, to confess our darkest secrets and most audacious hopes, and then to kiss under neon and moonlight and to fall in love, she will learn fairly quickly that what she might find attractive in me—Personal Best product placement power, *GQ* senior editor title, nice suits—are nothing but mere disguises. Deceptive advertising. A woman like Susan—a woman who looks like a major market weather girl and uses words like "subversive" without reading from a teleprompter—would never date the real me.

Consequently, the real me stays quiet while the *GQ* editor in the three-button houndstooth jacket and the powder blue Swiss cotton shirt with the French cuffs and the spread collar asks Susan if she'd like to have lunch on Friday.

Three days later, over sushi, I tell her I've commissioned a full page on the eyedrops she and her people represent. (Art accepts free clothes from designers that *GQ* covers; shouldn't I embrace the Conde Nast corporate culture?)

"Oh, that's great," she says. "My boss will love me."

She is wearing a gray skirt and a white button-down shirt and pearls, nothing fancy, but her beauty is irradiating the restaurant. The waiters and busboys are bustling and hovering over her, as I have never seen waiters and busboys bustle and hover. She is smiling her beer girl smile, but in a demure way. Susan is too classy to *flash* a cheap and tawdry beer girl smile.

I am not so classy. I have just traded editorial real estate for an impossible dream. I have just announced my intention to inform approximately one million credulous subscribers and newsstand readers that expensive bottles of chemicals will make them happier, all because I want Susan. I should be ashamed, but I'm not. Susan is the woman I have wanted since I was eight years old and my parents took me to St. Louis's University City High School to see the spring production of *The Music Man*. Susan is Marian the librarian, except taller and brunette and infinitely more carnal and having lunch with me. Harold Hill was a scheming con man who betrayed women and children and ripped the very hearts out of small towns in many states, and *he* found true love. Why not a simple man from Missouri?

Why not? I look into Susan's macadamia eyes for an answer. I tell her I hope I'm not being too forward, but I find her fascinating and am very attracted to her. Would she like to go to dinner with me that weekend?

She stares at me. The beer girl smile evaporates. It goes to that place where beer girl smiles always seem to go when I ask them to dinner. She looks down at the table, back at me. Still no smile.

Why not a simple man from Missouri? Because if Susan had a nickel for every simple man she had charmed into giving her eyedrops editorial coverage, she could buy gray skirts for the rest of her life. Because Harold Hill is make-believe, and I'm not only corporeal, but I'm also unprincipled, and I'm an idiot. That's why not.

"That would make me happy," Susan says, and I think I make a keening sound or lurch forward. I think this way because suddenly Susan is looking at me with concern. "But I live with someone."

"Oh," I say. *Just as well,* I tell myself. It would be terrifying to date someone who so effortlessly drives waiters and busboys insane. It would be taxing to live on high alert, to have to pretend I was worldly and wise and powerful and together all the time. It would be exhausting to constantly wonder about the fate of the flesh and blood Professor Harold Hill.

"That's too bad," I say, crushed but oddly relieved. "But you can't blame a guy for try—"

And then Susan—radiant, magisterial, the most beautiful woman I have ever seen who is not on a movie screen—surprises me.

"The thing is, he travels a lot."

Our second night together, Susan asks me what's wrong. I can't tell her I'm haunted by the notion that at any moment she will come to her senses and realize that someone who without even trying could be a Miss World finalist happens to be lying in bed next to a midlevel editor with dermatological issues. Even I, a lifelong whiner and blabbermouth, know enough to realize that such honesty will not help here.

So, on the nights I imagine her boyfriend, a big-shot lawyer, is busy crushing small family businesses and structuring multinational layoffs, I lie in bed with Susan and tell her about the fears I think she might accept. I complain about how I'm being mistreated at work, how editors are moving ahead of me because Art likes them more, how writers are getting assignments because they suck up to Art more, how I'm dying inside.

At first she strokes my face and kisses my recently rash-free neck and tells me not to worry so much. After a few weeks, she whispers that everything's going to work out, I should get some sleep, and I'll feel better in the morning.

Then after a month, on a cold and rainy night, when I'm telling Susan yet again how much I hate fitness and grooming and health and how I think the Queen of Mean is badmouthing me to the Big Man, and how what I really want to do is to be a writer, but David is too concerned with his own turf to help me, she rolls toward me (by now she has begun to turn away when I launch into my sad soliloquies), gently bites my ear, then reaches between my legs, and does some dexterous things with her left hand until I shut up.

"Steve?" Susan murmurs.

"Murgh."

"Are you paying attention?"

"Murgh!"

"Good. Because I want to tell you something. Put on some clothes and follow me into your living room."

Do I have a choice? By the time I'm dressed, Susan is sitting on my couch, in the black kimono she keeps at my place, spectacular legs folded beneath her, macadamia nut eyes blazing, inky tresses pulled back in a ponytail, legal pad in hand.

"What do you want, Steve?"

"Um."

"You need a plan. And that's what we're going to come up with. Now, what do you want? For Art to like you more?"

"Well, yeah, and—"

"To get treated with more respect?"

"That too, and—"

"And you want to write more, right?"

"Yeah, Susan, but you don't understa—"

"Shut up. Just for a change, shut up."

Shut up? That's a little harsh. But she's so beautiful. Regal. Barefoot. Ponytailed, long-legged, beer-girl-smiled. Plus, she knows me now, she knows the real me, the frightened and disgruntled me, and she's still here, at my apartment! Are all eyedrop flaks, behind their prim smiles and careful diction and polished high heels and cute little late-night ponytail holders, such complicated and alluring mysteries? So nurturing one moment, such growling tigresses the next? Innocent one instant, unabashedly amoral and insatiable the next . . .

"Are you listening, Steve?"

"Uh, yeah, Susan, I want to write and—"

"Yeah yeah yeah, I heard that. Now, what does Art want?"

"What does Art want?"

"Yeah, fathead, what does Art want? What does the guy who can give you what you want want?"

Fathead?

"Did you just say 'fathead'? Because I really have to say that—"

"If you ever want to touch me again, Steve, you will stop your daydreaming and focus."

"Okay." I am definitely focusing. "Okay. What does Art want? Art wants people who will suck up to him. Art wants me to pay more attention to

Personal Best, to care about health and fitness and grooming. Art wants, uh, Art wants. Art, uh. Art . . ."

Susan's kimono has fallen open. It's not *fair*. The sparkly teeth and pink gums, the slim ankles and long smooth calves and perfect thighs, and now this . . .

"Steve!"

"Oh yeah, Art wants me to be decisive! Art wants me to be well dressed! Art wants story ideas, but whenever I turn one in, he—"

"Okay," Susan says, "that's enough. Now, shut up and don't move."

Again with the "shut up"? I'm not sure I like this. But the kimono is still open. I don't move.

I stare as she scribbles on the legal pad.

"Here," she says, thrusting it at me. "Even you can understand this. You give Art what he wants; then he gives you what you want."

"But I—"

"It's a simple concept, fathead," she says. Did she just say "fathead" again? She is standing now, her kimono fully open.

"But. Yes. I mean. Can we . . ."

She moves toward me, touches me. "You make a person happy; that person makes you happy. Understand?"

"Murgh!"

"In English, fathead, just so I know that you understand, just so I know that you're going to start shaping up at work and quit whining so much."

"Yes," I gasp, "I understand. I understand!"

"That's good. I think there's hope for you yet."

I call April. Three weeks earlier I had told her that, of course, I missed her—of course, I thought about her, but didn't she understand that my work was demanding, that my time was often not my own? "Are you feeling better?" April asks. Susan doesn't ask if I'm feeling better. Susan tells me I *will* feel better. Susan tells me how to make myself feel better. Susan *commands* me to feel better. April is sweet. April restores eyesight for a living. April is pretty enough that St. Louis's sharpest television minds want to make her a medical correspondent. But I don't care for the shade of eye shadow she uses. It's too blue, not subtle enough. And there are the bows. Plus, she reads *Cosmo*. April is so . . . *Midwestern*. If I stayed with April, she would spend the rest of her life telling me everything was going to be okay, when it's clear that unless I take the appropriate steps, they won't be. I need someone decisive. I need Susan.

"April," I say, "I think we should give each other some space."

"Are you seeing someone else?"

"No!" I say. I shout, "No! Why are you always accusing me of things?" April has never accused me of anything in my life.

"Why is this always about you?" I demand. It has never been about her, of course.

"It's okay if you're seeing someone," she says. "See whoever you need to see. Do what you need. Because I'm not going anywhere. You're the one whom I love and—"

Are all Missourians so giving? So guileless? So unbearably solicitous? This is what I was like before I stood up to Yvonne in the department store. But I'm not like it anymore. I can't be with someone who is. I won't be.

"No, April," I say. "Stop. This isn't working. We're going different directions. I just need a break."

I take Ursula to expensive lunches, feed her oysters and steak, file the lunches on my expense reports under "story idea discussions," then stick the fashion closet ties in my gym bag when I leave for the day, and wear them when I take Susan to dinner. I arrive at work early, leave late, remark at least four times a week to Art how much I like his shoes or his shirts or his cuff links or his pens. Every time I compliment him, I worry that he's going to recognize my craven and obvious obsequiousness, but Alan is right. The imposing editor in chief known as El Jefe—perceptive, decisive, and discerning in all other aspects of his life—believes every compliment anyone throws his way. There is no ceiling on sucking up to Art. So I continue to suck up. I even compliment him on the box in which he keeps his pens.

I give Art what he wants because I desperately want to keep touching Susan. Her beauty has something to do with it, but so does her confidence. Also, I can't get over how when the expensive wool skirts and button-down blouses come off and the silk kimono comes out, the soft-spoken and polite eyedrop flak transmogrifies into something greedy and insistent. More greedy and more insistent since I've quit whining, no question about that. Plus, there's the fact that our time is necessarily limited and semisecret and precious because of the boyfriend. It occurs to me that maybe I am developing a dangerous appetite. I wonder if, when we have to end things, I will be doomed to chase PR flaks with mild multiple personality disorders and globe-trotting lawyer boyfriends.

But I don't spend a lot of time worrying. I can't. I need to be decisive. I need to be bold. I need to continue sucking up. I need to improve Personal Best. I need to bring energies and ideas to *GQ*. I need to do all the things Susan wrote on the legal pad.

I bring energy and ideas to an editorial meeting one Monday morning. The topic is covers, and Art wants suggestions on how to improve them.

"Less celebrities and more Holy Shit stories," says David, still the risk taker whose risks payoff. "I mean, who gives a fuck about Brad Pitt?"

"Actually, David," Marty replies, "four hundred and sixty-five thousand people seem to give a fuck. That's about fifty thousand more people than seemed to care about Paul Newman and about one hundred thousand more people than seemed to care about Ethan Hawke." Marty, the reasonable managing editor with the accountant's brain, who always keeps track of newsstand sales numbers and can recite them anywhere, anytime. Marty who, bless him, made me go to lunch with the Eyedrop People.

"Celebrities sell, David," Lisa says. She says this with the inestimable superciliousness that only the Queen of Mean can manage. By now she has become aware of David's rising stock with Art. Consequently, she takes whatever opportunity she can to demonstrate to Art that while David's bold suggestions might stir Art's manly blood, David's sensibilities pose a danger to the magazine. That they pose a danger to Art. "No one says we love doing them, but we have to do them."

"She's right, David," Art says. Score 1 for Lisa.

Art's not done, though. "But he's right too, Lisa. What I want to know is, how can we do them better?"

I see my chance. I will take the best of David and Lisa and offer something better than either. Then again, can I risk showing up either one of them, much less both? With my right hand, I rub my left Big Boy cufflink. I feel my neck rash flaring. I decide to keep quiet.

Then, unbidden, a vision appears to me. On a warm midsummer's day, in the middle of a *GQ* editorial meeting, I see Susan in the kimono. My quiet days are over.

"Uh, er, I have an idea," I say.

"Well, it's about goddamn time," Art bellows. "I was wondering why I ever hired you. What's your idea?"

Had my weaselly words about his pens and his pen holder and his cuff links and suits and shirts meant nothing?

"Well, look, like Lisa said, we all know that celebrities sell and that we need them on the cover—"

"Let me guess," Lisa says, "you want to put Mary-Louise Parker on the cover?"

Snickers and guffaws all around.

"No, no Mary-Louise on the cover, Lisa. You're right, Brad Pitt sells. But what I propose is that when we show Brad Pitt on the cover, we don't treat him like a celebrity. We treat him like what he is. We show our readers what's underneath the celebrity!"

It is bold. It is decisive. It is, I hope, my ticket out of health, fitness, and grooming and onto the editorial fast track.

"Huh," Marty says.

"Huh," David says.

"What the fuck are you talking about?" Art says.

"Yeah," Lisa says, with glee, "what the fuck are you talking about?"

I am my own worst enemy. Things aren't so bad. This, too, shall pass.

"What I'm talking about is inner lives, about craft. What I'm talking about is instead of just another celebrity shot of Brad Pitt, looking like every mook with perfectly tousled hair and more money than God, we put a shot on the cover that reveals *why* he's worthy of our adoration, *why* he's worthy of our cover." (I have started using words like "mook" lately because I think they make me sound bold and decisive.)

"He's worthy of our cover because he's a celebrity," Marty says. "Why else would he be worthy of our cover?"

"No," I say, "he's not just another mook. He's a celebrity because—"

"He's a celebrity," Alan repeats, "for the same reason that Mary-Louise Parker is a Babe of the Month, your creepy little valentine to her notwithstanding. Men want to do her. Women—and some men—want to do him. People find them very, very attractive."

Laughter all around, even from the Big Man. Then his booming baritone.

"Nice try, kid. But it doesn't make any sen—"

"But it *does* make sense," I say. Susan will be so proud of me. I have dared to interrupt Art. The kimono will come off tonight. I must continue my boldness, even though I can feel my neck rash flaring.

"Here's how it makes sense. We don't show a photo of him as a celebrity. We show him as an actor!"

"Are you for real?" Lisa asks.

"I think it would be fucking genius," David says, "if I knew what the fuck you were talking about."

"And how," Art asks, "do we do that?"

He says this in a soft voice. Art's soft voice is a scary sound. And the Man-Thing doesn't like fraidy cats.

How? This was a detail I haven't considered. How? I will have to wing it.

"How? Here's how. We don't show him with the unbuttoned shirt and the three-day stubble, the stuff we show every cover mook with." I *cannot* stop saying "mook."

"We show him with the stuff from his craft. People know Brad Pitt as a celebrity, but what they forget is, he's a serious actor. He *acts*. So we show him on our cover, but instead of with the unbuttoned shirt and the three-day stubble, we show him in Shakespearean garb."

There are a few moments in every man's life when he can spot disaster coming a millisecond before anyone else. The instant he feels the brakes fail on an icy stretch of country road, and senses in his gut the sickening slide to come. The second he recognizes the voice on the other line and realizes it is the boss's secretary, and there's only one reason she might be calling, and that it's not a good one. The moment he hears the deep, brassy clanging, the terminal bells, and he has no doubt for whom they're tolling.

"Garb" is out of my mouth before I can take it back. Where did "garb" come from? "Mook," okay, it's streetwise and decisive. It's bold. But "garb"? "Garb" is stupid. "Garb" is pretentious. "Garb" is indecisive and tortured. "Garb" is, well, "garb" is Shakespearean, but that's not going to help me. "Garb" is weak. It's silly. It's ugly to think it, but I can't help myself. "Garb" is gay. If there's anything *GQ* doesn't want to be, it's gay.

61

But maybe no one has noticed. Maybe Art appreciates my honest effort. Maybe I'm being paranoid. *I am my own worst enemy. Things aren't so bad.*

Art peers at me.

"Did you say 'garb'?" he asks. "Did I hear correctly that one of my senior editors just said 'garb'?"

Do not show fear. Do not show fear. Do not show fear. *Whatever knows fear burns at the Man-Thing's touch!*

"Yes, Art, I did, but what I meant—"

"This meeting is over," Art booms. He bellows. He has turned into a mighty, displeased and dyspeptic Wurlitzer. "Anyone who has cover ideas that don't involve Shakespearean garb, please let me know."

Much laughter. Much cruel, heartless laughter. Like the mime's crowd, but worse.

"And, Steve?"

"Yes, Art."

"Why don't you concentrate on Personal Best for a while?

"Sure, Art, okay."

"And, Steve?" He is not yelling. The Wurlitzer is purring again.

Still, I suspect what's coming. I hope that what I suspect is beneath Art. I also hope the cockroaches in my apartment will turn into ten-dollar bills.

"No Shakespearean garb, okay?"

CHAPTER 5

JOURNALIST OF TUNGSTEN

Susan doesn't leave her boyfriend. Art doesn't invite me to lunch. Mary-Louise doesn't call. (Nor does April. The break I suggested seems to have resonated deeply with her.) The cockroaches in my apartment multiply, and even though I could afford to move to a nicer place, the effort seems entirely too much. I can barely squeeze myself onto the downtown 1 train without whimpering.

I have visited three dermatologists for my neck rash and peeling fingertips, been prescribed five ointments, gained thirty pounds, bought ten suits, visited two tailors (I was ashamed to have the clothes let out twice at the same establishment). I have been in New York City for two and a half years. I would give up, but I'm not sure what would come next.

So on an autumn Monday morning so crisp and clear that a man who had never said "garb" might believe in happy endings, I shower and shave and slip into a just-altered gray windowpane number, with a spread-collared off-white shirt and a gray tie from the fashion closet. I approach the Queen of Mean in her office.

Now that Mary-Louise is long behind us, Lisa has become something like a friend. Whether that's because I have become more charming or because she'd rather have a pudgy obsessive starlet stalker around than a lean and hungry editor who might actually pose a threat to her status, I don't know. I don't want to know.

We go out for pancakes on weekend mornings, and she listens to me complain about my work and my life, and she tells me to quit whining; then we rollerblade together or eat ice cream. Basically, she is Susan without the sex. Actually, lately Susan is turning into Susan without the sex.

"Hey, boss," I say, shooting my cuffs.

"Steve," Lisa says, monotone. Not a good sign. Then again, with the Queen of Mean, I've learned not to read too much into flat and dismissive declarations, which—despite the rollerblading and ice cream—still covers most of her utterances toward me, excepting her more floridly hostile insults.

"I need help, Lisa. And I know you didn't love the Mary-Louise Parker piece too much, but—"

"You mean 'Confessions of a Stalker'?"

"I think one day you'll see the postmodern intent and—"

"What do you want, Steve?"

Why are all the women in my life asking me what I want? Am I not being clear?

"I want to write more. I want Art to like me. I want him to pay attention to me. I want—"

"You created this mess, stalker boy, and you're the one who—"

"Will you stop calling me a stalker? What I was aiming for was a meditation on the complex interplay between the famous and—"

"Like I was saying, you're the one who's going to have to fix it. Hey, new tie?"

"Yeah, new tie. But how can I fix it if—"

"There's one place in the magazine where you can write. There's one place in the magazine that Art doesn't read, and you can sneak stuff in. There's one place in the magazine where you're in charge. So start being in charge."

"The Personal Best section? But I don't want to write about health, fitness, and groom—"

"So don't. If you can convince yourself that a Babe of the Month is an essay on love and culture, then you can convince yourself that a piece on sit-ups is a reflection on God knows what."

"Oh, I think I see—"

"Now get out of my office. I have some real work to do."

Underneath all that frigid beauty and icy bluster, the Queen of Mean has a heart. What a surprising discovery. What a nice thing to know. In addition to wanting her and fearing her, I am discovering, after two and a half years, that sometimes I am actually fond of her.

"Thanks, Lisa, you're a good fr—"

"Yeah yeah yeah. Now get out of my office."

I turn to go, but before I do, she calls me back, asks me to come closer. She fingers my fashion closet tie, strokes the lapels of my silky two-button windowpane. She smiles appreciatively. At least one person at the magazine appreciates my sartorial efforts. That's nice, because I have been spending half my paycheck on clothes.

"Steve?" she says.

Can it be? Is the Queen of Mean actually smiling?

"Uh, yeah?" I say.

"Cool garb."

Emboldened by Lisa's friendly suggestion, I telephone the public relations director at a popular Upper West Side gym. I suggest she give me—for free—a ten-week session of intensive physical training and nutritional counseling that ordinarily costs $6,000. (As a Conde Nast editor, I already have a free membership.) I tell the PR rep that *GQ* takes fitness seriously, that *I* take fitness seriously. I tell her that *GQ* has a million readers and that many of them live in Manhattan (I think I read that somewhere), and I let her imagine all the new business the story will bring. I don't mention to the PR rep that since I arrived in New York City, what with the tragic nonaffairs and workplace humiliations and all, I have been eating a lot of pizza and ice cream. I don't mention the thirty-pound weight gain or the skin issues. I don't mention that my afternoons at the office—which often follow a lunch of a cheeseburger, fries, and a slice of apple pie à la mode, all billed to my expense account under "story ideas: nutrition" at Burger Heaven—are drowsy, grouchy affairs, saturated with a constant terror that Art and Lisa will yell at me for being lazy.

I also don't mention that in St. Louis we refer to fitness clubs like the one she works for as gyms, or that I have discovered that she's the one who ratted me out for mocking the Learn to Run program.

The PR woman calls me back ten minutes later. I can start the regimen the next morning. To celebrate, I walk home from work and stop for an ice cream cone. Behind the vats of flavored fat stands the ice cream man. In front of the vats stands me. I stand, and stand. I stand some more. The ice cream man ignores me. Does even the humble ice cream man smell my weakness, or is sullen anger a prerequisite for working at an Upper West Side ice cream counter, and should I not take it personally? In St. Louis, the ice cream man would have welcomed me; he would have asked how I was feeling, if I had enjoyed a nice day. He probably would have commented on the weather, the postseason chances for the baseball Cardinals. He might have complimented me on my Hawaiian shirt with the surfboards and palm trees and women in bikinis; he would have suggested a double scoop or a waffle cone before I had even expressed a desire for mocha chip or chocolate peanut butter or, if it were summer, cinnamon. But this guy? This crabby New Yorker with the thinning hair and the pockmarked face? He won't even *look* at me. I'm wearing my gold Joseph Abboud suit, with a pale gray shirt and a gold-and-gray tie and the Big Boy cuff links and this ice cream man, this *yogurt* jockey, he won't even acknowledge my presence. I cough. Still, nothing.

"Ahem," I say. I actually articulate the word "uh" and "hem." Not, "What is wrong with you? Have you no conception of human decency? Don't you see that we are brothers, you and I, that we both want nothing more than acceptance and love?" Not, "I miss St. Louis. I miss the friendly folks and April the ophthalmologist and the ice cream men who like my Hawaiian shirts." Not, "I hate this godforsaken and cruel and joyless city, and I'm going to get out of here as soon as I can." Just "ahem."

The ice cream man looks up. He looks through me.

"Next," he says.

That night, after a super chicken enchilada filled with avocado and loaded with sour cream and after I squash some cockroaches and after I drink some brown, brackish tap water, which I have complained about to the superintendent many times to no avail, my father calls.

He calls every week and asks how the job is going, and I tell him it's great. This has been going on for nearly three years.

"Does Art still like you?"

"Oh yeah," I lie.

"He still taking you to lunch?"

"Yep, Dad, every week."

"You working on anything interesting?"

"I'm getting set to do some long profiles, some features." I can't tell my father I've come to New York to write about weight lifting, that he has sired someone who might get his chest waxed. (The PR woman says graduates of the program often do so.)

That night I hang my suit and shirt in a garment bag; lay out my tie, shoes, and socks. I wake up at six thirty and walk to the fitness club in the predawn darkness. I spend an hour on the StairMaster, wearing a heart monitor, getting yelled at by a guy named Chris, who says chest waxing will be good for me; I eat some egg whites and tomato, recommended by the fitness club nutritionist. I return in the evening, which is when I work out with weights, and then walk to a neighborhood restaurant to eat sushi or a spinach burrito (hold the cheese, hold the sour cream, hold the avocado, no chips) and then home.

It hurts at first; then it doesn't. I'm hungry at first and then not so much. At work, I'm remarkably good-natured except for the morning I snort derisively at David, whom I witness shoveling a fatty Danish into his deluded, self-destructive mouth, and the afternoon when I see Lisa nibbling on a Snickers bar and I mutter, "Spike and crash, spike and crash, spike and crash," until she snarls, "You are creeping me out!" and slams her office door in my face.

I try to make friends at the gym, with female models; tall, leggy editors from *Vogue* and *Elle*; and flabby, sweaty guys like myself who, as I will discover, spend a lot of time pretending not to ogle the leggy editors and models, most of whom look bored or, when they see a flabby, sweaty guy looking at them, like tastefully made-up pit vipers.

When I approach one of the pit vipers and mention that I'm a senior editor at *GQ* and that I'm on the Peak Ten program and that I'm interested in the emotional benefits of exercise, she tells me she's an editor at *Vogue*, and she's interested too.

"Tell me what you have for lunch," she demands.

"California rolls," I say.

"But those have avocado," she says, in the same way she might say "Jesus, you're a toad!"

We're standing next to the lateral pull-down machine. I'm sweating.

"What else do you eat for lunch?" she asks.

"Sesame chicken."

"Drenched with oil. And dinner?"

"I pick up some grilled chicken and vegetables from a joint near my apartment and—"

"Fat free?" she spits.

"That's what the owners say."

"And you believe them?"

I do an extra set of abdominal crunches.

When Chris is busy (as he often is: a *GQ* editor is one thing. Female models are something else), my trainer is Roxanne.

"Quit being a wimp," Roxanne barks when I complain that some weights are too heavy and, in fact, cause what I'm pretty sure are dangerous muscle spasms in my shoulders. "C'mon! C'mon! C'mon!" she hollers as I struggle to finish a set of bench presses.

On the plus side, she possesses curly black hair, a dancer's taut body, and liquid black eyes. One day, after I've finished another grueling set of barbell curls for her, Roxanne steps back and looks at my biceps. She gives the left one a squeeze. It's a playful squeeze, I'm certain, transparent with intention.

She gazes into my eyes.

I put the barbell down and gaze into hers. This program might work out after all.

"Steve," she says.

"Yes?"

"You sweat more than anyone I've ever seen."

Eight weeks into the program, twenty-five pounds less but feeling more blubbery than ever (I suspect the models and *Vogue* editors' body issues have worn off on me), I schedule a session with a "body image consultant" whose card I see on the bulletin board of my apartment building's laundry room. She is a stout woman, and there are frightening dark stains on the front of her yellowing apron. Her office is in Chinatown, and I have to climb five flights of stairs to find it.

She tells me to lie on her couch.

Then she tells me to repeat to myself, "This is my body. This is where I, Steve, live." I can hear babies crying through the thin office walls and people arguing in Chinese and cars honking outside.

I had tried to break journalistic frontiers, had reached for beer-girl-smile love. I have ended up here. Now is not the right time to be reflecting on issues like dignity and self-respect.

"This is my body," I say. "This is where I, Steve, live. This is my body. This is where I, Steve, live."

I trudge down the steps, down more steps to an uptown subway, slink into my neighborhood grocery store to pick up some frozen yogurt, which sounds relatively healthy, but which I now know wants to hurt me, aspires to bring me even lower. I stop myself in the doorway, aghast. "This is my body," I mutter to myself. "This is where I, Steve, live." The security guard looks at me suspiciously. I leave, empty-handed.

A week later, I have made it to 184, down from a preprogram 220. My cholesterol has dropped from 217 to 160. My body fat has plummeted from 22 to 11 percent. My waist size is 34 now (four inches below my preprogram size), and I spend my lunch hour at the first tailor's, having all my trousers taken in.

But I think I need to lose a few more pounds. I mention this to Chris. I tell him I'd really like to have more defined abdominal muscles and if only I could get down to about 9 percent body fat and—

"The important thing to me isn't really how you look," he says, "but how this affects your health, how you feel."

How I feel? I feel okay, but that's because I've been focusing all my attention on my body, not on work or fame or love or redefining journo-frontiers or human companionship or any of the other things I had hoped might come my way when I accepted *GQ*'s job offer and left the heartland for New York City. Now my chief trainer is telling me that more muscle definition and less body fat do *not* comprise the secret to happiness?

When I start writing the story, I have some nonfat cookies, just to relax. I describe Roxanne and Chris and my new muscles, and it's stupid, so I have some frozen yogurt and take a nap. I wake up and start again, with a long description of the *Vogue* editor's left tricep, but it's weird, and I hate that I'm writing about fitness and that I lie to my father regularly and that Art still hasn't taken me to lunch. I consider making something up to improve the story, think about inventing some scenes where models who had sneered at me before had sex with me post–Peak Ten, and they all had one-hour orgasms. I know that Art would love that, and David too. I write a few paragraphs of made-up stuff and feel giddy and horrible all at once. I walk downstairs and buy a pint of Chubby Hubby—the hard stuff—and come back upstairs and eat the entire pint and watch cockroaches scuttle back and forth on the floor.

"This is my body," I say. "Fuck it."

In "Losing It," I stress the health benefits of exercise, the renewed sense of vigor, and calm that comes from regular workouts and a healthy diet. I don't mention how in my newfound obsession with slimming down and working out, I don't spend nearly as much time reading, or talking to my family back in St. Louis, or worrying about writing or writing. I don't talk about how close I came to lying in print, how the idea of manufacturing details for professional advancement still appeals to me on a theoretical level. Personal Best is not the place to get morose and postmodern.

I become even more bold and decisive. I had noticed during my ten-week fitness plan that a lot of serious gym rats treated themselves to regular massages. I propose a story on men and massage, a meditation on the subtle relationship between tender and tough. David likes my pitch, but not enough to pass it on to Art.

"You know what El Jefe goes for," David tells me. "Give it to him."

"You can talk all you want about shiatsu and Rolfing," I write in the revised pitch, "about the subtle relationship that exists among chi, chakras, and emotional well-being. But wouldn't you rather talk about strippers with loofah sponges and hot Czechs rubbing you down? Way down? Wouldn't you rather talk about sex?"

"Excellent pitch," David says. "You're learning."

"Green light," Art says.

In Maui, where *GQ* sends me for a week of massages, facials, and aromatherapy, I walk along the beach with a twenty-four-year-old blond travel writer from Nebraska who has just moved to New York City and who longs to write pieces that "really help people." I tell Maggie that *GQ* is always looking for freelance travel writers who want to help people, which I'm pretty sure is an absolute lie, and that she should call me when we're back in Manhattan.

I work hard researching the story. After Hawaii, I fly to Los Angeles, where I call an old flame who is a professional masseuse and tell her that maybe I could help her with some publicity. I do not tell her that she has been on my enemies list for some time.

I might be having trouble with the subways, women, and work of New York City, but I have always found the prospect of revenge invigorating.

When I sit down to write, the story seems to come easily.

The notion of lying still while someone rubs warm and fragrant vegetable extract into my skin fills me with excitement and shame. This makes me a typical guy. I am slightly more enlightened than many of my stout-hearted, beer-swilling brothers, though: I once dated a massage therapist. Meg taught me about energy fields and self-grounding, releasing negative vibrations, and the awesome power within. Then, on the second night of a week-long vacation in Colorado, she dumped me for a twenty-one-year-old French rugby player she had just met at the swimming pool.

My behavior isn't exactly noble. I know that. Using a journalistic essay to settle a romantic score wasn't something that would be taught at journalism schools in the decades to come. I know that too. But Meg *had* released some major negative vibrations in my energy field. And what was she going to do, write a letter to the editor?

Another byline. A "nice job, stalker boy" from Lisa. Two weeks of avocado masks and foreigners getting paid to make me feel good. Professional advancement, voluptuary pleasure, *and* a chance to strike a name from my enemies list. This big-time magazine job in New York City might work out after all.

I call Susan to share my joy. I call also because I long for her inky hair and her long legs and those flashing macadamia nut eyes. I have been back from my trip for a week but, because Susan's globe-trotting legal juggernaut of a boyfriend has been in New York too, I haven't been able to see her. But today he's supposed to be in Bogota. I tell her I miss her. I tell her I've been thinking about her. I ask if she's read my story.

"Why is everything always about you?" Susan says.

"Huh," I reply.

"Do you ever think about how I feel?" she demands.

"Of course, I do," I say. And it's true. On Susan, I've tried out a number of the various techniques touted by Dr. Sooth, Personal Best's pseudonymous sex columnist. They weren't purely for my benefit.

"I think we should stop seeing each other," Susan says.

"Huh?" I say. Maybe I bleat. "But. What? Why?"

"I'm engaged."

"Huh," I say yet again. I had thought of Susan's boyfriend as a kind of nuisance, nothing more. I had told myself that it was just a temporary thing, that it would never really lead anywhere.

"When did that happen?"

"Last week, when you were on your little story. I just think this is for the best."

I don't think this is for the best at all. She doesn't love him. I know it. How could she love him if she's been with me all this time? I know better than to suggest this. So I tell her I still have her kimono and ask when she wants to come by to pick it up. It's a desperate ploy. I'm desperate.

"Can you leave it with your doorman?" Susan asks. "I'll send a messenger over for it."

A messenger?

"And, Steve, I want to ask you something."

"Okay."

"Who would be the best person at *GQ* to pitch about a new line of moisturizer for men? Can I send you a press kit about it? I think it would be perfect for Personal Best."

I mope. I resume my two-a-day workout schedule at the gym. I sneer at the pit vipers. I join two basketball leagues. Most of the other players are lawyers and investment bankers with expensive haircuts and $100 Nikes and nylon tank tops, and I elbow them—even my teammates—as I jostle for rebounds because they remind me of Susan's fiancé (or at least how I picture him) and because my delts and biceps are jostle-ready now. After a while, even my teammates grow alarmed by the angry nihilism I exhibit near the basket, and they freeze me out and edge away from me. The exception is Denny. Denny is the league pariah. He wears high-top black Converse shoes and a ribbed white T-shirt and cut-off blue jeans shorts, and while the well-coiffed bankers execute precise cuts and grunt earnestly and flick up sharp little ten-foot jump shots that in their form and follow through would bring joy to the directors of the pricey suburban basketball camps the bankers doubtless attended as high school golden boys, Denny stands a few feet behind the three-point line and screams.

"Feed me, Rockefeller," he screams. Or, "Hey, J.P. Morgan, throw the fucking ball to someone who knows what to do with it." Or, "Yo, Wall Street, yeah, you, get the rock to a real man."

The bankers detest Denny, but eventually someone throws him the ball, if for no other reason than to shut him up. And that's when Denny swings the ball from his hip to his shoulder to a spot between his shoulder blades, in a spastic, convoluted series of movements that would make any basketball coach blanche and then flings it toward the basket, screaming, "Hate the shooter, but love the shot," or, "Watch and learn, banker boys," or, his favorite, "Give it to me hard." And most of the time, the ball ripples through the net, and Denny has timed his screaming, so he stresses "shot" and "boys" and, especially, "hard" just as he scores.

When Denny and I are on the floor one night and I elbow an opponent in the gut and grab the ball, Denny yells, "Kick it out, Carnegie," and when instead I shoot the ball myself, and it is blocked, Denny, who hasn't moved, yells, "Hey, take off the blinders, big spender, and try passing to someone who knows how to play the game."

And that's when I tell Denny to blow me, and he says, "Yeah, I bet you'd like that," and I shove him, and he shoves me back, and I grab his throat, and he grabs mine, and the ref blows the whistle, and the rest of our team huddles and decides that Denny and I should sit on the bench for a while.

I stare into space and listen to the screeching of rubber on wood, the referees' whistles, and the polite grunting of the players on the floor; and I wonder how I've ended up here. I came to New York to make a name for myself, to prove my father wrong, to find a beautiful girlfriend and success and happiness. Instead, years after donning the lime green suit, I've just been dumped by an engaged woman, am lying to my father, and actually contemplating making up things in a national magazine. And now I'm sitting next to a guy I've just tried to strangle, a guy who oozes class rage and who wears basketball shoes from the 1950s and who has the weirdest and one of the most accurate shots I've ever seen.

"Quit being a girl, and get a rebound!" Denny screams at one of our teammates, who has just missed a layup. Banishment from the game has done nothing to dampen Denny's contempt for the others still playing. Denny is not longing to look good or to be accepted. Denny does not seem plagued by what others think of him. Denny seems perfectly comfortable in his outrageous getup and with, his pariah-hood, squatting alone on his private real estate forever beyond the three-point arc, ranting gleefully at a world that despises him.

Maybe what happens next happens because I envy his solitary ease. Or is it because next to Denny, I really do look—and sound—like one of the high-functioning, well-groomed, by-the-rules men of Manhattan I long to be? Or is it that except for Lisa occasionally hissing at me and the ice cream man screaming "next" and my months of doomed and absurd coupling with Susan, I realize that my hateful embrace with Denny represents the closest I've come in Manhattan to any meaningful human connection? Who can solve the mysteries of friendship? Who can say when an adversary becomes an ally? Who can take the measure of a man's ghostly, conniving, needy heart?

"Hey," I say, offering my hand, "No offense intended back—"

"Get back on D—you fat-ass, fat-cat, lazy MBA monkey!"

I don't think Denny heard me.

I try again. "I really didn't mean anything. I just—"

"Forget it, banker boy," Denny says, still staring at the game. "You and the rest of the M&A punks are just jealous."

"I'm not a banker," I say.

"You look like one."

"Yeah," I say. "Well, you look like a roadie." It's the best I can come up with.

"Nah," he says. "Producer."

"Producer?"

"Yeah, I write songs. I used to be a bass player. You would not believe the pussy a bass player gets. Especially in this town. But you know, you grow up, you get older, you see you gotta grab the brass ring. You have any idea how much money you get with one song? You know 'Walk Away Renée,' that song?"

"Um, I think so. I thought it was 'Don't Walk Away Renée.'"

"Yeah, everyone thinks so. Ignorant dickheads. I know the guy who wrote that. Never had to work another day in his life. He's set. And he still gets lots of pussy. So now I'm a producer. Which means not only do I write songs, but if someone I'm producing writes songs, I also get some of their action. Hey, Rockefeller, lemme back in, I'm the only one who can put it in the hole."

"Producer?" I repeat.

"Yeah, what do you do?"

"I'm an editor at *GQ*, but what I really want to do more is write."

Denny swivels toward me. "Writer? We should do a song together. Why don't you come up to my place after we're done with the money boys tonight? We'll noodle around some ideas. I'm thinking of doing a musical based on Stalin, but calling it Svetlana, you know, after his daughter, 'cause Russian women are *hot*. Greedy hookers, but *hot*! And you work at *GQ*? Jeez, that must be pussy heaven. Is it pussy heaven? Maybe I can come visit your office sometime? Chicks dig producers, and if me and you team up . . . SHOOT THE FUCKING BALL, YOU HEDGE FUND DICKHEAD! "

That night, in Denny's studio, which is also his rent-controlled, one-bedroom apartment that he has lived in for the past twenty years, I tell him about Susan, how I miss her, about the lies I've told my father, and the fictions I've thought about passing off as fact in *GQ*. I want a confessor who won't judge me. I sense that might be Denny.

"You need some strange," Denny says.

"Strange?" I say.

"You really *are* from Nebraska, Abner."

"Missouri," I say.

By now, we've filled each other in on our life stories. Denny is forty-seven, grew up in Brooklyn, came to Manhattan to play in rock-and-roll bands and clubs when he was sixteen, had "more pussy than any man should ever have," and now has a twenty-three-year-old girlfriend, whom he cheats on regularly.

"Whatever. Nebraska, Alabama, Missouri. Same thing. You need strange. Strange, as in unfamiliar pussy. Susan sounds like she was hot, but she was playing you. She probably accidentally on purpose mentioned you to Mr. Moneybags a few times, until he took the bait and proposed."

"No, Denny, I don't think that's the way—"

"You need strange," Denny says again, "and if that doesn't work, I have a plan."

I'm not quite ready for strange. And I might be lonely and ready to be pals with this fearless and cheerfully offensive oddball, but I have enough sense to fear Denny's plans, so I call the personal trainer who thought I sweated so much and invite her to a movie. I tell her I'm fifteen pounds thinner than when we lifted together, and that I have a cover story in next month's *GQ* (which isn't technically true). Also that I edit the magazine's sex column.

"Wow," she says, seven hours later, as she's leaving my apartment at 2:00 AM. "You aren't nearly as flabby as you used to be."

I call Maggie, the travel writer, and invite her for lunch, where I listen to her talk about how journalism can help people and about mean old editors who only care about sensationalism and about how what's important isn't always shocking or titillating. I tell her that it's journalists like her who can make a difference, and I invite her to continue the conversation in my apartment.

I make it a point to attend every public relations event and product launch luncheon to which I'm invited. Susan, I have discovered, is not an anomaly among her species. It seems most female public relations flaks are prompt and well-dressed and exceedingly polite and friendly to big-shot editors and, when it comes to physical gratification, very focused and clear about what they want. I try to be good and decent, but I fear that I have become like the otherwise blameless killer lions of Tsavo who, through no fault of his own, has discovered a raging appetite for human or, at least female public relations, flesh. (In between my other activities, I continue to watch a lot of nature shows on television late at night, most involving animals eating other animals.) I find life as a flesh-eating lion much more satisfying than my former existence as a timid moth caterpillar.

I lift weights and have sex with Roxanne, the trainer. I talk about meaning and journalism and have sex with Maggie, who calls me "dude." I assign stories on hairbrushes and wrinkle cream and shampoo and then have sex with Jacqueline and Robyn and Kristin, high-heeled, silky-haired public relations junior powerhouses who don't mind at all when I leave after our romps. Strange, I guess, but respectable strange. I buy four new suits—two-button, double-vented solids that flatter my new slim physique. I commission ten custom-made shirts.

I cannot stop thinking about Susan.

Why? The kimono and the long legs and the sex, of course. Also the memory of the power I felt when I would walk into a restaurant with her and watch as otherwise implacable and haughty maître d's and managers would all but quiver and tremble at the sight of her gelid beauty. Her ponytailed, legal-pad lectures. Her calm and steady ardor in the face of my anxiety. Her artic certainty. Her confidence. Her absolute and unequivocal nonlimeness.

I call, suggest that until she's married, there's no reason we can't get together for a meal. I tell her that it will be fun to catch up. I tell her I miss her.

We end up in bed that night. She cries, says she thinks she might be making a terrible mistake by marrying. I rub her shoulders and tell her that whatever she does, everything will be okay. Just what April the ophthalmologist used to do to me. Just what I ended up hating her for.

"Why does everyone always say everything will be okay?" Susan says, sobbing.

"I don't know, honey," I say, "but really, you're here now and—"

"Will you please let me just feel how I'm feeling?" she cries.

I've been in New York City long enough to know that when women say things like that, the best thing to do is to shut up. Either that or to tell them how much you love them. Or to alternate.

April operated on retinas, and she loved me, and we haven't spoken since I suggested I needed a break. Maggie now cooks me dinner and wants to make the world better, and the only woman I'm interested in is scheduled to become another man's wife in six and a half weeks. So I let Susan feel how she's feeling and tell her how much I love her, and we continue sleeping together, and whenever I ask whether she has reconsidered the whole betrothed thing, she orders me to let her feel her feelings some more. After she feels them for a while, she tells me we're through and to please not call her again.

"Why?" I ask Roxanne one Saturday morning as we alternate dumbbell curls at the Equinox. "Why can't I be happy with Maggie? And why does a woman who's sleeping with me and crying to me and telling me how miserable she is—why is she going to marry someone else?"

"Quit jerking!" Roxanne says as I jerk the dumbbells from my hips to my chest. "Lift! Don't jerk! Lift!"

Roxanne still comments on how much I sweat and my relative flabbiness, and she yells at me when I jerk rather than lift. She also whines about her semipro boxer boyfriend who won't have sex with her two weeks before his bouts and the trainer she is having sex with on the side, who insists they go dutch for dinner. In exchange, I get to complain about Susan.

"Okay, okay," I gasp. "I'm lifting. What should I do? Should I tell her I can't see her till she's available? That might be a good strategy. Or maybe I should offer myself up as a husband—"

"Did your parents have glandular conditions? Look at those puddles!"

"C'mon, Rox, I'm in trouble here."

"You got that right," she says. "You need help. You should see a shrink. I know someone who's all about the mind-body connection. And for someone like you, with your sweating and stomachaches, I think she might be just the ticket. And I hear she specializes in writers, that people who see her start writing best sellers. Plus, she's psychic and so good at it that Yale paid her to sit in a room while their doctors took x-rays of her brain."

Her name is Rose, and she keeps an office in her midtown apartment. She has black eyes and black hair and dresses in tailored silk suits and velvety wool skirts. Except for the StairMaster I catch a glimpse of in the next room, Rose seems like she might have stepped from a fancy pastry shop in Budapest, circa 1928. She has serious and shiny black high heels and a purple suit, cut tight around her hourglass figure. The skirt stops a few inches above her knees. She has very shapely legs. She might be thirty-five. She might be sixty.

"So," Rose says.

"So I hear a lot of your clients are writers and that after they see you, their careers take off."

"Is that why you're here?" Rose asks. She is sitting in a black leather recliner chair and has her excellent legs crossed. I try to not stare at them.

"Well, that's part of it. But mostly I'm here because I've heard you're a really great therapist and also that you're such a great psychic that Yale paid you to study your brain waves, and that sounds really great to me."

"Actually, it was Princeton, and there were three of us involved in that study."

"Fine, Princeton. That's okay. In any case, I really think I could benefit from a psychic reading and from psychotherapy."

Rose frowns, recrosses her legs.

"No," she says, "I will only do one or the other for a client. To me, therapy is about helping a client gain control and mastery over his life. And when I do a psychic reading, even though I consider it serious and am aware of the talent I have, it's about a client ceding control for an hour or two, asking me to tell him about things."

"But I think—"

"Why is it important to you that I do both?"

"Because from what I know about therapy, it starts with my telling you the problems that are bothering me. But what if I'm not self-aware enough to identify those problems? And what if, even if I am self-aware enough, I'm not articulate enough to talk about them? Wouldn't it make more sense for you to do a psychic reading on me, tell me what my problems are, then we'll dig in on the therapy?"

Rose smiles. She has full lips. Those, with her aquiline nose and those midnight eyes, make me think of Hungarian witches or the peasants from *Nosferatu the Vampyre*, except better dressed, with sexy legs and a StairMaster in the next room.

"I understand," Rose says, "but I'm afraid this is nonnegotiable. So, if you'd like a psychic reading, I'd be glad to do one; and in that case, if you'd like, I can recommend some therapists. Or we can try therapy. You can think about it if you'd like."

I want to know if Art will ever invite me to lunch. I want to know if I'll ever get off the fragrance and body hair beat and get to do some real journalism. I want to know if Susan might call off the wedding. So, of course, I want the psychic reading. But I also want to stop my nightmares, to stop falling for bagel-noshing starlets and cohabiting publicists. I want to understand why I seem to have a thing for jettisoning available and attractive women and seeking out the Susans of the world. I want to make things right with my father, to make him proud.

"Therapy," I say. "I'll take the therapy."

"All right, then. Tell me about your mother."

Chapter 6

Missy's Earth Suit and the

Slavering Dogs of Midnight

My fingerprints have returned, but I still have trouble sleeping, and in addition to my chronic stomachaches, I now have recurring nightmares about large slavering dogs trying to bite me. So it's not a pleasant day. It's mixed at best. I feel the same about my social life. Even though the PR gals with their shiny hair and slim ankles and moisturized skin say how happy they are to be dating a *GQ* editor and even though my medicine cabinet is crammed full of hair gel and moisturizer and exfoliates and other swag that the PR gals and their corporate masters deliver by messenger to my doorman regularly, I wonder if they'd be quite so fond of me if they knew how much I worried, if they ever became familiar with my melancholy, striving-but-not-quite-arriving self. I have told exactly three women the truth. Mary-Louise had sent me a book of poetry and offered her wrists and then abandoned me. Susan had told me to stop my whining and informed me that she was marrying a lawyer. Psychic Rose asks about my mother, and while I talk about Susan and the editor known as the Man Thing, she listens and nods and crosses her shapely legs and refuses to do her psychic juju and then scribbles "generalized anxiety disorder" on a slip of paper so my insurance company will pay her.

What to do? I could dive into the work of the Russian novelists I've heard so much about, the ones who descended into the existential abyss and supposedly climbed back out with some answers. But that would cut into my workout time. I could go after some big-name writers and try to get them into *GQ*, which would please Art. But I'm not really interested in getting any writers other than myself into the magazine. I could write something serious and challenging. But that seems too serious. And challenging.

I leave the cockroaches and walk to the office one Sunday morning, intent on starting my new life by sorting through the mounds of press releases and pitches on my desk, earnest and pitiable notes from people who want to get their products and names into a section whose editor wishes he didn't have to edit it. That's when I find the letter from Hero-Quest, a California-based outfit offering a "journey to discover your higher purpose—the contribution that you were born to make and that only you can make." That's when I find the note from the Aspen-based Global Fitness Adventures, encouraging me "to say yes to your precious life" and offering in return "empowerment of body, mind, and spirit." That's where I see the brochure from Canyon Ranch Spa in the Massachusetts Berkshires, hawking something called a "Gateways to Spirituality" weekend.

I could stop having sex with multiple partners and search for love. I could start volunteering at soup kitchens on weekends and holding abandoned babies at hospitals late at night, all in an attempt to escape from the shackles of self. On the other hand, I could try to get my bosses to send me on an all-expense-paid couple of weeks' worth of back rubs, drumming workshops, and cozy "partnering" sessions with what I feel sure will be wealthy and intensely unhappy women.

"Don't we all wish for peace, serenity, a sense of fulfillment?" I write in a memo to David, my majordomo in all matters Personal Bestian. "Don't we all want to be happy? Don't even our most fit readers yearn for Something Better?"

Monday morning, he gives me the good news. The spiritual fitness piece is a go. Art loves it.

I have heard that the director of Global Fitness Adventures believes in past lives; I've been told that she recommends vitamin injections and regular enemas. I've been warned that she won't let me drink coffee. All this worries me. Still, when I arrive at the Global Fitness Adventures ranch outside Aspen, I can't help but notice that she also possesses startlingly high cheekbones, a dazzling smile, and precious little body fat. So what if she's deluded and fanatical? "Steve," this director, whose name is Kristina, exclaims, with an exuberance that I immediately distrust. She hugs me. This is wrong. My psychic psychotherapist never hugs me.

Then I reconsider. I *am* ready to say *yes* to (my) precious life. I *do* want a vacation that will "support and encourage empowerment of body, mind, and spirit."

Maybe the hug is part of it. "Yes," I whisper, getting into the spirit of things, eagerly encouraging body empowerment. "Yes," I repeat, "yes, yes." But she pulls away. I resolve to work on my tendency to objectify women, right after I become more open, pious, and uncynical. For help, I reach out to my fellow Global Fitness Adventurers on the first afternoon hike of our week together. I tell them that I want to trust my impulses more. I tell them I want to learn to live in the moment more. I tell them I'd like to *feel* more. Then because I need to bring a story back, I pump them for embarrassing personal information.

I learn that Joe, a forty-seven-year-old stock broker from Manhattan, would like to lose weight and meet a woman, and that Laura, a thirty-three-year-old nurse from California, who just broke up with her boyfriend, distrusts men. Wendy, a corporate executive from Boston who hates corporations tells me she was great healer in a former life, and Scott, an artist, writer, and "holistic teacher" from Louisiana, lets slip that he's arranged some colonics in town to help with his chronic stomachaches. I nod and smile and murmur and perform what an old girlfriend calls the "reporter as human being trick." It's lucky that I can perform this routine almost without thinking, the way Vegas dealers can cut cards, because at the moment, most of my spiritual energy is devoted to Missy, a twenty-six-year-old accountant from Ohio who is blond, giggles a lot, and who doesn't seem to be wearing a bra.

As the group gains elevation and loses breath, Kristina tells us to pump our arms, to breathe deeply, to hold our heads high. But my gaze is directed elsewhere. To Missy, I remark on the almost-ineffable beauty of the sky, the delicate quality of the light. To Missy, I comment on my high hopes for the week ahead, my sincere wishes for personal growth. To Missy, I confide about my biting-dog dreams. To Missy, I suggest that men who are most comfortable with their masculinity are men who are not afraid to *feel*. To Missy, I . . .

"Christ," Missy says when we reach the top of the mountain, "I need a cigarette."

The next morning, I stand next to Missy for our 7:00 AM yoga session. Kristina calls us "my little yogis" and "my little twinkly diamonds." "Shed your earth suits," she tells us as we assume the tree position, which I find much, much more difficult than the cynical reporter stance. "You are impeccable warriors," she says, "moving through life like cannonballs, pushing aside obstacles, but in an ethical, sentient way."

I steal a glance at Missy. She is remarkably limber. "Meet and comfort your wounded inner child," Kristina commands us, but I can't seem to locate the little guy. It could be because I'm distracted by Missy's earth suit.

Over the next few days, in between morning yoga sessions and afternoon hikes and early-evening massages and evening sing-alongs and drumming workshops and nutrition lectures, I work on my reporter-as-human-being trick. So when Laura says, during a hike, "*The Celestine Prophecy* taught me so much," I don't snort. When she cries during morning yoga because "it brings up a lot of stuff," I don't complain. And when the drumming guy tells me that if I can locate "the magical place in the rhythm," I'll be, generally speaking, a happier person, I don't laugh in his face and suggest that he keep his day job. I tell no one how lonely I am in New York City, how I want love and how I fear I'll never find it, how much I miss Susan.

Midway through the week, I invite Missy for a late-night Jacuzzi. In the tub, I tell her I think the world would be a better place if everyone could, as we have been forced to do, get outside a few hours every day, breathe deeply, quit coffee (after a couple days of splitting headaches and crushing malaise, I feel calmer), escape from the shadow world of commerce and meaningless concerns, and enter into the realm of what's *really* important. I tell her that work can be satisfying, but what truly counts is human connection. What really matters is love, I tell her. I actually say that. "What really matters is love."

Then lightning strikes the mountains across the valley, and we're lit up. What I see is a giggly twenty-six-year-old blonde sitting in a hot tub with a man old enough to be her father's untrustworthy junior partner. What I see is a man teetering on the edge of something sad.

Missy says she misses her car. "It's a black 300ZX twin turbo—and it's jammin', man." She tells me about the night she ran off the road, and I agree that, yes, it was kind of unreasonable for the authorities to demand that she attend an alcohol abuse workshop over the next two weekends.

"Really?" she says and moves closer. I know the next move by heart—comfort, commiserate, comfort some more, suggest a private global fitness adventure in my room—but something weird is happening. I can't do it. I remember my days in rehab, my few months of meetings in St. Louis. Sometimes I wonder if I should find some meetings in New York City, just for company.

"I used to drink," I say.

"Really?" she says again and moves so close we're almost touching. Her earth suit looks so fine. If ever there is a proper place for the reporter as sensitive human being routine, if ever there is an appreciative audience, if ever there is a perfect moment to snatch a twinkly little yogi from a hot tub, it is here, it is her, and it is most definitely now.

"Yeah," I say, "but it was causing problems in my life. It was causing problems with work and with people and even some problems with cars, kind of like you had. You ever think you might have a problem?"

As it turns out, she doesn't think so. She doesn't think so at all. Minutes later, she climbs out of the tub and marches to her room. I wonder whether I should blame the yoga or the ineffably beautiful sky or maybe my psychic psychotherapist.

At the next evening's sing-along, when Laura sobs during "You've Got a Friend," I put my arm around her and pat her back. When Scott asks whether he should agree to an interview about his art with a reporter in his hometown, I advise him to be careful. When Wendy tells me that "understanding past lives can help us heal our present ones," I don't run away screaming. The human being trick is starting to feel more human, less tricky. But will I be able to hold on to this newfound psychic equanimity away from daily yoga and mountain air? What will I do when I'm separated from these brave and few global fitness adventurers, when I'm thrust back into the midst of eight million or so brutes hell-bent on butting in front of me in bookstores, nabbing my seat in movie theaters, denying me ice cream, and otherwise violating the space that belongs to me and my earth suit?

The next morning, Kristina tells me the answer. "Don't operate out of fear," she says, "always go for how the spirit feels."

In a few hours, we will be driven to the airport, from which we will fly to our daily lives, our crowded movie theaters, our traffic jams, our dyspeptic ice cream countermen. But for now, Kristina tells us in the sun-drenched living room of the ranch house, for now and forever, we are all fish on God's hooks, and he is reeling us in. She actually says this. "You are all fish on God's hooks, and he is reeling you in." And if we fight, Kristina warns us, or swim away from God or the spirit, after a while, he will let us go, and that will not be good.

I consider life as a giant tuna, ferocious but obedient. I nudge Laura, whom I can't help but notice has dropped about five pounds and whose earth suit is looking kind of fetching. "Why's God such a lazy fisherman?" I whisper.

"You asshole," she hisses back. "Aren't you ever going to get it?"

In California, I am a giant porcupine. I make porcupine noises, scrabble in the dirt with my porcupine head, try to ignore my chafed knees and sore palms. I miss my inner tuna.

"Be your animal," a skinny guy in shorts tells me. "Feel what he is feeling."

The skinny guy is the founder of Hero-Quest, the wilderness encounter group, my second stop on the road to enlightenment. His name is Josh. Me, I have no name. I am nothing but a proud porcupine, self-sufficient but cheerful and amusing among my own kind; slow to anger but fearsome when provoked; willing to let bygones be bygones; but woe to the miserable canine stupid enough to fuck with me. I'm a spunky porcupine and inquisitive too, so I check out the scenery. I spot humans.

There, flapping her arms and pretending to be an eagle, is Rae, who is in her forties and who has said she "needs to let go of things." She's already let go of a considerable amount of money by attending EST, the Forum, Lifespring, and many other human potential groups. "I've already let go of so much," she told me earlier in the day, before I became a porcupine. "I don't have a job, I don't have a home, I left my husband and kids. All I have right now is my car and some bedroom furniture. I don't know how much more I can let go of."

And there, hugging a tree, impersonating a bear, is Moe, also in his forties, an independently wealthy engineer who thinks he's a failure because, after devoting much of his life to work, his marriage ended in divorce. And there, balanced on one leg—a flamingo, perhaps?—stands Carrie, a quiet woman with a gentle manner, who works in public relations but wants out. Five years earlier, she did every single exercise in *What Color Is Your Parachute?*, but failed to come up with any satisfying answers. And there, neighing and pawing the dirt, is Mary, a young filly with great legs and big white teeth.

I am crawling toward her, fully prepared to violate the age-old porcupine taboo against equine love, when Josh tells us to resume our human identities. Then he tells us to assume the role of childhood heroes, and presto, I'm the Silver Surfer. Later, Josh instructs us to transmute ourselves into famous historical lovers and people who irrevocably changed our lives and then into characters in self-invented narratives. So I spend the afternoon as King David and my junior high school English teacher with a taste for literature and young boys and the steely-jawed protagonist of the popular TV series *Lois and Steve.* I am resilient, resourceful and complicated, fearless and afraid, giving, dedicated and risk-taking, loyal, steadfast, true, and strong, though not always understood or appreciated.

These roles and the insights we gain from these exercises will help, Josh has promised in the letter we all received, on the "journey to discover your higher purpose—the contribution that you were born to make and that only you can make. After your trials and ordeals, you will bring back a gift—your higher purpose—to mankind. It is this higher purpose that will add meaning to your life."

After dinner, still in human form, we drive to a nearby hot spring. There, at the base of granite cliffs, next to a frigid river, beneath a canopy of brilliant stars, Mary, my favorite filly, leans against me and asks if I will rub her back. I remember the lessons of Colorado and the Jacuzzi. I rub, but at arm's length. She whispers that she was cold the night before. Is this a trial, an ordeal, or—oh, please, spirit master—my higher purpose? I invite her to share my tent. Later, as she nestles beside me, and the wind whistles outside, I nuzzle her back, porcupine-like. She tells me she is married.

The next day, we Hero-Questers discuss life themes, heroic qualities, and the things that are keeping us from achieving our most worthy dreams. The group decides that fear is a big impediment. I wonder if Mary's husband is big. Or jealous. Or violent. We all agree that we should try to be braver.

That evening, back in the tent, after dinner and desserts and more hot spring, perhaps emboldened by the day's activities, I nuzzle Mary again. She moans, tells me that her knees are shaking and that "you make me feel like a teenager." I consider that, chronologically speaking, she's really not too far removed from that state. I rub her neck some more.

She pushes me away, but gently. "You have to be brave," she says, "for both of us."

During the next couple days we talk about living better lives and discuss the excuses we make not to live those lives. Whenever we see a particularly beautiful sight, Josh says, "That's God," which really gets on my nerves. The moon rises. "That's God," Josh says. An owl takes flight. "That's God," Josh says.

On our last night together in the tent, I try to kiss Mary's neck, and she pushes me away. "But that's God," I insist. It gets a laugh but no action.

Finally, I am not an animal! During my one-on-one session with a personal transformation therapist at Canyon Ranch Spa, in the Berkshires of Massachusetts, I am merely another screwed-up human being. The therapist asks what I'm seeking. Peace of mind, I tell her. A sense that I'm connected to a universe outside myself. Focus, energy, a feeling that my life has meaning. The usual.

"Don't pathologize your anxiety," she advises. "If you're at all creative, of course, you're somewhat tense." Regarding the vicious canine nightmares, as well as frequent feelings of guilt and nervousness, she adds, "They come with the territory."

That makes me feel better. Reassured, I skip yoga the next morning to sleep late. I play hooky from tai chi to get a massage. Afterward, I decide that *GQ* readers should explore the healing benefits of Asian tea leaf steam baths and sea-salt body rubs, so I get one of each and bill the magazine.

I duck out of the breathing and meditation class so I can chat up a leggy physical therapist whom I invite to shoot baskets with me in the gym. Later, we take a walk in the woods, and then, because I want to check out the middle-aged widows and divorcees who will doubtless be there, we attend a grieving, loving, and living session, which I know will make good copy. And that's where—sitting with the physical therapist and nine other women, paying attention to their plump toes and sad eyes, thinking about how I will describe them, listening to the Canyon Ranch therapist tell us all to "say good-bye to someone we wish we could have had more time with"—I begin to shake.

I never saw Elaine after the night we shared chicken sandwiches. I never even talked to her again. I asked my dad a few times if I should fly back, and when he said no, that I needed to concentrate on my new job, on my career, I was enormously relieved.

I think of Elaine now, with her white Beatles boots and her white fingernails holding hair clippers and chicken sandwiches and gifts all her stepchildren rolled their eyes at, and I try to be dignified, to hold it in, but I can't. I convulse and blubber. I see the women looking at with me affection, and that makes me weep even more, and I close my eyes in shame. I try to concentrate on my breathing, and I feel something on my back. A hand. Then another on my head. And another on my back. And one on my arm. The women have gathered around me, these unknowing targets of my ugly wit, and they are all touching me, and that makes me cry even harder.

I drive back to the city the next morning and, after dropping off the rental car, head straight to the office. The traffic noise and honking, which usually makes me fantasize about shattering windshields with a baseball bat, today sounds like the lively and cheerful harmony of an enormous and chipper urban choral group. The people jostling me on the street—they are not my enemies, not would-be tormentors, just people, just people trying to get through the day, just people who have not enjoyed the organic, luxurious, nonpathologizing weekend I have just enjoyed. Art? The Man-Thing? To be such a bully, he must carry so much woe, so much terror. I will try to understand and accept his weakness. The Queen of Mean? Can I even begin to understand the loneliness that drives her, the bleakness of the Minnesota plains from whence she sprang? I have lunch with Robyn, one of the shiny-haired PR gals. She tells me that she feels stuck at work, that she deserves a VP job, but that her boss is sabotaging her.

"Instead of being ruled by fear," I tell her, "you should follow your spirit."

"You are really a pain in the ass," she says.

I chuckle, but it is pity I feel. My friend and occasional sexual partner is self-involved, wedded to her earthly problems, hopelessly stuck in her woefully three-dimensional earth suit. I, on the other hand, am doing my best to expand. That afternoon I spend a few minutes pondering my higher purpose. When I'm ready to mock or judge, I take a deep breath first. Instead of moving copy about ingrown facial hair and the shaving technology necessary to combat it, I imagine what kind of animal Lisa would be if she were an animal. I decide on killer whale, in captivity, slowly dying inside as she longs for the choppy waves and tasty mackerel of the Bering Sea. I get misty-eyed thinking of Lisa as a solitary swimming SeaWorld mammal.

I walk home and admire the long shadows of midtown. I stop in a bookstore and leaf through "The Road Less Traveled." So easy to mock, but there are some profound truths in its pages. I see the guy who yells, "Yo yo yo," outside my apartment at 2:00 AM every day, sitting on a piece of cardboard, and I smile and say hello, and he snarls at me.

Upstairs, I pour myself a glass of water. I had forgotten how brown it was. I sit down on the coach to do some breathing exercises.

I am in the moment, I think.

The phone rings. It's my father. I see Elaine again.

"How was the spa?" he asks.

"Good, Dad, good." A family of roaches scuttles across the floor.

"Did you have a good time?"

"Um, yeah. It was good."

I can't tell him about my encounter with Elaine's ghost. I have never been adept at sharing sadness or grief with my father.

"Are you going to get a good story out of it?"

"I hope so. How are you doing, Dad?"

"I'm okay," he says. "I'm playing golf."

"That's good. Are you still getting dizzy?"

"Yeah, but the doctor says I shouldn't worry too much. I wish it were him fainting, then I could tell him not to worry."

My father has always had a distrust of doctors. Since Elaine, he hates them.

"Yeah, well."

"Are you still eating at the Four Seasons every week with Art?"

I had told my father after my first hopeful week on the job that it was a rite of passage for Art to take new editors to his leather banquette, and when, a month later, my father asked about it, I couldn't bear for him to think I hadn't been deemed worthy. I told myself at the time it was because Elaine was so near death and I wanted to spare my father the woe of a professionally shunned son. Maybe it was just embarrassment. But I couldn't figure out a way to back off the lie, so I kept expanding it. Now, as far as my father knows, I'm feasting on foie gras and pasta with black truffle oil every Thursday afternoon.

"Yeah, Dad, pretty much."

"That's a pretty good life you have there, Steve, with truffles and spas. A pretty good life."

"Uh-huh. Yeah, it's pretty good. It's going pretty good."

Silence, then. What does my father hear when I speak?

"Well," my father says.

"Well."

"Good luck with your story. And tell Art your father wishes he could eat at the Four Seasons sometime."

"Okay, Dad. I'll talk to you later."

"Bye."

I hang up and take a gulp of the brown water, and when I put the glass on my desk, I see something tiny and black swimming in the bottom. At the same instant, more roaches scuttle across the floor.

"Be in the moment," I say out loud, an instant before I fling my glass at the wall, where it shatters.

The next day I call a realtor, and I tell her what I want. An apartment with clear tap water and no roaches. An apartment with a twenty-four-hour doorman and views of the Hudson River and the putatively peaceful hills of New Jersey beyond. An apartment with high ceilings and no visible families of insects. An apartment that some of the PR women might visit without wrinkling their noses in disgust upon entering. An apartment where I can eat healthy foods and where my earth suit and I can live in some peace and happiness. An apartment befitting a *GQ* senior editor.

I call my father with the good news.

"How much?" he says, and I tell him.

"That's more than half your monthly pay," he says. "That's craziness."

"Yeah, but, Dad, in New York City, most people pay—"

"Are you sure you're happy there?" my father asks. "Are you sure you're making the right move?"

"Um," I say. "Um."

CHAPTER 7

LOOKING FOR MRS. FRIEDMAN AND OTHER

REALLY BAD IDEAS

It is a simple plan. "It might sound sleazy," Denny says, "but it's not."

Denny is now my best friend, and it's his plan. These days Denny is, in addition to producing, giving voice lessons to a dental hygienist he met in a grocery store who aspires to be an opera singer. In exchange for the lessons, she gives him blow jobs. Denny's thinking always fascinates me, so I listen.

"The plan is foolproof," Denny says, "and it's only wrong if you think it's wrong."

"Uh-huh," I say.

"First we take out an ad in *Back Stage*," Denny says. "Showgirls always read *Back Stage*. Just a little ad. 'Looking for actresses/singers, twenty-two to twenty-nine, over five foot six, bring head shot.' And we give an address and a time."

"We?" I think. "Uh-huh," I say.

"We rent out a place somewhere in the theater district for one or two afternoons. Dingy is okay. We borrow a card table, some folding chairs. It makes it feel legit, kind of off Broadway. Actresses like that."

"Uh-huh."

"So there we are, behind the card table, and we get seventy or eighty showgirls coming in. Tall young showgirls. We take the head shots. Maybe we have 'em sing a song or read a scene or something. They want to express themselves, be artistic. Maybe you take notes or something."

"Uh-huh."

"Then we split 'em up, the head shots. We go back to my place, order some chinese, and go through the pictures. First cut. You take twenty; I take twenty. Then we call 'em. Say, 'Susie? This is one of the producers of the show you auditioned for yesterday. Look, we're still working on the financing, and it's not coming together as quickly as we'd hoped, but in the meantime, I was wondering if you'd like to have dinner with me.'"

"No," I say. "No way anyone will buy that."

"No way *most* anyone will buy that," Denny says. "No way nine out of ten people will buy that. But even that means each of us gets dates with two beautiful young showgirls.

"And these are girls who are very naive. Either that or they're willing to do what they need to do to get a role. It's a simple plan. Foolproof. We just have to work the numbers."

That night, finishing off the ad and a pepperoni pizza in my new insectless apartment with clear tap water, where I moved shortly after my not-entirely-successful quest for spiritual fitness, I decide that what I really need is a wife. Partly because I want children. Partly because I'm aware of the studies showing that married men live longer. Partly because my great-grandmother warned me years ago that "kissing fades, but cooking lasts," and after two decades of serial girlfriends and way too much pizza, I realize I've been starving.

Mostly, though, it's because when I take a break from polishing the line about head shots (I can't decide between "Bring photograph" and "Photo a must"), what I see in the living room mirror terrifies me: a forty-two-year-old bachelor whose most recent bedmate called him "dude," a would-be writer who pimped eyedrops for sex, a man who pretends he is seeking brutal big truths while groveling for massages and free gym memberships, a seedy middle-aged coconspirator in a pitiable and possibly illegal fraud.

I should be beyond this. I have been in the city almost five years now, and I want to be beyond this. I think of Denny and the hygienist-soprano. I *must* get beyond this.

So I come up with a plan. "The Plan" is how I think of it, not to be confused with Denny's plan or other similarly repugnant schemes. Here's how the Plan will work: I will identify a target demographic. Literate, childless, sexually desirable, trusting and optimistic, interesting job, somewhat ambitious, kind, understanding are my starting points, though not necessarily in that order. Also, I want kids. This cuts off women older than about thirty-five.

I will search for the future Mrs. Friedman in bars, at clubs, on the Internet, down memory lane (I'll call some old girlfriends, in case they're still available), and in my heart. Blind dates will be accepted. Attractive strangers will be approached. Meals will be purchased, bon mots proffered, confidences exchanged. Sex, I hope, will be had. But it will be had only as part of the process, an integral element of the Plan, not as an end unto itself.

I will be confident and selective but realistic about my market value. Consequently, the Plan demands that I approach my search for a wife in much the same way I might approach the quest for a new job. So I vow to be polite. To return calls promptly. To shave and dress nice.

Eventually, after the requisite paperwork and civil or religious ceremony, depending, I will impregnate the successful candidate, and we will live happily. Forever would be nice, but who knows?

I meet Candidate Number 1 in line at a late movie on Sunday evening. I can't help thinking that only a certain type of woman would be attending an eleven o' clock screening on a Sunday night, alone, much less talking to and sharing popcorn with a strange man. I figure such a woman is confident, open to the mystery and magic of life, and so rich and/or bohemian that she would have few hang-ups about supporting a man while he works on artistically challenging but commercially uncertain ventures.

Harriet is almost twenty years younger than I am, and she's from the Midwest, which on the trusting and optimistic index is good. She has until recently been dating a drummer in a rock-and-roll band, which I take to mean that she's highly tolerant of philandering louts, which is valuable information.

She is a dancer. She writes in her spare time, which might eventually prove threatening, but why worry about the future? She is a waitress too, and I have always been partial to women who bring me food and carry large wads of small bills.

On our second date, I learn that her father taught high school math for years before ditching the job to become a golf pro. I consider my heirs, scholar-athletes, powerhouse combinations of brains and athletic prowess.

On our third date, over cheesecake, she tells me, in a dreamy voice, "Sometimes on Sunday mornings, I think how great it would be to have a boyfriend. Sharing a coffee. Holding hands. Walking the dog."

"Yeah" I say, and I reflect upon, I must admit, the Saturday nights that inevitably precede those Sunday mornings as the rain precedes the flowers, as the acorn precedes the mighty oak, as the—

"But then," she says, interrupting my religio-sexual musings, "I think of his hands around my neck, choking the life out of me, squeezing my life force, killing my self, sucking my chi, and I see what love really is."

On our fourth date, she says, "Sometimes I think you're just looking for someone who's gymnastic in bed and inventive in the kitchen and has a twenty-four-year-old body."

"But . . . ," I say.

"I'm all three of those things," she says, "and they're really not that important."

On our fifth date, she says, "I think we'd be better off as just friends."

"Why did you put up with her for as long as you did?" Bridget asks me at dinner one night. Bridget lives across the hall from Denny, who has invited her along this evening. Bridget is thirty-six, the mother of a three-year-old boy, and in the midst of a divorce from her husband of eleven years.

When I'm with Denny, I feel better about myself, even though he's been sulking since I backed out of the *Back Stage* scheme. Bridget's life also seems more screwed up than mine, which is reassuring.

"She was pretty. And she seemed nice." I don't mention Harriet's long legs or alleged gymnastic talents. I have learned that even the most empathic women have a hard time understanding such things. And Bridget, pushing forty and facing life as a single mother, shows no indication of being particularly empathic.

Bridget shakes her head and laughs. It is a raspy sound.

"She's a little snot who has admitted that love frightens her, that you don't interest her, and that men in general are disgusting playthings. Why are you pursuing her?"

I don't have a ready response, so I give my standby.

"That's what my therapist asks me. I dunno."

Denny, who has been ogling a waitress, turns to us.

"Has your therapist seen Harriet in a miniskirt?"

Candidate Number 2 is sitting next to me on a flight from Salt Lake City to New York City. She is returning from the Sundance Film Festival. Her eyes are as green as a lime Popsicle. Her hair is the burnt orange of an autumnal maple leaf. Also, her T-shirt is tight, and she says "fucking" a lot.

"The film festival has become one big fucking celebration of hip wannabes who are really nothing more than fucking bourgeois yuppie stroller lovers who think that art means quick cutting and fucking feeling good," she says.

"Fucking-A," I say.

I get her number. We go out for dinner in New York. I learn that she has lived with seven men. She is thirty-two.

We go to a movie. She mentions that she's engaged but that she recently discovered her fiancé is still married. I wonder, not for the first time, why so many young married or about-to-be married women in Manhattan seem so available.

I suggest that we should not date anymore, at least until she and her fiancé are no longer engaged and/or living together. I have learned something from Susan.

"You're a fucking control freak," she says.

A week later, after she and the married fiancé have split up, we meet.

At the end of the evening, I move to kiss her. "What the fuck are you doing?" she asks.

"Er, trying to kiss you?"

"Do I look like a toy?" she asks.

I wonder if this is a trick question. I shake my head.

Two minutes later, she says, "I really want to fucking kiss you."

The next night, we are walking down a street in Greenwich Village. I take her hand.

"For fuck's sake," she says, "what are you trying to do?

"Hold your hand?" I venture. Softly. Cautiously.

"Do you ever think about what I want?" she demands.

"Of course, I do. But I thought, you know, it might be okay to hold hands walking down the street."

"You're so fucking bourgeois."

"What took you so long to dump her?" Bridget asks me.

"She seemed interesting?" It comes out as a question.

"Interesting?" Bridget repeats. Lately she has been referring to Danny and me as "you two children." This is because, I'm convinced, Denny's latest scheme involves telling his girlfriend he's out of town (are all twenty-three-year-olds so credulous?) and offering waitresses money to have sex with him.

"Do you have a thing for lunatic women?" Bridget asks me. "Or are you just an idiot?"

We are at Bridget's apartment, Denny and Bridget and I. The three of us have been spending a lot of time together, lamenting about our respective love lives, if they can be called that.

"What's wrong," Denny wants to know, "with saying to a waitress, 'How much do you make on your shift?' then offering her $50 more to give me a full-body massage?"

"Why don't you just hire a hooker?" Bridget asks.

"What kind of person do you think I am?" Denny demands.

"I think you're the kind of person who wants to pay waitresses for hand jobs," Bridget says. "You're just a little more honest about your emotional life than Mr. I Want a Wife here."

I make a mental note to tell Denny that he and I should really spend more time together without Bridget.

Our discussion is interrupted by pounding and yelling. Bridget's three-year-old son has waddled into the living room, where he pounds on the floor with one of his plastic dinosaurs and screams, "Goo!" For reasons that mystify his doctors and teachers, the little boy barely speaks. Other than an occasional "bye-bye," the only sound he utters is "goo," which is shorthand for juice, which he sucks down from four-ounce paper cartons. Woe to anyone who doesn't give the kid goo when he demands it. He is demanding it now.

Bridget laughs and walks into the kitchen. The kid evidently thinks the whole thing is rather amusing, so he laughs too.

"Shut up," Denny says, which just makes the kid laugh more.

Then I laugh. I love to tousle the little fellow's hair. He quits laughing and starts screaming.

"No," I say. "It's okay, Milo. It's okay." "Milo" is the kid's name.

"Blaieee!" Milo screams. "Fleeeoooo!"

"Shhh. Goo is coming," I say. "Mommy's bringing goo."

"Blaieee!" Fleeooooo!"

"Will you please shut him the fuck up?" Denny says, which makes Milo cry.

I move to hold the child, to comfort him.

Milo stops crying and slaps my wrist.

"Sittu," he shouts. Then he points at the couch on the other side of the room. "Sittu."

It's a new one, but I get the point. I retreat to the couch while Milo stares at me through narrow distrusting eyes. Together, Milo and Denny and I wait for Bridget to bring the goo.

Maybe the Plan will work just as well without children.

Candidate Number 3 is a television producer with a trust fund, who says, "I'm sorry, I just don't have any patience for people on welfare. Don't they know how to take responsibility for themselves?"

Candidate Number 4 is a blind date. "I'm sick of men who are afraid of commitment," she tells me five minutes after we sit down. "I'm just not going to allow men like that to hurt me anymore."

Number 5 is married and has not had sex with her husband in three months.

"He doesn't take anything I say seriously," she tells me over cappuccino after a late lunch. "It's like he thinks I'm stupid or something."

I tell her I don't think she's stupid. And it must be awful to live with someone and not have sex for three months. I frown, while crinkling the corners of my eyes. I read in a book once that this sends the message that the crinkler is warm and accepting. I murmur the phrase "horribly lonely." I sip my cappuccino, hoping that she will put my sentences together, consider my crinkled eyes and sympathetic frown, and arrive at the appropriate conclusion. To help, I take her hand. She begins to cry. This is not what I intended, but who am I to judge? "Do you want to come up to my place and have some tea?" I ask. "It can be very calming."

Two hours later, walking her to a taxi, I ask why she doesn't just leave her husband.

"You're so naive," she says and, to my horror, actually chuckles. She pats my arm. Then she puts two fingers in her mouth and whistles.

Psychic Rose tells me I need to come to grips with what she calls my "free-floating hostility" toward women. The Queen of Mean orders me to "grow up." An old friend from college suggests "figuring out what you want." And more than a couple of relatives tell me to "quit being so picky."

Only Denny wraps his wisdom in a Zen koan.

"How do you think a waitress would feel," he asks as we shoot baskets one afternoon, "if I offered her $50 to blow me?"

"Degraded?" I suggest. "Dehumanized? Objectified? Pissed off?"

"You and your cold Midwestern logic," Denny says. "That's your problem. Why can't you ever loosen up, stop thinking? Why can't you just live for a change?"

Number 6 is sort of chunky. Number 7 is a lesbian. For Number 8, I call the woman from the flight, the redhead with the tight T-shirt who says "fucking" all the time. Maybe I *was* a little bourgeois. Is hand holding really that important? I decide it's time for me to just live for a change.

When she arrives at my apartment, I offer her a glass of nice, clear water. Or maybe she would like some ice cream? As a teetotaling bachelor, these are my staples.

She declines, then chooses the seat across the room, farthest from me, and glowers. Is anything wrong? I ask.

"You're in your forties, and you've never been married," she says. "Do you have any fucking idea how fucked up that is?"

I feel a chill. A cold Midwestern chill.

"Actually," I say, "I do have some idea. It's probably in the same place on the fucked-up spectrum as being thirty-two and having lived with seven guys, including a fiancé who was still married."

"So fucking funny. So fucking, fucking funny."

"Look," I lie. "I'm not making any judgments, but—"

"You think you know me?" she asks. "You think you fucking *know* me?"

Before I can formulate a firm but nonthreatening answer, there are a few more things she'd like to know.

"You invite me to your apartment, and you offer me ice cream or water? What the fuck is the matter with you? Who the fuck are you?"

Candidate Number 9 is in her twenties, an aspiring journalist. Tight black dress. Stiletto heels. Maybe just a little too much perfume. I take her for fancy Italian. Deep eye contact. Inviting smile. "Can you introduce me to some editors?" she asks.

For Candidate Number 10, I accept Denny's suggestion, with hope and just a little self-loathing. She's a Russian dancer and a friend of the singing hygienist. I suggest lunch. She would really rather have dinner. "At a nice place, please. And please, you will pick me up at eight, in nice car."

When I get home that night, I log on to the Internet and track down a Texas-born radiologist to whom I had proposed the day I quit drinking. She lives in California, practices medicine with a private group. I remember her kind eyes. I figure she's netting about three hundred grand a year. She baked excellent Toll House cookies, as I recall. I punch her phone number. It's been more than a decade. Is it anyone's fault that my proposal came from a hospital rehab center pay phone?

She's happy to hear from me, I think. After a few minutes of catching up, there is a pause. It seems to me a happy, hopeful pause.

"Can I ask you a question?" she asks.

"Sure," I say. I close my eyes and wait. I can see my future life in the Golden State. Five years has been enough. Settling my accounts in New York should take only a few weeks. The radiologist probably has a nice place already, so we'll live there. Less pizza for me. More hand holding. A couple of kids. I'll work on my novel, and I'll stuff it with brutal big truths. But redemption too. Lots of redemption.

There is noise on the phone.

"Huh?" I say.

"I *said*," the radiologist says, "why are you calling me?"

Sometimes I feel like the only one who understands me is Milo, with whom I now spend Wednesday nights, which is when his mother goes on dates with investment bankers. Tonight a hedge fund manager is taking her for dinner downtown.

"He's kind of shallow, but entertaining," she says as she checks her lipstick in the mirror. "But a girl's gotta get out. Don't wait up."

Milo still doesn't talk much. And every time I try to engage him in some friendly banter (usually with bribes of stuffed animals or food or by patting his head, which if he'd just stop his damn screaming and let me do it, I'm sure he'd get used to), he raises his hand and points to the couch. He has graduated from "sittu" to "sittin'." He has also added "see you" to "bye-bye." He continues to drink freakish amounts of goo, which he now calls "jew." He counts. He likes to name his animals, repeatedly. Tonight he said "cow" fifty-seven times in a row. I keep track, because I have nothing better to do, and I figure if I ever am going to have kids of my own, I should bone up on the behavior of children, even weird ones like Milo.

I'm trying to read a detective novel when something hits me in the head. It's one of Milo's cartons. He has flung it across the room, and he is stamping his feet and chortling.

"Bye-bye, jew," he cries, delighted. "See you."

This unsettles me a little bit.

"No, I'm not gonna fix you up with anyone," a former girlfriend (not April) from St. Louis tells me. "Do you really think I hate any woman that much?"

"Maybe you don't really want to get married," Rose tells me and then adds, "and there's nothing wrong with that." Is it my imagination or has the good doctor dropped a few pounds? She is looking very fetching lately.

"Accept it," Bridget tells me. "You're nothing but a pathetic old bachelor."

"Pig!" Milo chimes in. "Pig! Pig! Pig!" He is deep into the animal-naming phase. Whenever I'm around, he seems to focus on the porkers. I try not to take it personally.

Even Denny is of little aid.

"We want women in their twenties, because they're cute and frisky and smell good," Denny says. "But we're not into the same things that a twenty-five-year-old is. I mean, hell, they want to get up on Saturday mornings and go to the museums. We've *been* to the museums."

Why is the Plan not working? It can't be because of flawed methodology. Are my motives impure? Am I seeking a wife only because I fear bachelorhood? I tell myself my longing is for true love, but maybe I'm just trying to establish a cagey negotiating stance with a grim and not altogether secure future. Can't I be single and not devolve into Denny?

I resolve to quit looking for Mrs. Friedman, to spend more time looking for myself. Maybe that's what I should have been doing all along. I spend a couple of weeks looking. They are very long weeks.

"Jew!" I hear through layers of sleep. "Jew!"

Something is tugging at my head. Or am I dreaming? I open my eyes. Attached to my ear is a meaty, sweaty little fist. Attached to the fist is Milo.

"Jew!" he hisses. "Jew!"

"Shhhhh," I tell him. Next to me, sleeping still, is Bridget, whose raspy laugh I am still getting used to, after nearly four months.

"Jew!" Milo insists, louder. And then, when I move a little too slowly, he adds, "Sittin', jew."

So I sit, then get out of bed, and walk with Milo into the kitchen, where I fix the kid some juice.

Later on, after Bridget wakes up, after Milo names all his animals four hundred or five hundred times, maybe we'll all go for a walk in Central Park or look at the dinosaurs in the Museum of Natural History. Bridget and I will hold hands. Milo will no doubt scream for more jew, which probably will alarm passersby.

And after that, I'm not sure. My plan hasn't worked out quite like I thought it would. None of my plans have.

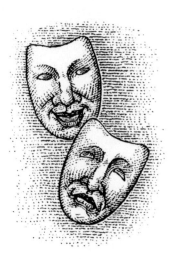

CHAPTER 8

YOU GET WHAT YOU GET

Playing father is fun. I growl at Milo until he laughs, and I wrestle with him on Bridget's bed while she orders us Chan-Do chicken and steamed vegetable dumplings from Shun Lee Café and bustles about in the kitchen and screams at one of her three sisters on the phone. When the Chinese deliveryman arrives and we sit down to eat, Bridget tells Milo and me what she's been screaming about. One of her sisters sleeps till 2:00 PM every day, hasn't held a job in five years, and for most of that time has been working on her taxes for the year she *did* have a job. Bridget tells me that Ruth—the sister—is angry that I am with Bridget, because Ruth believes that Bridget drinks too much and sleeps around and is an amoral slut and that Ruth is the one who deserves love. Another sister majored in women's studies at Wesleyan and spent the summer between her junior and senior years in Texas stripping. She says it was "empowering." She is Bridget's mother's favorite. Leah, the feminist stripper, who is also the youngest of the Johnson sisters, has bounced for the past few years between progressive political campaigns,

111

an organic farm in Upstate New York, and an experimental lesbian dance troupe, and has borrowed more than $100,000 from Bridget, whose husband (they're separated but haven't even started divorce proceedings) is a hedge fund manager. "And," says Bridget, "the little slut tells me *I'm* irresponsible with money!" The only sister who doesn't call her siblings sluts is Lulu, at forty-seven the oldest. Lulu is married to an accountant and expresses disapproval by pursing her lips and sighing. Behind her back, Bridget and Leah refer to their oldest sister as the Little General.

I like hearing about the crazy sisters. I like Bridget's raspy laughter. I like dipping my pork dumplings into sweet sauce and listening to tales of the Johnson matriarch, whose response to all woe, no matter how niggling or vast, is, "You get what you get!" When Ruth got fired from her last and long-ago job because of her sleeping habits and was crying over the fact that her whore of a sister was sleeping with the guy who should have been hers, Mrs. Johnson told her, "You get what you get!" When a neighbor child who lived down the street in the small town where the Johnson girls grew up was kidnapped when Bridget was seven, and Bridget cried about it at dinner the next evening, same thing. "You get what you get!" I like that kind of granite, if unhinged, stoicism, especially compared to the quiet melancholy and sour, impotent rage at which I'm expert.

What I like best of all is the way women look at me when I hold Milo's hand walking down Broadway while Bridget is straightening up her apartment and yelling at her sisters on the phone. They are looks ripe with admiration and longing—why can't the men in their lives be as kind to children as this man?—and sometimes I imagine myself in a J. Crew catalog, wearing a powder blue V-neck sweater and creased pants that stay sharp even as Milo is tugging at them with his sweaty little paws. Because I am heavily invested in the ripe looks, sometimes I bend down to whisper something fatherly and bighearted to my fake son.

"This is the boulevard of broken dreams, Milo," I say. And he looks at me with bewilderment and yells "Teeb," which, I think, the women like. I am such a good-hearted, child-friendly broad-shouldered pretend Daddy, and I spend so much time seeing myself through other women's eyes and conjuring up visions of my miracle crease pants that it takes me awhile to notice some troubling little things around the apartment.

For example, Bridget's yelling and screaming on the phone seems to get louder and more slurred the later in the day it gets, and for all the many, many hours she spends straightening up her apartment, there always seem to be chunks of old cheese left out in the kitchen, piles of sweatshirts on the living room floor. For another example, even though Milo is now four years old, he still hardly talks, is prone to tantrums, and insists on calling me "Teeb" or "Jew." He spends most of his time watching *Tom and Jerry* cartoons on a television that Bridget has set up in his bedroom because "it's the only way he'll go to sleep." He also likes Animal Planet, especially when it shows programs involving animals eating other animals. We watch Animal Planet together. When we're not watching television, I growl and make faces and chase Milo around the apartment. One night, playing monster, I slip and find myself prone on his bedroom floor. That's when I spot the pile of moldy spareribs underneath his bed.

"I found a bunch of spareribs underneath Milo's bed," I tell Bridget after she hangs up from Shun Lee. I figure it's best to be straightforward about things like this. I don't mention the mold.

"You want to clean my apartment, be my guest," Bridget says.

"No, I didn't mean—"

"Why is it that every person I know feels perfectly entitled to judge me and the way I live?"

"I'm not judging, I just thought you would want to know about the spareribs."

"Fuck you!" Bridget screams. "Fuck you and your cold Midwestern logic!"

Has she been talking to Denny? What is it with New Yorkers and their trouble with logic? Isn't a pile of moldy pig meat underneath the bed of a four-year-old who still doesn't talk a cause for—if not alarm—at least a little bit of concern?

I tell Bridget I meant no offense. I'd like to report that I told her to treat herself to a massage at the health club down the street—on me—or to take a walk, that I would take care of dinner, and that I would get rid of the spareribs and mop Milo's floor, but that would be a lie.

"I'm sorry," I say. "I have no idea what your life must be on a daily basis. I'm just trying to get to know you, and Milo. Just tell me what I can do to help." As I say this, I'm thinking, *No cleaning, please, no cleaning, please, no cleaning, please.* I hate cleaning. I suspect I might be fundamentally lazy.

Bridget starts crying then—long, convulsive sobs. She pulls a bottle of wine from her purse and takes a long pull.

"Did you just pull a bottle of wine from your purse?"

"Shut up and come here," Bridget says, and I do.

It occurs to me, a few minutes later, that a real J. Crew daddy might feel some concern if he were having sex with his drunken girlfriend at 6:00 PM on a weekday night while twenty feet away and two closed doors away, her four-year-old son sat in bed eating a day-old pizza and screaming with delight at crocodiles chomping on helpless wildebeests on the television set his mother had set up against one wall, while underneath, like a vestigial prehistoric reproach, old spareribs lay moldering.

"Sweetie?" I whisper to my girlfriend, the mother of the boy I have come to love. We are in that happy postcoital place. Or at least I am. "Sweetie," I whisper again.

But Bridget is passed out. It is not yet dark. I clean up her kitchen. I remove the ribs from beneath Milo's bed, take the bottle from Bridget's purse, and while I'm at it, I snoop through the piles of mail stacked next to her telephone in the kitchen. There are dozens of unopened bills and bank statements and a letter from a doctor. I read it a few times, skim the "tests" and "therapies" and "diagnostic tools" and come back to the word. I peek into Milo's room, where he is gnawing on a pizza crust, chortling over the adventures of *Tom and Jerry*. Apparently, he has changed channels. I tousle his hair.

He laughs. "Teeb," he says.

"Show me which one is Tom," I say.

"Teeb!" Milo screams. He hits me in the arm and points to the floor, in the corner. "Sittin'! Jew!"

I sit and point again at the screen.

"Is the mouse Tom? Or is it the cat?"

"Teeb!" he screams again. "Teeb!"

It takes two hours to get Milo to go to sleep. Every time I turn off the television, he screams, so I let him keep it on. When he is breathing evenly, I turn out his light, check to make sure that Bridget is breathing, and let myself out the door.

The next evening, after a day editing a piece on hair gel—with sidebars on the best places in New York City to get combination haircuts / neck massages by women in negligees—I meet Denny for tuna burgers at Josie's, a restaurant that serves organic food and that employs attractive young waitresses who aspire to singing careers. Denny is trying to lose weight, and he can't afford the Peak Ten Fitness program I got for free. He doesn't think that's fair.

I tell him about the spareribs, the bills, the wine bottle in the purse. I tell him about Milo's diagnosis and *Tom and Jerry*. I tell him that Bridget seems in some jeopardy.

"It's because you don't love her enough."

"What?"

"All she wants is love. You need to love her more."

"Did you not hear what I said about the old spareribs and the bottle in the purse? Plus, I really don't think that Milo being autistic has anything to do with my love."

"You need to make a decision," the deranged bassist says. "Do you want a real woman, with real problems, and a real life?"

"Passing out in the afternoon isn't just real. It's drunk."

"Or do you want a cookie-cutter girlfriend to go with your cookie-cutter life?"

"I'm talking about a little boy eating pizza and watching cartoons while his mother has drunk herself into a stupor."

"It's your fault. She told me that you're not sure about her, that you never make her feel safe, that she's having a really hard time trusting you."

When had she told Denny all this? Why hadn't she told me? Was I missing not just secret drinking and hidden food caches but also some critical yearning at the emotional core of the person who had, over the course of the past few months, somehow morphed from Denny's fun, wisecracking, banker-dating single-mom pal into a potential Mrs. Friedman?

"Trusting me? Trusting *me*? She was the one dating a different banker every night. You're the guy tricking singers into blow jobs. How can you two be talking about *my* trustworthiness?"

I continue yelling. Yes, I had almost joined Denny in the card table scheme. And yes, Bridget had witnessed firsthand my long and determined search for Mrs. F, which had involved sex. But shouldn't my last-minute recusal from the "head shots a must" plot and my abandonment of the many possible Mrs. Fs for Bridget have been enough to persuade her that I was in it for the long haul?

I tell Denny as much.

"Hey," Denny says. "You're always looking for the next best thing. You're never satisfied. You think some imaginary love is going to save you, and you can't see that the greatest thing in the world is right in front of you. And she picks up that uncertainty, so she drinks."

"How's she picking up any uncertainty? I'm sleeping over there a few nights a week. I take Milo to see the dinosaurs. I even washed the dishes once."

"She's invited you up to the family farm for Thanksgiving, and you haven't committed yet. So she doesn't think you love her."

"What do you know about love?"

"I was married, *GQ*," he says. Denny knows how I hate it when he calls me *GQ*.

"You were married to a Danish grifter, and she needed a green card, and it lasted four months."

"She was an artist exploring postindustrial attitudes toward currency and wealth and—"

"Denny. She got busted trying to buy beer, with money she tried to make at Kinko's. She was a counterfeiter. And if you don't mind my saying, a monumentally stupid counterfeiter."

"Why do you always want to label everything? Why can't you just let yourself love? Why can't you surrender to love?"

These are legitimate questions—even if Denny is asking them—and I consider them as we chew on our tuna burgers. I would consider them more deeply if the man posing them wasn't at the moment chatting up our waitress/actress, who looks to be about twelve years old, asking if she has any head shots, promising her that he's very friendly with some very important producers, that he *hangs* with them, and that he'd be happy to make the appropriate introductions. Maybe, later on, after her shift, they could lay down a few tracks in his apartment.

I stare at my tuna burger, as if the fish might give up some answers to the questions plaguing me. Why am I listening to this guy? Why am I blaming myself for the spareribs underneath the bed and the wine bottle in the purse? Was it so wrong that I hadn't committed yet to Thanksgiving, even though it was only the end of October? Wasn't it better to be cautious? I had bought the lime green suit in an instant of impulse, and that hadn't worked out. I had courageously, spontaneously, expressed my bottomless, eternal love for Mary-Louise Parker, and that hadn't worked out either. True, my first half decade in the center of the publishing universe was drawing to a close, and none of my plans had come to fruition, including, apparently, the search for Mrs. F, so maybe I needed to adjust my approach. But wasn't it wiser to take things slowly, to trust in the universe, to have faith that as long as I wasn't overtly dishonest, or sleazy beyond measure, love would blossom, and then delight would bust out all over, like Kudzu was always busting out in the gothic Southern murder mysteries I'd lately taken to reading, to take my mind off my troubles? Wouldn't spending five days with my boozy girlfriend and her screaming kid and the entire clan of Johnsons—where little mishaps like kidnapped neighbor children were treated with "you get what you get"—represent an unacceptably risky move for someone with such a delicate constitution as yours truly? Wouldn't it be better, and wiser, to tell Bridget that I loved her, and her son, but that I needed to wait until we knew each other better before we spent such a long time together? I look again to my tuna burger for answers. Nothing. I take a bite. I regard Denny, who is scrawling something on a piece of paper for the poor, trusting, hapless soprano. I pity the spindly-legged, soft-eyed wildebeests delicately traipsing into the Namibian river, where Milo's favorite crocodiles lurk.

What had happened to my dreams of literary incandescence and transcendent love? Was I doomed to be forever assigning stories about flat abs and miracle razors, dating women who were married, or nuts, tossing aside partners who really could make me happy, like April the ophthalmologist? (We hadn't spoken in four years now.) Denny is no help. The tuna burger is useless, but tasty.

"This, too, shall pass," I mutter to myself. "This, too, shall pass." The waitress glances up from her tête-à-tête with Denny and looks at me. She gestures to a busboy, who refills my water glass.

I will be smart this time. I will be wise. I tell Denny I need to use the bathroom, and from the rear of the restaurant, I telephone Bridget, but she doesn't pick up. It is seven o'clock. I imagine her passed out on the couch, in the living room, clutching a bottle of wine. I imagine Milo crying in a corner, gnawing on old meat. I need to be prudent.

"I love you," I say after a beep. "I want to make you trust me. I'm in for Thanksgiving. I can't wait."

Something is terribly wrong. I've just woken from a dream of wildebeests wearing lime green suits and crocodiles who talk like ice cream vendors. I am sweating, and my stomach hurts. I hear birds, but no traffic, and no "yo yo yo." I smell something, and it's not car exhaust or spareribs. It's bacon and eggs. After some time in New York City, all this normalcy unsettles me. Then, from downstairs, voices. I turn toward Bridget, but she's not there. I throw on jeans and a sweatshirt, wander down the stairs of the Johnson family farmhouse, and there, in the living room, are Bridget and her sisters. It's Thanksgiving morning, and they're all in running clothes. Denny is there too.

We arrived yesterday afternoon—Bridget and Denny and me—just in time for dinner with the family. I had met Bridget's get-what-you-get mom, Glenda, who, in between milking cows and shoveling shit and cleaning five bedrooms, managed to make a dinner of fried chicken, hamburgers, lasagna, and salad. I had met the paterfamilias, Max, who had bellowed when the table was set.

"Goddamit, Glenda, why can't you ever get the meat and the chicken on the table at the same time?"

I chuckled, looked around the table for everyone else to acknowledge the joke. No one was laughing.

"I'm sorry, honey," Glenda yelled from the kitchen. "It's coming, it's coming."

"It wouldn't hurt you to lay off the chow, Dad," said Ruth, who, as it turns out, really does think Bridget is a slut. (She had told her so when we arrived. "I can't believe you got the good bedroom," Ruth said. "Especially considering all the guys you've brought up here before. Oh, hi, Steve.")

"Lay off your sister, Ruth," Ruth's father said. "She's been married and had a kid. I've got a wife. But you're still single. And unless you slim down a little and cheer up, you're going to stay that way."

I turned to Bridget. She smiled at me and raised her eyebrows.

And now it is morning, and Bridget and Ruth and Leah, whom Glenda likes best, and Lulu, the Little General, are getting ready for a family run. Denny too. I have nothing better to do, and Max and Glenda scare me, and I don't want Milo to wake and start screaming at me, so I shrug into gym shorts and join Denny and the Johnson women at their driveway. We head up into rolling hills and bursts of color.

"That was a good dinner last night," I say, about a quarter mile into the run. I always aspire to be a polite guest. "Your mom's a really good cook."

"She's a fucking slave," Ruth says. "I hate how she lets Dad order her around."

"Someone didn't get enough sleep last night," Leah says. And then she adds, "Oh, I forgot, Ruth, it's before noon. Of course, you're tired."

"How's the fake-lesbian ex-stripper lifestyle?" Ruth says.

"At least she's having sex with someone," Bridget chimes in.

"Will you guys stop!" That's Lulu, the Little General, keeping order.

"Hey, gals!" Denny says. "Let's play the Circle of Love game."

I'm not sure what alarms me more, Denny's use of the word "gals" or his weird-sounding game.

"Circle of Love?" I say.

"Yeah. Someone says someone's name, and that person named is in the circle of love. Then everyone has to go around and say three things they love about the person in the circle."

I suggest we start with Bridget. That seems like a good boyfriend move.

"Doesn't seem to be troubled with generally accepted notions of morality," Ruth says.

"C'mon, Ruth, be nice to your sister," I say.

"Can have sex with a bunch of guys at once and lie convincingly," Ruth continues.

"How are the taxes going, Sleepy?" Bridget says.

"Oh yeah, and number 3," Ruth adds, "doesn't let a little thing like motherhood interfere with her fun lifestyle!"

We jog—slowly—over plump, gentle hills, through shallow valleys where we can see our breaths. We all get turns in the circle of love, which seems to me more like a circle of resentment and vicious hatred, but with all the hilarity and laughing, I'm not sure. I throw in some sincere-sounding compliments for everyone. Ruth gets "faithful to a moral code," and Little General Lulu, "commanding." Leah is "spunky and not crushed by society's dictates," and Denny is "inventive." I lay it on thick for the woman I want to trust me. "Beautiful, funny, and generous," I say when Bridget is in the circle of love.

"How many girls have you told the same thing to?" Denny asks, and everyone but me laughs.

"Should we talk about your Fund for Starving Singers, fat boy?"

"Hey, *GQ*, I'm not the one who screwed a bunch of women and told them he was looking for a wife."

"That's when I was stupid and listening to you."

"What?"

"Before I surrendered to love."

That's a little much, even for me, but it seems to work. All the Johnson women look at me with moist eyes and something that resembles the admiring glances I get from the females on Broadway when I'm with Milo. The phrase "surrendering to love" seems to be just about as potent as a cute toddler when it comes to inspiring trust in women. That's good to know. What's better is how I actually believe what I'm saying. What's best is how it makes me feel. I'm with my girlfriend and her family and my friend, the deranged bassist, and I don't need to remind myself that it's a pleasant day. Because it actually *is* a pleasant day.

I don't know whether it's the fresh air or the humpy little hills. It's *more* than a pleasant day. Bridget is sober, and Milo is safe, and today is Thanksgiving, which will be cooked by Glenda, who, whether she's a slave or merely an old-fashioned, hardworking farm wife, will almost certainly be laying on quite a spread. And after dinner, Bridget and I will retire to the good bedroom, and we'll fall asleep holding hands, and in our dreams we'll float down humpy hills through happy valleys.

After the run, and after we all shower and gather in the living room for football on television and a light lunch, and after I play monster with Milo, Leah asks who wants to drive to the indoor tennis courts in Oneonta for some tennis.

The enthusiasm and exuberant joshing of the Johnson household has taken root, kudzulike, in my usually fearful and halting heart. I feel like part of the family.

"I'm in and I'll kick your ass!" I yell. "And I'll kick anyone else's ass who dares to step onto the court!"

Denny says he's going to stay at the house and play chess with Father Max. The Little General wants to help Glenda in the kitchen. Ruth hates tennis, and besides, she needs to take a nap.

"That leaves us, honey," I say to my girlfriend. "Grab some rackets and let's go show your little sister what grown-ups can do."

"I'm going to stay and help cook."

"C'mon, the Little General and your mom can handle it. Besides, you hate cooking."

"Oh, now I hate cooking? I'm a slob and unfit mother, and I hate cooking? Why are you with me at all? Why aren't you with someone *spunkier*?"

I have become expert at spotting trouble. This qualifies.

"Hey, you're the one I love, and you're the one I want to be with. I'll just stay here and help you guys out in the kitchen."

"Don't be silly. Go play tennis. Have a good time with the little communist."

Leah and I play two sets, and I do, indeed, kick her ass. She asks if I'd like to stop for coffee afterward, and even though there are soft, dull clanging alarms going off in my head, I agree. Leah doesn't have any obvious drinking problems. She smells like Bridget, which is nice, and doesn't yell at me about how I don't appreciate her, which is even nicer. After coffee, where I mostly ask about organic farming and the lifestyles of lesbian dance troupes, we drive back to the Johnson farmhouse where we find everyone, except Glenda and the Little General, sprawled in the living room. Denny and Max are playing chess, Milo is running around screaming, and Ruth and Bridget are yelling at each other about something.

"I kicked her ass," I announce as Leah and I enter the living room.

Silence.

"What's everyone been doing?" I ask.

"Just talking," Denny says. "Just talking about things."

I notice three empty wine bottles.

I walk into the kitchen, ask Glenda and the Little General if I can help with anything, and they say no; and the Little General makes the pursed-lips hissing sound, like I've done something wrong, which I try to ignore, because it seems so unfair.

"Just be at the table on time for dinner, Steve," Glenda says. I think these are the first words she has ever spoken to me.

I shower and shave, and since it's an hour till dinner, I crawl into our bed—I think of it as our bed now, my girlfriend's and my bed in the good room—and I call my father to wish him a happy Thanksgiving. I tell him I'm at my girlfriend's family's house, and that makes me triply happy, because I like the sound of the phrase "my girlfriend's family's house," and I like that it probably makes my dad feel better, because I know he worries about my inclination toward solitude and anxiety. And I like the dense, textured reality of staying at my girlfriend's family's house for a major American holiday. I like the swirling waves of decades-old family resentments and jealousies especially because they're someone else's family. I am moved by the stronger undercurrents of love. I like the smell of food and tennis with Leah and the prospect of sex after turkey with Bridget. I like it all. I tell my dad I love him, and he tells me he loves me, and after we say good-bye, I read a few pages of my kudzu-soaked thriller, and then Bridget walks into our bedroom.

"Get in bed," I say. "Grab a book and let's lie next to each other and read."

She grabs her book—it's *Captain Corelli's Mandolin*, which she's been reading since I met her five months earlier—and slips into bed, and we lie back to back, and everything should be great, but something doesn't feel so great. I'm not sure what, but the deathly bells are clanging again, not quite so softly this time. "Is everything okay, sweetie?" I ask.

She turns toward me. The phrase "purple with rage" occurs to me. I'd always thought it was just a figure of speech.

"If you are going to fuck my little sister," my girlfriend says, "at least have the decency not to do it in front of my entire family."

"What?"

"You heard me."

"We played tennis. You told me to go have a good time."

"You want to fuck her, fuck her. Just don't humiliate me."

"You're being insane. Really. This is ridiculous."

"Oh, really? I drink too much, and I'm a pig, and I'm not spunky. And now I'm insane? Then how come my mom said she noticed you looking at Leah? And how come Denny told me this afternoon when you and Leah went to play tennis that he'd seen you in action before, and this was exactly what you did when you were trying to get into a girl's pants."

"That's ridiculous. First of all, it's untrue. First and a half, you're making that up about your mother. She's not *that* insane. Second, there's no way Denny would say that, because it's untrue. Third, even if he did say it, you know about all the girls he pays for blow jobs. How can you believe someone like that?"

"He's honest with me. He never lies to me."

"I'm not ly—"

And then, a voice from below. A voice that, ordinarily, would be trumpeting the glories of professional football, togetherness, and the opportunity to obscenely overeat without censure, but that at the moment signals what I fear might be at best a temporary reprieve, at worse a descent into get-what-you-get terror. It's Glenda's voice, Judas as farm wife, tinny and swollen with false cheer.

"C'mon, kids. Thanksgiving dinner is ready!"

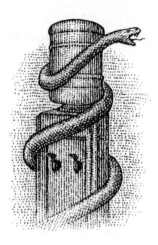

CHAPTER 9

"MAKE IT MEANER"

"I'm looking good," I whisper to a press release sitting on my desk, a document detailing the health risks of improper nose-hair removal.

Thanksgiving had ended not so well. Back in New York City, I called Susan, who told me if I did so again, she would consider a restraining order. Psychic Rose keeps asking about my mother. I'm a senior editor at a major magazine, living what is supposed to be my dream, which feels more like a low-level nightmare. I don't *feel* any better, so I whisper my other mantra again, a little louder, "I'm looking good!"

I gaze at the wall where I wish there was a window. Outside, the city is blinking and braying, honking and hollering—a gorgeous, bejeweled beast, a vast and writhing monster swallowing thousands of puny humans every minute, shoving them into its heaving belly, vomiting them up its concrete steps. Outside my wall, handsome and hardworking family men with corner offices and expense accounts and nose-hair-free schnozzes—indomitable metropolitan monster tamers!—are barking orders to their loyal and sensible-shoed assistants, telling them to take a little extra time at lunch, to pick up some Chanel No. Five at Saks for the family man's beautiful wife, who is at the moment squirting rich, meaty juices on the pot roast and mashed potatoes and candied carrots that awaits the family man when he arrives home. Outside my wall, Valentine's Day approaches, pleasant memories of someone else's holiday season linger like the gentle scent of nutmeg, spring waits just a few weeks away, and fame and fortune accrue to the deserving, the courageous, and the pious.

I wad the nose-hair release into a ball and pitch it toward my wastebasket. I miss. My phone rings, but I ignore it, hoping against hope that my not-so-loyal assistant might actually do her job for a change and take a message.

For Christmas I had returned with Bridget to the Johnson family farm, where I avoided Leah, put Bridget into the circle of love every chance I could get, and played monster with Milo for hours a day. Except for Lulu breaking into tears on Christmas morning because her father said, "Don't you think you should lay off the holiday ham, Little General," which prompted the Little General to scream, "You're a fat bully, and I've always hated you!" which prompted Milo to burst into laughter, which prompted Bridget to start sobbing along with the Little General, it was fun. New Year's Eve, Bridget got a babysitter, and the two of us went to a fancy dinner downtown and then held hands on the cab ride home. She had only had two glasses of wine at dinner, but was slurring her words. I asked if she was okay and then, while I was kissing her, felt up her tiny purse, in which I could detect the shape of three airline-size bottles. I asked her if she didn't think she should cut back on her drinking. She told me she knew I wanted to be with someone younger and prettier and without a child.

"You think that I don't feel love," I said, cradling her face in my hands.

She mumbled something. She had closed her eyes, was breathing slowly.

"But what I feel for you is real love."

More mumbling.

"Don't think that I don't need you. Don't think I don't want to please you."

She stopped mumbling long enough to smack me on my chest.

"What?" I demanded. "What? Didn't you hear me?"

"Yeah, you schlimy fucker, I heard you. I heard you quoting me the lyrics from 'Love Child.' Leave me alone!" Then she passed out.

New Year's morning, while Bridget slept and Milo watched TV, I walked across the hall and rousted Denny. We went out for pancakes, and after I shared my problems, he told me I should let Bridget be free, that while he respected my stealing lyrics from a Motown hit, Bridget was too smart for that, and besides, I couldn't care for her like she needed to be cared for. I had told him that his filling her booze-soaked brain with my imaginary lust for Leah hadn't helped the matter, and he had replied that Leah was hot, anyone could see that, who *wouldn't* want to do her? And then we had walked to the gym and played basketball with men richer and more powerful than we would ever be. And now here I was, inside a windowless office, while outside the filthy and irresistible city beckoned. My phone was still ringing.

"Hey, you think you might take a message?" I yell.

Three months earlier, when Art informed me that Personal Best was going to expand and that I should find a good candidate for my assistant position, I immediately thought of a female freelancer who had sent a pitch letter to me—out of the blue—about Fearsome Forearms and then, after I assigned her the story, had written a piece as informative as it was droll. We had talked on the phone through the editing process. She had called me "boss" and "handsome" and "chief." She had helped me forget all about mean ice cream men. When I called to tell her that there was a job opening on my staff—I actually said "my staff"—she replied, "Who do I have to blow to get hired?" Or maybe it was, "Are you fucking kidding—how could you even consider anyone else?" or, "Stop looking, I'm your girl!" She was audacious. She was bold. She was everything I wanted to be.

Within a month of hiring her, I learned that Allison was also focused. That's because by then, she was channeling all her audacity and boldness (not to mention her mordant wit) toward Art. Himself had transformed restaurant hostesses into feared and semifamous editors, slovenly sportswriters from weekly rags in Alabama into best-selling authors and dandies. His generosity and eye for talent were legendary. And now, both were being heaped on Allison, who, on her third day, had ceased calling me "boss," "handsome," or anything other than "Steve." Her third week on the job, Art was assigning her features. Not Personal Best features. *Real* features.

My phone continues to ring.

"I wish I could," Allison yells back. "But I'm busy on assignment. The Big Man told me I should concentrate on it."

I inspect an Ecuadorian owl-tooth eyebrow brush sitting on my desk. I comb my right eyebrow. Allison is writing a long piece about why jocks are lousy lovers. Art wants her to pose for the accompanying photograph. The shot will involve a latex dress and a locker room.

I switch to my left eyebrow. I was supposed to be critically acclaimed by now. There was supposed to be an adoring pot-roast squirting wife at home by now, who didn't accuse me of lusting after her sister and, clutching at her apron, at least one or two cute, slobbery kids, who screamed neither "Teeb!" nor "Jew!" I was supposed to be slouching into cocktail parties in my worn but elegant brown tweed sports jacket, watching pretty brunettes in expensive glasses approach me while I smiled with bemusement as they placed their elegant palms on one of my forearms, near one of the leather elbow patches, and I listened attentively while they told me how much my books had changed their lives, how they had no idea a man could be so sensitive *and* so powerful. My assistant was supposed to be sucking up to me, not Art.

A noise distracts me. Not Art's chilling vibrato—I would have jumped from my seat and been clutching my stomach had it been the Man-Thing. No, this is a pleasant noise. It is a melody, in three parts. "Oh, Stee-eee-ve." It is Art's editorial assistant, Kiki. Horse-jumping Kiki. Hamptons-summering Kiki. Sun-dressed, miniskirted purring Kiki, who graduated from Sarah Lawrence with a degree in French, whose cheekbones are high and whose neck is cruel and aristocratic. Kiki is the one person at *GQ* whose presence reduces even the growling and snarling Man-Thing to longing, dreamy silence. I try not to look directly at Kiki, who stands in the hallway outside my windowless office. Looking at Kiki is like looking directly into the sun. Allison doesn't look at Kiki either. Nor does Kiki look at Allison. One has spunk and talent. The other has a beauty so effortless that even the macadamia-eyed Susan would probably tremble before it. Allison and Kiki hate each other. Sometimes I imagine them hating each other inside a rubbery pit, surrounded by a chain-link fence, covered with lime green Jell-O. I'm not proud of this, but all the nose-hair and eyebrow grooming is wearing me down. I find diversions—however transient, integrity sapping, and doomed—wherever I can.

Again, the melody. "Oh, Stee-ee-ve."

I turn toward her.

She is standing in my office doorway. She winks at me. *Kiki winks at me!* Stomach cramp. Neck on fire. *It is a pleasant day.*

I clear my throat. It takes three tries. I straighten my hunter green tie.

"Hey, Keek."

She cocks a Sarah Lawrence–educated horse-jumping hip, and I try to hide a shudder. She smiles.

"Cool garb," she whispers.

It is a pleasant day. I am still looking good. The neck rash might be flaring up. The dog dreams might be getting worse, the teeth sharper, the snapping jaws more ravenous. And now even Kiki, even an editorial assistant who, her gravitational carnality notwithstanding, scrabbles and claws at the bottom of *GQ*'s swirling and sartorially resplendent but fiercely Darwinian aquarium . . . now even Kiki finds it safe to mock me. I am looking good. I am looking good. It's a pleasant day. *Things aren't so bad.*

I lower my head to my desk, and rest. I could stay here forever. No one will mention my garb if I keep my head on my desk. Then again, Lisa had caught me napping once, and that had not gone well. I lift my head, apply some jojoba-based moisturizer to the skin behind my ears. I rub some strawberry-scented lip balm on my lips. I consider how I might package the moisturizer and the balm in the pages of Personal Best, primarily because both products were given to me by a PR woman named Krista whom I met at a party a couple weeks ago. She had nice bangs.

I want love. I long for serenity. I need acclaim. And riches too. And an office with at least one measly window. And a boss who might occasionally utter my name, or nod his head at me, or maybe even invite me to join him at his corner leather banquette at the Four Seasons, the one he invites all his other employees to.

How is it that I've failed so miserably? Will I ever feel banquette leather beneath me, the brunettes caressing the leather patches on my elbows?

"I will have the tie now, please."

"What?" I say.

"I said," Ursula says, "I will have the tie now, please." While I had been muttering my self-affirmations and brooding over the vast distance between my life as it was and as it should be, the German had crept into my doorway.

"Oh, hey, Ursula, I didn't hear you come in. Hey, have a seat. Long time no see. *Wie geht es dir?* How about a nice package of foot soap for my favorite Fraulein?" I pull a package from my pile of grooming products. "I think the oil's extracted from the fur of river otters. Have you ever seen a river otter with dirty feet?"

I'm talking fast. Maybe if I talk fast enough, the writhing metropolis will not swallow me whole, will not vomit me back to Missouri. Then again, maybe Missouri wouldn't be so bad. Maybe, in this sixth year after the lime green suit (ATLGS), it's time to admit failure, to abandon my dreams, to leave glory and fame to spunky women in latex dresses and to cruel-necked debutantes who have destroyed better men than me. Or is it I? (The copy editors had been yelling at me lately about sloppy grammar in Personal Best.)

Ursula remains standing. She thrusts out her fat lower lip and says, "Ach," while she shakes her head.

"Ursula?" I say.

"Ach," she says again. I haven't taken Ursula for lunch in more than two months. What with the holidays and worrying about Bridget and my discovery that among female public relations employees, Susan was not alone in her naked ambition and apparent willingness to trade sex for editorial coverage, I have been attending every product launch and grooming luncheon I can find. I tell myself it's because I'm grieving for the loss of Susan, because I'm struggling to deal with the difficulties involving Bridget and Milo. Plus, *GQ* needs product. That's not my fault.

"The tie, please," Ursula says, still scowling.

"But, Ursula, I'm *wearing* the tie. You know that Art likes his editors to be well dressed. "

"The fashion department wants the tie, please, now. And the fashion department wants all the ties. You will please to bring them all to the fashion closet tomorrow morning."

Is it my imagination, or is Ursula sounding more and more like a *Wermacht* lieutenant?

One more "ach," one more protruded lip, and Ursula marches out of my office, clutching silk.

I decide at that moment I have hit my professional bottom. De-tied by a fashion department location coordinator. Defamed to my hard-drinking girlfriend by a jump shot–shooting sociopath who preys on headshot-holding waitresses. Demanned by a twenty-two-year-old whose ancestors probably denied my ancestors access to the hedge-lined country clubs where her ancestors ate toast points and complained about the vulgarity and relentless *striving* of my ancestors.

Then again, maybe it isn't absolute bottom. Maybe the search for Mrs. Friedman, which hasn't paid obvious dividends yet, is merely taking a little longer than I had imagined it would. Maybe I was just getting what I was getting and that, in time, I would get Mrs. F. She could wait. What cannot wait is professional advancement. What I will not—cannot—be patient with any longer is my stalled writing trajectory at *GQ*.

Just a few hours earlier, at lunchtime, I had told Art I would be interviewing a plastic surgeon about jowl-reduction surgery, but instead I had shuffled five blocks to Rose's office, where I bleated to the psychic psychotherapist about dog dreams and my jealousy of Allison. *I will not feel guilty*, I mouth to myself, back in my office, so Allison won't hear. (The phrase is a new one, not recommended by the rehab unit shrink, but lately I've found it useful. It started when Bridget accused me of still being in love with Susan, which I denied, and then screamed, "I will not feel guilty!" Now I say it to myself. I've grown fond of it.)

This afternoon, I'm supposed to assign a piece on gum pinkeners and another one on ear dandruff. But why *should* I assign them? Art's supposed to nurture me, and he hasn't done that. My assistant is supposed to answer my phones, and she hasn't done that. Kiki is supposed to treat me with respect, and Susan is supposed to come back to me, and Ursula *certainly* is supposed to let me hang on to my fashion closet clothes. Milo is supposed to be talking like a normal kid, and Bridget is supposed to accept my love and cut back on the sauce. No one is doing what they're supposed to be doing, so why should I?

I give both eyebrows a final brush. I close the door. I flex my fingers.

"To Art, David, Lisa," I type, and as the words appear on my computer screen, I almost believe I can tame this wondrous, cacophonous wriggling conurbation called Manhattan.

"From Steve"

Yeah, I think. "Yeah," I say.

"Re: How I can contribute."

The memo is forceful, but not arrogant. Spunky, but not childish. I promise that if I were unleashed on some meaty assignments, I would deliver. I pitch a story on a serial killer in St. Louis and a reported essay on blue-collar rage and the inevitable consequences of an oppressed underclass. I pitch a piece on the identity crisis of a professional bowler laboring in the shadow of his famous father.

"In the stories of these men lie the stories of all men," I write, but I don't really believe. But it sounds good. I look good, and it sounds good. "Yeah!" I say again, flinging the eyebrow brush from my desk onto the floor. I spend all afternoon and evening on the memo, and when I leave the office at 10:00 PM, I place copies on the desks of David, Lisa, and Art. (First, I replace the eyebrow brush on my desk.)

The next day, after lunch, as I'm applying some more moisturizer and lip balm, my phone rings. Through the receiver I hear the familiar three-note siren song.

"Hey, Kiki," I say. I try to sound disinterested.

"Art would like to see you."

"Right. Sure he would."

"Should I tell him you said that?"

Something in her voice makes me sit up straight.

"No," I say. "No no no no." I can't stop saying no.

I hold my breath as I walk past Kiki—I can't risk her scent distracting me. I have already muttered a few self-affirmations, reminded myself that whatever gory thing is about to happen will happen fast, and then it will be over, that whatever merciless toying El Jefe is about to do with me will be short-lived. My eyebrows are well-groomed, and even though I am tieless, I am wearing a suit that is not lime green. I am a senior editor. *I am looking good.*

I stride into Art's office. I want to creep. My instincts scream at me to hunker and shuffle. In my heart and soul, I am dragging my knuckles and gazing upward, like Quasimodo, well-intentioned but fully aware of the fate that befalls misshapen outcasts like me. But I can't let my knowledge show. I know what happens when the Man-Thing senses fear. I puff out my chest. I try to swagger.

Art is slumped in his chair, writing something in the little black book he keeps in the top left-hand drawer of his desk. The desk is made of wood so impossibly dense, so burnished, so glowing, it looks like it was extracted from the kind of prehistoric African tree that once grew only on the rich and loamy banks of crocodile-infested Congolese rivers and was harvested by tribes of oiled and high-haunched Amazons who ate the babies of tribes that weren't as good-looking. He continues scribbling. He doesn't even acknowledge me. Is he drunk? It is afternoon, and he has been to the Four Seasons for lunch with Lisa, so he's probably at least a little drunk. But it's a point of pride with Art that he can function drunk. (He suggested I run a piece in Personal Best on just such a subject—Heavy Drinking Needn't Be Horrible.) So why is he ignoring me? Or has he not noticed me?

Art keeps scribbling. I decide I will take a seat. When I'm halfway to the couch, he booms.

"Are you happy here?" he says.

Me? Happy?

GQ men are supposed to be silver-tongued rascals, wondrous wordsmiths, as comfortable around convoluted and convincing linguistic constructions as they are around platinum-inlaid, gold-tipped fountain pens. But all I can choke past my strawberry-balm-slathered lips is this: "Me happy." I sound like Tarzan.

Art stares. *It is a pleasant day.*

If Art liked me, *GQ* would be a magazine like no other. A place of leathery lunches and growling confidences and testosterone-charged bonhomie. A place of editorial assistants who look like exotic dancers, of Lisa's smooth rippling flanks, of goose liver and oft-stroked (by bespectacled brunettes) elbow patches. Why did I say, "Me happy"? I might as well ask myself why I still erupted in rashes, why I had such a delicate digestive system, why I daily battled powerful and at times overwhelming urges to put my head on my desk and to sleep for a long, long time. Me at the moment not-so-happy.

Art continues to stare. Longtime staffers trade tales of the Man-Thing's malevolent gaze the way the ancient Greeks must have trembled over stories of Medusa and her head snakes. Once, the story goes, when they were locked in a bitter argument over whether "winter white" was a legitimate fashion choice after Labor Day, a top fashion editor tried to match Art in a staring contest, and the editor fell into an epileptic seizure on the Big Man's couch. The next morning, Art had a new couch, and *GQ* had a new fashion editor. True? Who knows? Terrifying? Definitely.

"I mean," I lie, "I'm happy. I'm very happy."

Art continues to stare.

He stares at me as the man-eating leopard known as the spotted devil of Gummalapur stares at the doomed villager who has foolishly wandered to the edge of the forest from nearby Devarabetta. The spotted devil continues staring, patient, with naked malevolence just waiting for the limpid-eyed

Indian to turn and bolt so the sleek killer can then leap from behind his wood-logged-by-high-haunched-baby-eating-Amazons desk and sink his fangs into the trembling flanks of the harmless and frightened villager who never wanted to hurt anyone, who just wanted some respect, who wanted an assistant who answered his phone every once in a while.

I wonder what Milo is doing at the moment, if he's thinking of dinosaurs. I haven't seen him in a few weeks. I think of the pleasant hours we shared watching Animal Planet. I wonder if he ever thinks of me, if he ever asks where Teeb is, or whether I'm forgotten the instant I leave, like the summer forgets the spring. I wonder what will happen to Bridget and me. I wonder if I'll ever find Mrs. Friedman. I realize with shame that I'm about to start sobbing.

"Do you want to know the secret of being a manager?" Art growls.

Trick question! my mind screams. *Trick question! Trick question! Trick question!*

"Sure," I squeak. "Yeah. Definitely." Has Allison been complaining about me to Art? Has she been whining about how I'm a *bad* manager, when all I've been doing is asking her to pick up my goddamn phone every few hours and take a mother-fucking message? In my mind's eye, in a very happy place where I wish I could spend more time, my feckless assistant is slathered all over her body with honey-based scalp conditioner, tied to an anthill somewhere in the sun-scorched African veldt. I picture myself standing over her, gently inquiring, while insects feast on her well-conditioned flesh, "Don't you wish you'd answered my phone now and taken some messages, like assistants are *supposed* to?"

Art continues to stare. Hadn't I told him that, yes, I wanted to know the secret of management? Hadn't I answered in the affirmative? Hadn't I written a manly memo? I decide that if I were ever going to return to drink and drugs, today would be the day. As soon as I escaped from the Big Man's torture chamber, I would walk out of the *GQ* offices, down the block to one of the Irish bars with warm, shadowy interiors and tough Irish barmaids who lived in Queens and cussed out of the corners of their mouths, and I would order some scotch. Maybe I'd invite Bridget.

Still, the staring. I'm sweating, and I know it's showing.

"Learn the Stare," the Big Man booms.

"Learn the Stare," I repeat. *What the fuck?* I think.

"When people are whispering in the hallways, 'Friedman has the cruelest eyes I have ever seen,' when people start sweating and stammering just because you're looking at them a certain way, then you'll know you've arrived as a manager."

I know something important has just transpired between Art and me. Something insane, but important.

"Thanks, Art, I appreciate that."

He goes back to scribbling. I sit for a while. And awhile longer. He must be drunk. This can't be brilliant managing, can it? I get up to leave. I'm at the door, on my way to the Irish bar and a lifetime of ruination when he booms again.

"Nice memo. You showed me something."

I turn.

"So I'm assigning you a feature. You're flying to California tomorrow. You're going to meet Barbara Hershey."

"The actress?" I say. *Another Babe of the Month?* I think.

"Yeah, the actress, and you're going to love her. I'm slotting this as a feature, so you'll have 1,500 words. This is your chance."

She is Barbara to me, and I, Steve to her. We are not subject and object, nor actress and journalist. We are not merely our jobs. We are man and woman. After spending some time with Barbara, I see now how my infatuation with Mary-Louise Parker was just that—an infatuation, a schoolboy crush. Barbara and I discuss the sad plight of the actress over forty in the authenticity-crushing machinery of Hollywood. She tells me she is considering moving to Italy, where she will give up acting and paint. We share tuna sandwiches. I tell her about my problems with my disloyal assistant and my scary boss. I ask—delicately—about the collagen-injected lips, which she got for *Beaches*, and why she changed her name to "Seagull" when she was young, and why she named her child Free, and she tells me those are silly things, beneath me as a journalist and as a man, and to focus on them is to miss the point of what she tries to do in her work and what she has to offer as a woman.

When I leave her bungalow in the Hollywood Hills after two afternoons, I say good-bye and thank her. I have learned a great deal. She embraces me and kisses me on the lips. I am too stunned to move.

Back in New York City, I call Barbara to ask her some questions to which I don't need answers. I tell her I have thought a lot about what we talked about. I mention that I'm working on the piece.

When we hang up, I wonder, not for the first time, why I didn't kiss Barbara when I had the chance.

At my weekly appointment, I ask Rose too.

Rose doesn't know. Why do I think I didn't kiss Barbara?

I ask Rose if she thinks it's possible that I might find love with Barbara, in Italy. I tell Rose I think it might work. She would paint, and I would write a novel. It could work. Barbara doesn't drink like Bridget. I really think it could work. Rose nods and says, "Mmm-hmmmm."

I write 6,000 words, even though the piece is only supposed to be 1,500. I spend most of my nonwriting time with Bridget, who, when she's not drinking, is exuberant. I have grown to love her. She is exuberant in every aspect of her life, and it makes me feel exuberant. She loves throwing parties, which is a nice antidote to my hermit tendencies. There is the sex, to be sure. But there's also those wonderful mornings before she's started drinking, when she'll make coffee and tell stories about her family, when

Milo will run around screaming and I'll play monster with him and think about how life might be great if things were just a little bit different.

The Barbara piece will make things different. It will give me more acclaim at *GQ*, and that will make me better equipped to make Bridget feel secure and loved, and that will make her drink less. That's the plan. But first I have to boil down my six-thousand-word, uncuttable essay into something that's not superficial, that's not Babe of the Monthish. How can I convey Barbara's beauty and enormous talent, and my appreciation of both, and hint at the connection with God we all seek, in just 1,500 words? Rose is no help. I can't ask Bridget. On Saturday evening, I call the Ascot, who in his most recent piece argued for the return of the short-sleeved dress shirt to the executive suite. I call Eddie because many years after the garb incident, many of the other editors still move away from me when I approach as healthy and high-stepping gazelles move away from their lame and diseased gazelle brothers. (I probably should cut down on my Animal Planet watching time.)

I tell Eddie I've already written seven drafts. I confess my difficulties, my ambitions. I tell him about my imaginary life in Italy with Barbara. I tell him that I know that I let my worst instincts get the best of me with Mary-Louis but that Art promised me this assignment wasn't just a Babe of the Month, that it was a *feature*. I tell him that I'm struggling.

"Never mistake motion for action," Eddie suggests.

"What?" I say. I hear a rustling on the other end of the line. What are you talking about?"

"There are some things that cannot be learned quickly, and time, which is all we have, must be paid heavily for their acquiring."

"Goddamit, Ascot!" (He hates when people call him Ascot. He finds it demeaning.) "Quit quoting Papa and help me out here."

On the other end of the line, a book slapping shut and a sigh.

"Dude," the Ascot says. "Remember, she's an actress."

The nights when I'm not at Bridget's, we talk on the phone. If she doesn't answer, I'll sometimes call Denny and ask him to go across the hall to check to make sure that everything's okay. Denny has a girlfriend now, a twenty-four-year-old bisexual dancer named Trudi. Sometimes she brings women home to Denny's, where they have threesomes.

I still shoot hoops with Denny. I ask whether he really thinks threesomes with Trudi and her lesbian girlfriends is going to make him happy in the long run. I also ask whether Trudi using an *I* instead of a *Y* in her name doesn't drive him nuts. He tells me I don't know myself, that I should cut Bridget loose, that I'm wasting the best years of her life.

The story runs at 1,500 words, a terribly watered-down version of my vision. I call Barbara afterward, but she doesn't call back. I call Barbara the day it hits the stands, but she doesn't answer. Is she angry? I want to tell her that I *had* to mention the collagen-filled lips! Art made me.

"Nice babe piece," Allison says to me when I'm on the way into my office one morning. On her desk, in plain sight, is a personal note from Art. "Attagirl!" it says. "Men across the country are hanging up their jock straps after your essay."

"It wasn't a Babe of the Month," I say. "It was a reflection on celebrity and—"

"Yeah, whatever."

I would like to kill her—as the aging but still-proud Indian elephant kills those who vex him—by kneeling on her head and then leaning forward, till her skull explodes. I saw that on a special called *When Animals Kill.* Instead, I practice my managerial technique. I stare. I stare and stare.

She looks up from her desk, stares back. Has Art been telling her the secret of good management too? We continue staring at each other, as both our phones ring. I will *not* lose the staring contest.

"Hey," Allison says, "your left eyebrow is bushy. You should comb it."

"What?" I say, looking upward, reflexively smoothing the offending hair. "Huh?"

Then I realize her cunning. She has won. I enter my office, close the door. It is as quiet and sad as an elephant's graveyard.

Bridget and I argue every night, often over the phone. She asks me why I can't love her like Denny loves Trudi. I explain that if she were sleeping with women and bringing them to my apartment rather than drinking herself into a stupor so often, her request might be easier to fulfill. That's a mistake. We discuss breaking up a couple times a week, then have sex, then she passes out, then we talk about her family over bagels and fruit and coffee in the morning. Once, after Milo has left for school, she asks me what a "wimee popowus" is.

"What?"

"It's Milo's new favorite phrase. It's all he was saying when I walked him to the bus this morning, 'Wimee popowus, wimee popowus.' Then he said, 'Teeb!' What kind of things are you telling him? Are you guys still watching Animal Planet when I'm sleeping?"

Passed out is more like it, I think. And while we have been watching Animal Planet a lot, I can't think of any animals that sound like what Bridget is claiming Milo is saying. I ask her to repeat it.

"WHY ME POP OH US," she sounds out.

"I have no idea," I say, but I can feel the neck rash, the rumbling guts. This is a low point even for me. "Wimee popowus" is Milo-speak for "writhing metropolis." I've been talking about my visions of the bejeweled beast and my lofty ambitions late at night to a kid who can't tell Tom and Jerry apart. And what he has taken from my soul-baring is "wimee popowus." I tell Bridget that I can't have coffee with her this morning, that I need to get to work.

At the office, David tells me that he has persuaded Art to turn me loose on another profile. A *real* profile. It will be part of a package David had conceived, about the degradation of American culture, the national celebration of tackiness.

"We're calling it Cheese Nation," David tells me. "Get it?"

"Yep. I get it. We're going to show how cheesy everything is, right?"

"Right! And you're going to do the main profile in the package. John Tesh, the *Entertainment Tonight* guy, who plays that god-awful Christian music. Call his people and set it up."

Tesh's people are happy that *GQ* is doing a profile on their man. But they are not stupid. They know that Tesh—with his religious music and his born-again Christianity and his highly publicized year of abstinence with his once cocaine-using, but now also born-again Christian wife Connie Selleca—is not exactly what *GQ* celebrates.

"Is this going to be a positive story?" one of his people asks me.

"Sure," I say. "I mean," I add, quickly qualifying, "I mean, I love his music, and I want to write about not just John the entertainer, but John the musician. I want to learn about the guy behind all the publicity. I want to write about John the man!"

I can justify the most horrible misdeeds with the easiest and most facile qualifiers like the one I just made. I didn't technically lie. Tesh wrote, in addition to the execrable and mock-worthy Jesus crap he plays at outdoor stadiums stuffed with white-haired, overweight Midwestern grandmothers, the theme song for the National Basketball Association. I like that song. Sometimes, I hum it.

The Tesh handler buys it. I fly again to Los Angeles.

If I were a superhero, I decide somewhere over Iowa, my name would be the Qualifier, a lonely, well-meaning but awesomely flawed earthling banished to a strange and forbidding planet of clear judgments and passionate action, a seminebbishy man-child who can't help but see twenty sides of everything, who is most at home in the dangerous gray hollows and canyons that others dare not enter.

I was going to take down an entertainer whose handlers I had lied to. But it was okay, because that was what journalism demanded. Besides, I could write a fair piece. Critical and scathing, but fair. The Qualifier would triumph.

To my great surprise, Tesh is funny. He is also self-mocking and open. He tells me he's been eating a lot lately, that he can't stop eating, and he thinks it's because his mother has emphysema and he's worried about her. He tells me when his father died, it hit Tesh that "we're all going to die, so we should seize the moment, we should stop putting off difficult decisions. What are we scared of?"

He makes fun of his yearlong abstinence and all the resultant publicity. He buys me dinner, where I meet Connie, who is more closely guarded than Tesh, less voluble in her answers, more inquisitive about why exactly *GQ* is interested in her husband. Connie might be born-again, but she is very shrewd. The Qualifier might even describe her as cynical.

But she needn't worry. I might be the Qualifier, I might be a liar, I might be duplicitous and cowardly and double-dealing and self-seeking. But I like this big-headed blond lug, who is about to quit his luxurious gig as *Entertainment Tonight* host and embark on a music career. Why can't I quit *GQ* and concentrate on my writing? I envy Tesh—his courage and his apparent serenity. I tell him so, and we have a few heart-to-hearts about what it means to be a man. He invites me to join him for church services. I decline, but I admire the delicacy of his proselytizing effort.

On our third day together, he asks me to meet him in the parking lot of the studio where his band is practicing. He tells me that he can't meet me the next day, because his mother has died. I think he just learned in the past hour.

Of course, I say. I understand, I say. I tell him how sorry I am.

"But if you need anything else," Tesh tells me, "please call. You've really been honest with me, and I want to help you with your piece."

I thank him, and then we talk about life and death and mothers and meaning and how we need to be bold, how life is short, how we can't be seduced by worry and misery. Not only do I admire him, but I also want to be like him. Not in the born-again way or the terrible music way, but in the way he is open to others, helpful even in time of crisis, living a life filled with pain and loss—sure, all life is filled with pain and loss, but living it in a way free of fear. That would be a much richer life than the one I lead now, in my secret identity as the Qualifier.

It's the best thing I've ever written. That's what I think. I open on a tender holiday scene: Tesh as a young boy, awakened late one Christmas Eve, when his father summons him downstairs to play "Silent Night" on the family piano for a group of grown-ups who are celebrating. Little Johnny plays carefully and with great feeling, and afterward, there is a moment of silence, then glasses clinking, and gentle applause, broken only when Johnny's father rumbles, "Play it again. This time without the mistakes." Little Johnny has to play it four more times until his father is satisfied.

I cry as I write the story. I cry as I polish it, and polish it again. I mention the terrible music that the adult Tesh plays, but I pay more attention to the little boy and all little boys, and the man and all men, and all our dreams. I talk about fathers and sons and choices and death and life. It's Tesh's story, but it's really the story of all men. I believe this.

I turn in my tenth draft.

The next day, that draft lies on my desk, with a note from Art. "If we like this guy so much, how come he's in Cheese Nation? Make it meaner!"

I reach for the eyebrow brush, the lip balm. Then I push them away. I won't take the easy way this time. Tesh was walking away from millions at *Entertainment Tonight* to follow his dream. I could at least exhibit a *little* courage. I would make my stand here.

"To Art," I type.

Yeah, I think. "Yeah!" I say.

Then I stop. I rub some jojoba moisturizer behind my ears. That soothes me. Tesh is deeply religious, a man of convictions. I am the Man in the Lime Green Suit. Tesh reads the Bible. I watch Animal Planet. Tesh's faith is so deep, his belief so potent, that he forgoes sex for twelve months in order to spend his remaining days on earth with the woman he loves. I have never even uttered the word "marriage" to Bridget.

Still, the Qualifier has his ways. He is not *all* craven self-interest. I won't tell Art he is wrong or that I refuse to allow him to reduce my nuanced and complicated and admiring story on a man and manhood in general into a caricature, the way I had allowed him to reduce my pieces about Mary-Louise and Barbara into your-tits-make-me-hard shtick. The Qualifier will be more subtle. I will do a rewrite as ordered, but it will be a sneaky, artistic rewrite. I will salvage Tesh's dignity, and mine.

But how? It is Tuesday, the rewrite is due Wednesday, and I'm not seeing Rose till Friday. The Ascot would just quote Hemingway. I know I can't ask Lisa or David for sympathy. I'm not sure they really get my odes to men's dreams.

I'm stuck, again. I'm helpless. Again. I'm dithering and worrying while others are doing and getting. What should the Qualifier do? What would Tesh do?

Suddenly, in my airless office, on a summer morning in New York City, midway through year 7 ATLGS, staring at my windowless walls, I know the answer.

Tesh would not fret about a single song or a single boss or even a single career move. He would see the big picture, the one that encompasses others, and dignity and faith. He would know that a lot of things matter in life, but that only one thing *really* matters.

I crank out some Personal Best ideas for future issues ("How to Give Her an *Even Better* Orgasm," "Why Women Dig Guys with Pedicures," "Neck Beards, Lose 'Em!"), and then I tell Allison I'll be taking a long lunch.

The doorman at Bridget's knows me by now, so he lets me take the elevator to her floor without buzzing. I'm going to surprise her. I'm going to tell her how much I love her, that sure, Milo's a handful, and yes, her drinking isn't something I exactly approve of and I don't drink anymore myself, but I want her to feel safe. I will make her safe. As I'm in the elevator, I think of our mornings together, of a lifetime of mornings, and holidays at the Johnson family farm. Tesh has shown me what's it like to live as a man, to make difficult choices, and now I'm going to make one. I'm going to become a father to a little boy I love, a husband to a woman who occasionally guzzles wine from her purse, but whom I also love. That's what Tesh has taught me—that our jobs and our passions (*Entertainment Tonight* and music, respectively, for him, *GQ* and writing for me)—are just manifestations of who we are. But who we *really* are is the people we love. I will love Bridget and Milo, and I will do my best on the Tesh piece, will do a rewrite that won't be perfect, but I will stop looking for perfection. I will get what I get. I will settle for being human. The Qualifier is done qualifying. The Man in the Lime Green Suit is going to strip off his protective coloration. The moth caterpillar is about to flap and soar. He is going to ask Bridget to be his wife.

I turn the handle to Bridget's door. She always leaves it open, what with Denny constantly coming in and out, often accompanied by bisexual Trudi with an *i*. But the door is locked today. That's weird. I knock. I hear Milo screaming. I knock again. More screaming. Now I'm alarmed. Might Bridget be passed out in bed? Is Milo bleeding? I hammer both fists on the door. Finally, footsteps.

The door opens and standing there, shirtless, is Denny. I can see that Milo's door is closed. Milo is screaming from inside his room.

"Is everything okay?" I ask. One of the dumber questions I've ever uttered. It's dumb because standing behind Denny, emerging from the bedroom, wearing one of his button-down shirts but nothing else is Bridget.

I make it mean. I cut the little-Johnny-at-the piano opening to a couple paragraphs. I cut out the dead mom and the search for transcendence. I write a lot about the size of Tesh's head. I refer to him as "Frankenstein in a purple suit." "Benign bilge," I call his music. "Reflect upon the fact that as his popularity rises," I write, "the decline of Western civilization must surely be hastened."

Art loves it. I get an "attaboy." Allison starts taking messages for me. Ursula offers me more ties. Kiki asks if I want to have lunch sometime. Maybe, I tell her. We'll see. My lunch hours are already busy with Robyn and Kristin and Brooke and all the product-pushing, fragrant PR women. I have sex with as many of them as I can. I write a lot of Personal Best copy and I write it with a sneer. I write a column for the magazine called *The Single Guy*, and I write it with a sneer too. I start calling women in print "chicks" and "the ladies."

April the ophthalmologist calls from St. Louis. How long has it been since we've talked? Five years? She has been reading some of my stories, she says, and she wants to know, is everything okay? Of course it is, I tell her. April's so sweet, like a lot of people who haven't figured out how the world works.

My father visits. We walk to Barney Greengrass "The Sturgeon King" for bagels and lox, and he asks if everything is okay. Of course, it's okay. Why is everyone asking me if everything's okay? I'm getting attaboys from the Big Man. Other editors envy me. I'm having sex with a bunch of well-groomed, good-looking mercenaries who read enough women's magazines to know all the bedroom tricks that, as the cover lines promise, "will drive him wild in bed." Many work.

"I wish I had been more approving of all my children," my father tells me over nova and cream cheese on a toasted sesame. "I wish I had been less critical."

That's sweet, I think. That's kind of sentimental. My father has recently started dating again. It's been a few years since Elaine died, and he seems to be coming out of his mourning. I don't think I'll ever have to go through that. Marriage or mourning.

"Don't worry about it, Dad," I say. "No harm done. I'm doing great."

In May, I find a cream-colored envelope on my desk, addressed to me, with the words "personal and confidential" written in elegant script across the right-hand upper corner.

It's a note from John Tesh.

I apply some moisturizer behind my ears, touch up my lips with the strawberry balm. I brush one eyebrow and then the other. I open the envelope with the hand-carved ebony alligator letter opener sent to me from an Australian PR rep working for a Kenyan ecotourism lodge.

"You are a liar and a cheap imitation of a journalist," the note says.

I smack my lips. The strawberry tastes good.

Does he think I don't know that?

CHAPTER 10

DEAR DIRTBAG, I IDENTIFY WITH YOU

The Qualifier needs another girlfriend. He is embittered and angry and, in print, sneering and clever, and of course, he can understand Bridget's crippling moral weakness and Denny's irredeemable evil, because he's the Qualifier, and he can understand everything, but in his not-so-secret identity he is still human. He still wants female companionship. I meet Kitty on a blind date, arranged by the Ascot, who is the only other *GQ* staffer still waiting for a lunch invitation from El Jefe. When the Ascot isn't reading Hemingway or writing about the career-killing perils of pocket protectors, he's in my office, theorizing with me about why the Big Man won't recognize our literary gifts. The Ascot tells me that the woman he's dating knows an actress who just broke up with her boyfriend and she was just in a movie with Paul Newman. Did I want to meet her?

Like Mary-Louise, Kitty talks about poets. Like Barbara, she rails against the cruelty of her business. She also cries during sex, which I like, because I'm sure it signals her intense emotional involvement in the act and, just as important, with me. On the downside, she yells at me when I ask too many questions about her most recent boyfriend, the guy who keeps calling her and who sends her flowers three times a week.

"I need to hear him out. I need to find closure," she tells me. "Why can't you understand that?"

I can understand that. But does closure really need to involve regular meetings with the ex? I mean, didn't she say she loved me the last time we slept together? Or had I misunderstood, because of the blubbering?

"Stop trying to control me," she says.

A reasonable request, I suppose, but of course, I can't satisfy it. The Qualifier might be overly analytical, pusillanimous, and awesomely passive-aggressive (to himself as well as the world at large), but one thing he is not, is easygoing about old boyfriends trying to worm their way back into their ex's affections, particularly when the ex is the Qualifier's current. He knows how these guys work. He knows that "I've been thinking about you" is the ostensibly sweet and harmless opening remark, which, if entertained, is followed by "I wish I would have been smarter, kinder, and more open when we were dating," which leads inevitably to the beseeching little kicker: "Please please please, let's try this again." I know this because I've delivered these loathsome (but persuasive) oratories myself.

I could tell Kitty that she can't trust the ex, that shortly after he gets what he wants, he won't want it anymore, that he is nothing but a remorseless and fib-dripping ball of longing and inchoate need, that he will hurt her and hurt her again, and that by agreeing to this thing the lying fib ball calls "closure," she is asking for more hurt. She is inviting it. But I don't tell her that because to do so, I would have to admit how I know such things. I would have to tear away my fake superhero uniform and reveal to Kitty the baggy, saggy, wheezing chambers of the Qualifier's gray and flaccid human heart. I suspect that might be a mistake.

Post Bridget, post Denny, the Qualifier has become slightly cynical.

"I want you to get closure too, Pork Chop," I tell her. "If you get closure, you'll be more available to me, and I want us to be available to each other." I learned to frequently use the word "available" with females by reading some of the women's magazines published by Conde Nast. I read them in my office, with my door shut, when Art is at the Four Seasons with Allison and Lisa and David and Kiki and everyone else who has ever worked at *GQ*. (He even takes *former* staffers there.) I read them as I stuff double hamburgers and bags of french fries down my gullet. I also read that using nicknames inspires trust in women.

"You do?" Pork Chop says. She is staring at me over her glasses. She has widened her eyes. But she's slightly frowning, suspicious. It's how a smoldering, languorous assistant district attorney might look when she stumbled on evidence that the handsome serial killer she had been planning to send to the electric chair might actually be innocent, but probably wasn't. Actually, it's *exactly* that look. I remember when she played the hot assistant DA in a television role before the Paul Newman movie.

"I do, Choppie," I say. "I do want us to be available to each other. And that's why I fully support closure. All I ask of you is that you let me know the times you're getting together with Bruce to seek closure."

She doesn't know when those times might be. She doesn't think she would like having to report to me. Something about this doesn't make her feel right. Why can't I trust her? Pork Chop knows she is being maneuvered into a corner, and she responds with all her actressy tools. She widens her eyes some more, then squints, then widens them again. She works the frowny mouth. She tells me that love is all about trust.

The Qualifier understands. The Qualifier empathizes with her discomfort. And of *course*, the Qualifier loves her, and trusts her too. But the Qualifier insists. The Qualifier's attractive, frowny-mouthed, wide-eyed, quite-possibly-unfaithful little Pork Chop might have played an assistant DA in a crappy little TV show, but the Qualifier could out-argue the Grand Inquisitor. The Qualifier has been fucked over by his last serious girlfriend. The Qualifier has been fucked over by his former best friend. The Qualifier has been fucked over by his boss and his boss's assistant and his own assistant and by an "ach"-spouting tie fetcher. True, the Qualifier has fucked over John Tesh, but it was not enough. It just whetted the Qualifier's appetite for fucking over people. The Qualifier possesses an exquisitely calibrated justice-measuring gauge, and he has deduced that in order to balance the cosmic scales, he needs to not be fucked over any more, by anyone. He really loves her, and he really understands her, and he wants to be available to her, and her to him. But the Qualifier would really like it if Pork Chop would tell him—beforehand—about any closure-seeking sessions with Bruce.

She agrees. She gives him more frowny mouth, and she doesn't cry when they have sex that night, but she does agree. The Qualifier considers this a victory. The Qualifier is, of course, a moron.

The next week, we arrive at her apartment door. There, leaning against the frame, a large bouquet of yellow tulips.

"Do you want to discuss this?" Kitty asks.

"Nope. If there was anything to discuss, we would have discussed it already. We had an agreement and you promised—"

"You don't understand anything about my pain!"

We have entered her apartment. She is placing the tulips in a vase. I stand next to the door. The Qualifier is considering his options. The Qualifier always considers his options.

"Um, excuse me?"

"Do you ever think about me? Do you ever think about how hard this is on me?"

"Well, sure, Pork Chop, I think about how hard this is on you. I want you to be available to me. And it's not your fault that he left you flowers.

You're beautiful and tender, and you have so much to offer. I don't blame Bruce for wanting you back."

I'm so glad I spent those lunch hours with *Allure* and *Vogue*. While I have gained back most of my pre–Peak Ten flab and developed what I suspect might be acid-reflux disease from all the double burgers and fries, I know how to talk to women.

Kitty is weeping.

"Chop? Choppie?"

"I saw him twice this week. Last night he was here for three hours. He was on his knees, proposing."

"Um, I thought we had an agreement and—"

"Can you tell me why you think it's your business what I do?"

"This is about an agreement we had, and there's no need to yell at me."

"I'm not yelling," she yells. Then she cries. "This has been so hard for me," she says. "Why can't you see that? Why do you always have to be so controlling? Why is it always about you?"

The Qualifier is . . . where is the Qualifier? Suddenly, I can't seem to find my superhero alter ego. I stare at my girlfriend, the woman who had cried during sex with me, my little Pork Chop. I stare at the woman whom I have trusted (for the most part) and whom I bullied a little more than I should have but whom I said "available" to a lot, certainly more than most men would have. I stare at her as she cries, and as she yells at me some more, and as she tells me how selfish and *narcissistic* I am. That's a word the women's magazines seem to like too, especially regarding men.

I try to see Kitty's side of things, to take into account her pain. I *want* to see her side of things. I request a consultation with the Qualifier, but he seems to have taken a vacation. I'll have to handle this myself. So I do. I remind myself that we are all struggling—even two-timing actresses and drunken unfit mothers and lying friends and insubordinate assistants and cruel bosses. I don't need to upset myself with others' struggles. I need to remain calm. It is a pleasant day.

I notice the tulips—slender, graceful, lovely. They are twitching. It might be the breeze from the open kitchen window. I'm well aware of the fact that flowers can't think, that they have no inner lives. But if tulips *could* chuckle, these yellow tulips would at the moment be chuckling. They would be snickering. They would be enjoying a laugh riot.

"Goddamit!" I yell. Then I make a fist with my right hand, and I smash it against Kitty's door.

["It was my hand,"] I type a month later at my office. ["My right hand, and for four weeks it didn't move. Every morning and every night I thought of her while I looked at it, broken and bowed and swollen and crammed into a cast. I had smashed it on an oak door. The door belonged to my girlfriend-at-the-time. She is a hyphenated being to me these days. Girlfriend-at-the-time. Woman-I'm-still-trying-to-work-things-out-with. In-all-probability-soon-to-be-former-significant-other. And in those moments when I struggle to tie my shoelaces or button my shirt, nut-job-who-single-handedly-led-me-to-single-handedness."]

Yeah, I think as I type. *Yeah.*

"Once upon a time, we called each other 'honey.' But they were ironic 'honeys,' weighted with winks and nods. For the Single—which is to say Unmarried—Man in a Serious Romance, nicknames, like our most earnest attempts at love, are fraught with ambiguity, redolent with the scent of never-ending bliss, which can smell an awful lot like impending disaster."

I write about Bruce. I write about Kitty's perfidy. I write about my search for true love. I describe some of the sobbing sex and arrive at a place of sad wisdom. All in 1,500 words. If that's not a Single Guy column, I don't know what is.

Art gives me an "attaboy" note. Kiki says she liked the story. What she really liked, I suspect, is that the piece got teased on the cover. I confess my suspicions regarding Kiki's soulless careerism to Rose, who tells me I should be more generous with myself, less skeptical of women's motives. Then she asks if I remembered my checkbook.

Every week I receive ten to twelve submissions for the Single Guy column, because now I'm the editor in charge of it. The manuscripts go into a pile on the back right corner of my desk, behind the jojoba moisturizer and the river otter fur oil-based foot soap. Do the would-be single guys think I'm going to put their stories in the magazine, when those stories would be taking space otherwise filled with my words? This is a zero-sum game. The Qualifier might feel for the hacks' thwarted little ambitions, their puny hopes, and doomed pitches. But the Qualifier never did return after the Night of the Tulips. The Qualifier is dead. He doesn't wear the cast on my right hand. No, the man who wears that cast is someone else entirely. He is bold and ravenous for female flesh, and he doesn't wear lime green suits or put up with double-dealing girlfriends or frowny-mouthed, two-faced actresses. He doesn't use words like "available," and he employs exactly one nickname for women he dates (sweetie), and he dates lots of them, simultaneously. He needs to because—in addition to being angry, needy, hurt, and selfish—he must have material for the column he has seized for his own, the column that has granted him a new identity.

He needs to write columns about blind dates and about sex and about lusting after other men's girlfriends (that particular column is called "His Girl," and it gives him a dark thrill that worries Psychic Rose). He has a regular column now, and his byline is in the pages of a leading national men's magazine. He is a new man, and, unlike the Qualifier, who was sure of exactly nothing, the new me is sure of most everything.

My phone rings. Allison doesn't answer it. Of course, she doesn't. The Man in the Lime Green Suit would have puffed up with impotent rage. The Qualifier would have been miffed at Alison's failure to serve, but he would have empathized. He would have *understood* his assistant's sleazy professional longings and her obvious and perfidious, whorish-but-effective massaging of the Big Man's tender ego. The Qualifier would have qualified. The new me, though, does not. The new me is decisive. Yes, the new me might occasionally fantasize about Allison being seized by one of the Namibian crocodiles that the new me still enjoys watching late at night on Animal Planet. The new me might smile wistfully as the mighty croc takes the ambitious rubber-dress-wearing assistant into the crocodile's fearsomely named death spiral, as Allison's mouth forms a perfect O of terror and she is suddenly enveloped with regret that she never answered the new me's (*or the old me's*) phones—

The phone is still ringing.

The new me picks it up.

"Hello," I say, but what I think is that I'm grateful to Kitty and her persistent ex and my broken hand. Could the new me have been born without them?

Single Guy lures a waitress many years younger than himself up to his apartment and gives her lots of wine and has sex with her, and afterward, when she is sleeping, he notices with some discomfort that she snores. He notices with much more discomfort that she wears a toe ring. He isn't positive why this distresses him so, but as he flosses and brushes his teeth and listens to her raspy breathing, he suspects that the toe ring represents for him the idiocy of youth, the slavish and misplaced devotion to glittery and silly fashion. He, of course, is slavishly devoted to pretty young women even though he is in his midforties now. Maybe this is why he is so distressed. To work out his issues, the Single Guy writes a column about sex with younger women.

After that, Single Guy dates an Iowan who has recently moved to New York City and who likes to tell people she's just "a simple gal from corn country." She graduated Phi Beta Kappa, and when she has a lunch appointment with a man she thinks might help her career, she wears a low-cut blouse. "Time to get the guns out," she says, twirling in front of the mirror. Lucy scares me. Still, there are the big guns, and she is clever, so we become a couple, and it is nice, until I decide we should break up. Why? Psychic Rose asks me this, and I have no answers any adult would consider reasonable. I just think it should be so. Lucy and I break up, and we get back together. We break up, and we get back together. We do this four times, during which time my rashes return, and I suffer terrible indigestion. When we break up for good, I write a column about breaking up. I'm as usual the rational but befuddled hero of the piece. I aim for gentle, mildly self-lacerating humor. I leave out my rashes and digestive issues.

Psychic Rose has a suggestion regarding my physical discomfort. She tells me that my anxiety regarding illness has always been far worse than any actual ailments that befall me, that, in fact, my anxiety probably is the cause of my skin and stomach issues. She tells me that since I have such a "rich imagination" (I've confessed to Rose my love of the Man-Thing comic book series and Animal Planet and my visions of elephant and crocodile revenge on my assistant), I should use that imagination to help myself.

"But how?"

"Think of yourself as a big blue cell," Rose says.

"A big blue cell?" I silently tote up the sums I have spent over the past eight years on my psychic psychotherapist. It's a large-enough number to bring on a bad stomachache. "This, too, shall pass," I mutter to myself.

"What?"

"Nothing."

Rose has never bought in to the whole self-affirmation thing. She thinks it might be a way of distancing myself from the core of my real pain, which she's pretty sure involves Mr. Hass, the molester. Also, my mother. But at the moment, she wants to focus on my future as a big blue cell.

"I want you to picture yourself as a big blue cell," she says, "and every time you feel sick, picture a little brown particle that comes into the cell, some germ or virus, and then it's inside the big blue cell for a while, and then it passes out of the big blue cell."

I'm paying money for this advice, I think to myself and hope that Psychic Rose's mind-reading powers are not set to supersensitive today.

The Big Blue Cell roams the streets of Manhattan, muttering to himself, as usual. But now he mutters that he's a big blue cell. He buys lots of new clothes, partly because Ursula has cut him off from the fashion closet and partly because he is earning lots of money. He shops at Bergdorf Goodman for men and at Barney's, and on his shopping expeditions, just to be on the safe side, he searches for and notes the city's finest public bathrooms. In the basement of Henri Bendel, on Fifth Avenue, he discovers marble chambers worthy of a Babylonian potentate. Each bathroom is furnished not merely with the gleaming toilet and the brass handles and sparkling, capacious interior—the lavatories ("bathroom" seems too cheap a word for these magnificent palaces) also each have their own antechamber, also marble, equipped with a telephone.

I trip merrily down the steps at Bendel's during my lunch hour, fairly singing, "I'm a big blue cell, I'm a big blue cell." After expelling the germs and plague vectors that no longer terrify me, I spend thirty minutes or so in the antechambers, calling writers, conducting business, sometimes just studying the patterns in the pretty marble. Some of the shopkeepers look at me funny when I enter the store, but I'm invulnerable. I'm wearing the Egyptian cotton shirts and the elegant suits of worsted wool, and I'm looking good, and besides, any pathogens that enter me will not be with me for long, because though the Big Blue Cell looks cheerful and slightly round and while he might have not only gained back all the weight he lost during the Peak Ten program but added a few extra pounds as well, and while his suits might be pinching, he is remorseless and predictable when it comes to dispatching germs and pathogens, and women too. The foreign bodies come; the foreign bodies go.

The column on breaking up begets a column on reconnecting with old girlfriends. That one gets me a call from the husband of an ex, a woman in another city I dated long ago and whom I had lunch with during a trip to that city. In the piece, I imply that we slept together, which is untrue, but which helped with the narrative tension to which I always aspire and the sad wisdom I pretended to gain. My ex's husband, unfortunately, buys it. He calls me in New York City. He suggests he fly up and we meet. I decline.

"I am a big blue cell," I fairly screech when we hang up, as I race to the bathroom. "I am a big blue cell."

While not defecating in the marble sanctuaries of fancy department stores and betraying women in print and watching Animal Planet, I hang out at the *GQ* fax machine and occasionally tap into the magazine's e-mail system. I do this in the same way that the mountain weasel (who is sometimes referred to as the pale weasel) roams the peaks and alpine meadows of Kazakhstan, sniffing out danger before danger sniffs him out. Sometimes I rifle through the boxes of the Queen of Mean and David and Marty. I do this because I yearn to discover the secret to happiness and success at *GQ* and in New York City and in the world and because I have learned that if the secret involves boldness and/or mastery of the Stare, there's no way I'm moving up the ladder. I'm hoping that through my spy missions, I might learn some shortcuts to fulfillment.

What I learn is that other editors pay their writers more than I pay my corps of back hair and gum pinkener scribes, that David orders very expensive wine during the lunches he expenses, that Kiki is sleeping with a guy older than me (and much, much richer), and that one of the other assistants is sleeping with the Ascot, who e-mails her quotes from Hemingway while suggesting to her what she should wear when she comes to his place that evening. Some of this is disturbing, some amusing. What gives me a sharp pain is discovering that Allison has recently worked out a contract to write six features stories a year for a sum greater than my salary.

When he feels threatened, or neglected, the mighty but imperiled black rhino launches doomed and frenzied searches for a mate, because even though he possesses magnificent power and fears no other animal, he is a sensitive beast and sometimes doesn't really get the big picture. I learned that on Animal Planet. Or I dreamed it. Since a short bout of painkillers for my broken hand, I've been having trouble discriminating between my television bouts and sleeping visions. In any case, when I return from the Bendel's basement one day, I launch into a frenzied search through my calendar where I circle upcoming product launches and magazine parties. I'm feeling threatened and neglected. Single Guy hungers for fresh material.

Candy sports the requisite PR gal silky brown hair, the standard creamy skin. Her smile is more dazzling than most—equally as radiant as Susan's, but wider and more cheerful. As much as I abhor the word "adorable," and think it should be reserved for overweight-but-not-yet-morbidly-obese toddlers and certain breeds of trained pigs, Candy has the most adorable pug nose. Her eyes are dark brown and large, and though I always mistrusted writers who described eyes as expressing intelligence, Candy's seem to.

She's tiny, no more than five foot three. She's wearing a clingy black dress and strappy high heels. Candy is telling the woman next to her about the causes and treatments for melanoma. She's throwing around words like "basal" and "subdermal." What kind of talk is that from a PR gal at a sunscreen product launch? The words and the look don't add up. It makes no sense, not to the Qualifier or the Single Guy or the Big Blue Cell. Then I figure it out. The corporate strategists for the new sunscreen—the PR gals' bosses—must have combed the city's hospitals until they found a sexy dermatologist and then brought her here. Brilliant move. Sleazy, but brilliant. I respect that.

"So, Doc," I say, sidling next to her, more water moccasin than moth caterpillar, "How much are they paying you to shill?"

The eyes flash. I notice how full her lips are, how sexy her little grin.

"Paying me?"

"You're a doctor, right?"

"No, I'm the health editor for *Elle*. Who are you?"

When I tell her, the smile widens; the eyes flash some more.

"Oh yeah, the Single Guy. Poor baby."

I express my admiration for *Elle*. I confess my respect for health editors. I signal my sincere affection for the many products that hardworking health editors bring to the attention of their readers. I all but shout that the Single Guy she seems to have heard about is merely a literary persona, that he in no way resembles the decent, polite, well-mannered moisturizer-rubbing GQ senior editor gazing sincerely into her smart eyes.

I ask if she'd like to get together for lunch later that week. I suggest a place near Bendel's.

She puts her hand on mine. Her skin is very soft. They must get great product at *Elle*.

"Sure," she says. "But you have to promise me something."

"Of course."

"You have to promise that you won't write about me. I don't want to be reduced to a literary cliché."

Candy is more beautiful naked than she is with her clothes. She likes hamburgers and laughs easily. She has a great vocabulary. She uses words like "ostensible" and "jejune" and "archetype" and "crepuscular." She uses words like "meretricious" and "obviate" and "preternatural" too. She also claims to have invented the word "ginormous," which I find doubtful, but she looks so serious when she says it and is wearing a low-cut blouse and skin-tight jeans, so I accept that at least she *believes* she invented it. It makes her even more adorable. She listens to me rail about Allison and Rose and my life as a Big Blue Cell. We like the same movies. She agrees that Art doesn't appreciate me. She is entertaining no marriage proposals from ex-boyfriends of which I'm aware. She tells me I'm wonderful, that I should try to relax, that I should try to appreciate the joy within my grasp. I think she means her. She *never* gives me the frowny mouth, no matter how much I whine about my life. Sometimes late at night, when I'm at her apartment, and I can't sleep and I'm up late watching Animal Planet, she'll get up and pad behind me on her little feet and see that I'm studying the crocodile death spirals. She'll kiss my neck and say, "Are you okay, Cellie?" On those evenings, I feel something large and moist moving in my chest, like a boulder dislodging from a place it's been stuck for a long time, and then I feel Single Guy's flaccid gray heart skip a few beats.

One night, while we're holding hands on her couch, watching the wildebeests get ambushed by the crocodiles (it's one of the channel's most televised episodes), she asks how I'd like it if she cooked dinner for Valentine's Day.

I'd like it a lot. Trouble is, Single Guy thinks it seems a little hasty. That it might lead to expectations. That it seems fraught with romantic holiday, promise-making, gift-necessitating implications. But I'm trying to ignore Single Guy these days. I'm trying to live life not as that cad or as the oversized blue amoeba thing. The Man-Thing is *not* hunting for me. I am *not* the titmouse to the hungry ferret. I remind myself of these things. Rose would be so proud.

Sure, I say, Valentine's dinner sounds great.

When I arrive at her apartment, she is wearing a black cocktail dress, a necklace of pearls, and high heels. She wears an apron too, and when I enter, the smell of the steak and potatoes and green beans, and the sight of her makes me gasp. She looks like a young June Cleaver in a Maxim spread. Or maybe June Cleaver's younger sister who got into drugs and had to earn money for her terrible habit by stripping before finding religion and getting healthy again. A dash of Marian the librarian, certainly. I nuzzle her from behind when she sets the table, like the marmot from Animal Planet nuzzles the other marmot, when marmot number 1 is feeling particularly affectionate, right before both are killed by feral pigs. Or were they bobcats? I can't remember.

While I'm feeling affectionate and grateful, my neck starts itching, precursor to rash. Why would my neck start itching at a time like this? I'm safe and loved, about to be fed, and I'm nuzzling the very probable future Mrs. F, who will help make me happy *and* expand my vocabulary. Then I realize why my neck is itching. It's the same reason the humble yet misunderstood Norwegian rat's neck tingles when he approaches the fragrant and tantalizing hunk of cheddar that seems to beckon him, that seems to promise delight, the beautiful morsel of orange paradise carefully nestled in the spring-loaded instrument of the innocent little rat's annihilation.

I back away from marmot number 2. Why's she being so nice to me? What's with the balanced meal and the sexy June Cleaver getup? That's not right. Who would get out her pearls and then go to this trouble for such a rash-ridden, television-animal-loving, hamburger-gobbling moron? What's she after? The neck tingles. The rat is hungry, but he must practice caution. His survival depends upon it.

We eat and chat, and she kicks off one shoe under the table and rubs my left calf with the miniature but perfectly formed high arch of her left foot. She uses the word "rapturous," and then she smiles at me. Life is good. And then, the trap is sprung.

"C'mon," she says, "before we go to bed, help me do the dishes."

"Do you really think Candy went to all that trouble just so she could trick you into helping her with her dishes?"

"I don't know," I tell Psychic Rose. "Maybe."

What I want to say is, "How can a man ever understand you people?" but I don't.

"It sounds like Candy loves you," Rose says.

"Then why'd she try to make me do the dishes?"

"Steve, a lot of women ask their boyfriends to help with the dishes."

"A simple request would have been one thing. But luring me with the pearls and the cocktail dress and rubbing my foot under the table?"

Rose looks at me. I look at her, and I can't believe what I'm seeing. My psychic psychotherapist is giving me the frowny mouth!

"What?" I say. "What? Did I say something? Are you seeing something psychically disturbing?"

"Maybe you need to look at why you use the word 'luring' to describe Candy's dinner invitation to you."

I say nothing. I give Rose the frowny mouth. Two can play this game.

"Maybe you need to look at why you're so suspicious of your girlfriend, why you're so suspicious of women in general," Rose says.

"Well, maybe Bridget sleeping with my best friend has something to do with it. And Kitty seeking *closure* a few times a week with her old boyfriend."

"I understand," Rose says. "I do. But Candy is not cheating on you. She's not lying to you. She's making you dinner and looking sexy for you. For you! Asking you to help with the dishes is not a form of manipulation or betrayal."

"Not to you," I grunt.

"It sounds like you love Candy," Rose says. "Can you allow yourself to feel that?"

"But, Rose. Candy says she invented the word 'ginormous.' Don't you think that's weird? I mean, wouldn't it be dangerous for me to be involved with someone like that?"

Rose stares at me. She takes a deep breath.

The next day, I break up with Candy. I don't mention the dishes. I say something about not being ready to settle down, about respecting her too much to lead her on. I paraphrase something I read in one of the women's magazines about men who can't face their own terrors. Candy looks at me with her intelligent big eyes, which fill with tears, and she tells me that I am about to make a mistake, that I should believe in what we have, and be brave enough to work it through with her.

I tell her it's not a question of bravery and that we're through.

I write an essay for an anthology called *The Bastard on the Couch*, and I call it "A Bachelor's Terror." I don't mention the Big Blue Cell or the Qualifier or the Single Guy. I avoid mentioning Animal Planet and visions of rat traps. I write about Candy, breaking my vow to her, and while I'm at it, I turn her into a marriage-obsessed and scheming caricature. I transform her into the cliché I promised I wouldn't. The author comes across as wounded and confused, but brave. Very brave.

I tell my father every week on the phone that I'm fine. I tell him I'm really getting tired of the Four Seasons, that I think I need to cut back on all the rich lunches with Art. He congratulates me on all my Single Guy columns and asks—again—if I'm happy, and maybe that's what prompts me to walk into Art's office one spring morning.

"Art," I say, "I need to talk with you."

He is scribbling in his little black notebook, bent over his impossibly burnished, high-haunched-Amazon-harvested desk.

"Art?"

He continues to scribble, and when, after what seems like five minutes, he looks up, I give him the Stare. He gives me the Stare. We give each other the Stare.

"What?"

I tell Art I've loved working at *GQ*, that I really appreciate the opportunity he has given me, but that I want to write more, that I've always wanted to write more. I tell him that I'm going to try life as a freelance writer.

He gives me the Stare. I give him the Stare. I don't think he can quite believe that I'm quitting. I don't think I believe it myself.

"But I want you to know that I have a lot of myself invested in Personal Best and that I'm going to leave the section in great shape."

Have I always been such an emotional and convincing liar, or have I improved since working here? I tell Art that I will stay as long as he needs me, that I'll make sure the section is assigned for at least a few months, that I'll help find a new editor to assign the back hair and gum pinkener pieces everyone is counting on.

He continues to give me the Stare, and then he nods a little and smiles. I think the Man-Thing is admiring my decisiveness. I think he has been waiting for me to do something manly—to complain about Allison, to demand he respond to one of my meaty story pitches, to do *anything* other than cower and qualify—and that my bold, if unbelievably self-destructive, announcement pleases him.

"I understand," Art says and offers his hand. "How would you feel about a writing contract with the magazine?"

How would I feel about it? How would the mighty black rhino feel if he were allowed to roam the vast and grassy plains, free from fear and poachers? Pleased? Delighted? Flabbergasted? Art proposes that I write a few features and a few columns for the magazine. The columns will be for Personal Best, which I loathe, but the features will be meaty, manly stories. And I'll get a monthly retainer from the magazine, almost as big as the one Allison is getting. And I can keep an office there too. On my way out of Art's office, I give Allison the Stare, which she ignores, and I prepare to live my dream. Which turns out to be kind of a nightmare.

For my first manly contract writer feature, I fly to Roswell, New Mexico, to report on the fiftieth anniversary of the night that aliens allegedly landed on earth, leaving behind mysterious remains of a spaceship and some alien bodies. For a man who tends toward the gleefully cynical, who revels in the contemptuous bon mot and in offhand character assassination, interviewing Roswellians is like picking off purple-suited Frankenstein monsters in a barrel. The woman who has driven from Boston and who believes aliens abducted her and implanted things in her flesh, the larcenous locals who serve flying saucer pancakes and sell paintings of aliens to the credulous tourists, the wisecracking hacks from other magazines who gather at a local bar every evening and try to outdo one another with alien probe jokes. The story has everything a savage and dyspeptic writer of manly, meaty, mean features stories could want.

Art sticks "Aliens Among Us" in the columns section in the front of the magazine, rather than among the features, which I think is unfair, but rather than complain, I redraft my pitch about the professional bowler and his father. I mention to the Big Man that the bowler has been in and out of drug and alcohol rehabilitation centers for the past ten years and that, against all odds, he is winning championships again. If that potent combination of pain and redemption doesn't move El Jefe to make the assignment, I also point out that bowling is increasingly popular with men in their twenties making over $100,000 a year. I have no idea whether that's true or not, but it could be. It *should* be. After my story, in which I intend to illuminate not only the painful story of the bowler's life but also of *all* men's lives, it will be.

Art gives me the assignment, and I spend a week with the bowler at the Tuscon Invitational, where I hang out with other pro bowlers and their wives and girlfriends. I take the bowler and his wife to Tony Roma's for spareribs, and I spend time with them at the bowling alley bar and smile with understanding as the bowler sucks back many seven and sevens, and I yell along with them and everybody else as a bowling ball representative sings "Mac the Knife" at the bowling alley's karaoke night. I also visit the bowler and his parents in St. Louis, and I spend some time with him at the country club where he spends a lot of time drinking and golfing. I tell the bowler that my story will trace his development as a professional athlete and as a man. I tell the representatives from the Professional Bowlers Association who help me get set up in Tuscon that I want to explore bowling's evolution as legitimate sport, that I want to offer readers a peek into the difficulties that the organization's finely tuned athletes face.

This is how I start the piece:

> "I am not a dick," says the greatest bowler in the history of bowling. He has had a couple of beers, and he's now on his third seven and seven. When he's not bowling, he golfs. When he's done golfing, he drinks. Sometimes things seem clearer after a few drinks. "When I have a little buzz on, my eyesight gets better" is how he puts it.

The bowler might not be overjoyed with that, but few men see themselves with the clarity of a seasoned journalist. That's not my fault.

> Many of the bowlers throwing strikes this afternoon are built like Fred Flintstone. This undercuts the PBA's insistence that bowlers are finely tuned athletes. All the bowlers who chain-smoke don't help the PBA party line either. And not that facial hair has anything to do with athletic performance, but many of the bowlers sport mustaches that call to mind porn stars from the seventies and

dentists through the ages. Dentist / porn star mustaches simply do not scream "finely tuned athlete."

It's journalistically above reproach. But it's got attitude. The Big Man loves attitude. I lay on some especially pungent attitude when I turn my journalistically above-reproach eyes to bowling fans or, as I call them, "sluggish little pockets of hunched white-haired men and women who move from lane to lane watching, many of them chain-smoking, some missing teeth, a few with walkers. The air reeks of cigarette smoke and stale beer and disinfectant and sweat."

I suspect that the PBA people and the bowler will hate the piece. Big deal. I didn't spend a week of my life inhaling beer fumes with senior citizens so I could make some mustachioed fatties happy. I did it to plumb the murky depths of a particular bowler's soul, to investigate the sticky ties that bound him to his bowler father. I wrote it to take a hard, unflinching look at the pain that had led the younger bowler to drink and near-ruination and improbable glory. I wrote the story to tell the bowler's story but more critically to tell the story of *all* men's lives. Most importantly, I wrote the story to impress Art and to jack up the amount of money he was going to pay me in my new multiyear *GQ* writing contract. With the Roswell Piece and a few things I had cranked out on power push-ups and perfect sideburns and a couple more Single Guy columns, the year had skipped by. My current one-year contract was ending. This story fulfilled it.

Two days after I turn in "Up from the Gutter," Kiki calls me at home, where I'm staring out the window, thinking of the trinkets I'll buy with my raise. I'm considering some new cuff links. Kiki tells me the Big Man would like to see me in his office.

I swagger in. Looking good. Feeling good. My days of slinking and shuffling are behind me. No one will ever again order me to make anything meaner. The truth is often mean and painful. I have learned that, and now the bowlers and bowling fans will learn it too. Why should I feel bad about that? It's the truth—the attitude-filled, gracefully written truth. And isn't that exactly the elusive and precious commodity that will help to wise up the world and that will free me from ever again being forced to search for an adjective to describe moisturizer? The truth, in the form of my journalistically-above-reproach bowling opus, is what's going to incite Art to give me the fat multiyear contract that I have so long deserved.

"Steve," Art says just as I sink (without asking, because I am feeling so good) into his couch. "I'm worried about your productivity."

My productivity? I betrayed John Tesh for you. I savaged an entire city in New Mexico and mocked some possibly mentally ill people who have nightmares of aliens. I spent the past eight years of my life learning about emollients and eyebrow maintenance for you. And I just deconstructed the personal and painful relationship of a father and a son and told the story of all men's lives—for you!

This is what I should say to the beast who has terrified me ever since I first heard his growl. If I were the man I wanted to be, it's what I would say. But I'm not that man. Was I ever?

"You are?" I squeak.

"Yes, and that's why I'm not renewing your contract."

"You're not?" I whisper.

"No, I'm not. But maybe you could write some for us in the future. Keep in touch, okay?"

"But didn't you like the piece on the bowler?" I see the manuscript, sitting there forlornly on the desk that was polished by my imaginary but vivid high-haunched Nubian beauties.

"I haven't read it yet."

"You haven't?"

Art doesn't seem to hear, so I try again.

"You haven't?" What comes out is a soft, dying sound. I think of the polar bear cub I had watched the other night on Animal Planet. The furry youngster would have—*should* have—grown up to be one of the proudest and most fearsome predators ever to lumber across the polar ice sheet. But he hadn't found enough food his first winter. Had he spent too many hours in his fevered little bear brain, daydreaming of fleshy salmon, and not enough time foraging for berries? Had he been too slow? Too anxious? Too timid? Or had he just been unlucky, doomed from birth? I had watched the cub collapse on a snowbank, exhausted, crying for the help that would never come. His cries had grown softer and softer, until finally, they were barely sounds at all.

"You haven't?" I ask, again. It's as if I'm whispering into the howling arctic wind.

Art rises from the burnished desk, offers his Man-Thing hand. "Good luck," he says. He gives me the Stare. Behind it, I think, is a malevolent grin.

That night I call the deli across the street for Chubby Hubby. The next night, the same thing. I stay up late, watching *Law & Order* reruns and pay-per-view pornography on television. I start sleeping in. I go to the gym less, and when I do, it's to flirt with the women who hand out towels. I ask one of them to dinner. When I talk to the Ascot, one of my few remaining friends, I refer to Valerie as "Towel Girl," even though she's studying astrophysics at Columbia University. I also spend every Tuesday night playing backgammon and having sex with Kim, a yoga instructor who is married to a man she complains "has no conception of my feminine power or the power of chi." Kim drinks a bottle of wine by herself each time she comes over, and a couple times, she demands that I go out and buy her a second bottle. Twice, she asks me to rip her blouse as part of foreplay. I comply. Why not?

With no steady income from *GQ*, my savings dwindle, and because no one else is assigning me stories where I might tell the story of all men's lives, I start taking some assignments strictly for pay. I do a relationships column for one website. I write an astrology column for another. I write admiring short profiles of actresses, and because my *GQ* affiliation is still recent enough to exploit and to mention on contributors pages, an essay on "What Guys Really Think" regarding what an editor from *Allure* tells me is the latest craze, namely, "Grooming as Foreplay."

"Sure," I say. "I can do that. Any particular activities you want me to be sure to mention?"

"You know, like painting her toenails—"

"I think that's disgusting. Can't she do that herself?"

"Well, we want your opinion, but maybe a little more nuanced."

I'm trying to silently suck sugar off an afternoon apple fritter during our phone conversation. My consumption of sweets seems to be spiking. The pause in our conversation allows me to come to my senses.

"Sure, nuanced, I can do nuanced."

I do nuanced. I expound on the great joy men derive from massaging their girlfriends' hair, how happy it makes them to paint their special someone's toes.

I order ice cream every night, and I rarely rise before 10:00 AM, and by the end of the year, I am fatter than ever and cranky and approaching a zero balance in my bank account.

I know I need help but am not sure where to look. I consider a return to the meetings I attended after rehab. I know New York City has them. But such a return would represent more desperation than I care to admit.

On the afternoon before Christmas, the end of my ninth year in New York City, I call the woman who helped me get the *GQ* job. She has climbed from editorial assistant to senior editor to executive editor. Now she is editor in chief at *Elle*. She is Candy's boss, in fact. But Robbie wouldn't hold my behavior with Candy against me, would she? It's Christmas Eve, after all. Aren't holidays the time when old friends are supposed to reconnect? I find her at the office.

"What're you working on?" she asks.

I hate that question. I had planned to have a fat multiyear magazine contract. I had also planned to have written other nonmagazine things. A novel. Some short stories. Manly, meaty stuff. Maybe if things got tight, a screenplay, but just to pay the bills. No one *plans* to become a whore.

In the past ten months my most ambitious project had been a magazine story about a starlet whose laughter I'd compared to a melody. "Her laughter is like a melody," I had written, though, for the life of me, I couldn't remember what tune I had been thinking of. Which made me not only fat, not only a hack, but also a fat, forgetful hack. And Christmas was the next day. And I was alone.

What was I working on? Well, there was my weekly Internet dating column—due in a couple days. I typed it late at night, while I watched porn. I commanded my readers to be honest and giving. "She is a precious gift from heaven," I instructed, "not a toy." There was the monthly online horoscope for another website, which, after I discovered how labor-intensive it was to actually research planetary movements and patterns, I decided to simply make up. I ordered my readers to quit being such selfish hogs. "Don't be a gimme pig," I thundered. "Mercury says there will be ugly consequences unless you become more charitable. Try giving for a change, instead of taking all the time." I also strongly advised caution. "Dark forces are at work in the cosmos this week," I warned, "so don't take any unnecessary chances." There was the "Grooming as Foreplay" piece, in which I had pronounced that "nothing turns a man on more than making his beautiful girlfriend even more beautiful, while she simply lies back and enjoys a private, intensely personal pedicure."

What was I working on?

"The usual whore work," I say.

Wrong answer. My friend takes her position seriously. In her world, actresses laugh melodiously all the time.

"That's a nice attitude," Robbie says.

"It's honest."

"You know, you're getting a reputation among a lot of people as a hothead."

"What people?"

"I'm not going to tell you that."

"Why?"

"I don't want to get in the middle of anything."

I think I hear holiday music and laughter in the background. Probably an office holiday party. I hadn't been invited.

"You're supposed to be my friend. This is my professional reputation on the line. You won't be in the middle of anything."

"Steve, you called women 'psychotic harpies' in your grooming piece. For a *women's magazine!* You didn't think that might affect your reputation?"

"I was making a rhetorical point. Besides, that phrase got cut."

"It got cut after you told your editor that she was a 'tone-deaf martinet.'"

"Is that who's been spreading lies about me? Is that who, because if she—"

"No, I'm not going to put myself in a position that—"

"You're not just an editor, Robbie. I consider you a precious gift from heaven and—"

"Nice try, Steve, but save it for your relationships column. I'm not giving up a name."

There it was again, in the background. Unmistakable this time. "Jingle Bells."

"Look, if you're talking about that bald, fat-assed, weasel-headed Iago over at—"

"You really need to work on your anger. You are becoming someone who is not pleasant. And I have to get back to work."

I hate it when people with office jobs tell me they have to get back to work. I picture Allison writing a suck-up memo to Art, Lisa twirling in one of her tight skirts. I close my eyes, and there are the sad but proud bachelor lions on Animal Planet, exiled to the patchy scrubland of the Serengeti, skulking about and roaring listlessly after their challenges to the alpha lion (which I'm sure seemed like a great idea to the bachelors at the time) were met with torn ears and terrible wounds and defeat and exile. I miss the office.

After hanging up, I grab my laptop and open my latest astrology column. It's due in a couple days.

"Reevaluate so-called friendships," I type. "The holiday season is an excellent time to let go of things, to cut the dead wood from your life, to clean the closets and open the windows."

Too many metaphors? Not for the her-laughter-is-a-melody guy.

I put my laptop aside. I call family members. I get recordings at my mother's, father's, and older brother's. I don't leave messages, because I don't want them to think I'm so pathetic I need to reach out to my family on Christmas Eve. My little sister, a ceramicist, massage therapist, and waitress in a small mountain town in Southwestern Colorado, picks up the phone.

"Happy holidays," I say.

"Same to you," Ann says. "What's new?"

"The usual." I don't mention how terrible the usual has been lately. I haven't seen my sister for a year, since she moved from San Francisco to the mountains. She moved there after a breakup. She wanted a fresh start. Now she lived in a village of gun owners and rock climbers. No need to upset what I imagine is her hard life. Then, in the spirit of holiday politeness, I ask, "What's new with you?"

"I'm pregnant. I'm pregnant! I'm so happy. I don't know if I've ever been this happy!"

"That's great!" I choke out. "Um, who's the father?" Since the breakup, I didn't think my sister had been dating.

"His name's Matt," she tells me. "We met a few months ago, when he was driving through town, on his way to Mexico. He's got an MBA and used to work in banking, but he gave it up to follow his passion."

"His passion?" *Uh-oh*, I think.

"He's spending a few years skiing and rock climbing. Right now he's in Scotland, which is where he's from. He's having some trouble with a green card."

"That's great!" I lie. I know better than to ask my free-spirited sibling about wedding plans. I try to keep things neutral, but hinting-at-joyous. "Is Matt excited about becoming a father?"

"Well, he wanted to know if it's going to interfere with his rock climbing."

I laugh, because I can't imagine another response will do anything but make me weep. I wish Ann happy holidays. I stare out the window of my apartment. I pull my laptop back onto my lap, open a new file.

I begin.

> Dear Matt,
>   I don't blame you for falling in love with my sister or for impregnating her or for throwing away a career so you could indulge your most infantile appetites. I've been there. I identify.

No, that's too transparently hostile. I need to gain his confidence before I impart wisdom to which he will listen.

I try again.

> Dear Matt,
>   Congratulations! I know that you hardly know the mother of your child to be, but . . .

That's not quite it either. I push the laptop away. I need human companionship. I call Kim, the married yoga teacher. No, she says, she cannot come over. It's Christmas Eve.

"But I was going to cook something special for us," I say. Total lie.

"I want to. I really want to. And next year, when I'm divorced, we can spend the entire day together. We can spend every day together."

Four lies. Four total lies.

"I'm thinking of starting a yoga practice," I lie. "I've been thinking how all the answers I've been seeking outside might lie within."

"Bullshit!" she hisses. It comes out as "bullshissssssh!" She's been drinking. But at least she's finally telling the truth. It's more than I can say for myself.

"C'mon over," I say. "I understand your chi."

"Quit being a baby."

"But it's Christmas."

"And you're Jewish." It sounds like "Juiceshissssh."

"You should really try giving for a change," I say, "instead of taking all the time."

She laughs. Nothing like a melody. Maybe like the part in the "The Devil Went Down to Georgia" when Satan takes the fiddle into the bar and makes the ugly, raspy, spooky, screeching sounds. But not a melody.

"Screw you, Astroboy," she says. That's a surprise. Robbie was reading my relationships column, and now Kim is familiar with my work charting the sun signs? Maybe I have a wider readership than I imagined. I should ask for a raise.

When we hang up, I grab the remote control and the phone and call the deli across the street.

The Pakistani guy who answers recognizes my voice on the phone. "Ah, apartment 40-F," he says, "perhaps another pint of Chubby Hubby tonight, am I correct?" On the rare evenings I had human company, I imitated him, which invariably got a laugh and made me despise myself even more.

Christmas Eve. About a year since my contract expired and I started watching my savings disappear and my dream of meaningful work remain deferred. I did whore work. Which made me a whore. A porn-watching, Chubby Hubby–sucking, Christmas Eve–alone whore. I needed to figure something out.

I take a few deep breaths. I clutch the remote control to my sickly breast. I pull my laptop back to where it belongs, my lap.

"Dear dirtbag," I write.

Yeah, I think. "Yeah," I say.

The next day, I call directory assistance, and I get a number, and I call that number and get some other numbers, and then an hour later, freshly showered and shaved, I walk out of my apartment building into a chilly, crisp Christmas, then a block east, and then down some ancient stairs into the basement of the local YMCA.

I put myself into a plastic chair between a muttering white-haired woman and a guy in tight shorts and a tank top who pats me on the shoulders and says, "Welcome, newcomer."

The old lady and the tank-topped man are, like me, seekers of serenity, fellow travelers on the long, torturous path to, if not happiness, at least a respite from self-loathing, fear, anxiety, anger, and all the other things that have led me to psychic shrinks, deli men who recognize my voice, cranky ice cream vendors and drunk quasi girlfriends who call me baby, but not in a good way. Writing to the father of my sister's unborn child last night—identifying with him in some ways, hating him in other ways—had gotten me to thinking. I had decided that I needed help. This group had seemed like my best bet.[1]

We are in a windowless room, in a circle of plastic chairs, most of which squeak whenever anyone squirms. Remorseless fluorescent light bathes us all—the sad and the lonely, the fat and the tank-topped (he must be cold!), and, most interesting of all to me, the tall blonde with the sparkly green eyes and the freckled neck and the swimsuit-modelish-looking body. She reminds me of Susan, except more Icelandic.

She is telling the group a story. She is describing to us ten years of a successful European modeling career, during which she grossed half a million dollars annually. It was a time filled with sleepless nights, loveless sex, notions of suicide. I notice other people are nodding, so I nod too. Finally, she says that she found this group. She started sharing honestly. She started living "the principles of the program." And now she is happy.

We applaud. One fat woman I'd guess to be sixty says she identifies with the beautiful blonde's pain. A man wearing leather pants praises her courage. Many weep quietly. Others smile radiantly. Some do both. I can't stop thinking about the yearly take.

Half a million dollars, I think as I try to smile at the woman. *Half a million dollars. Half a million dollars. Half a million dollars!* A big sodden thought balloon, filled with "half a million dollars," is wobbling over my head, much like the thought balloon with the doughnut in it forever wobbles above and plagues Homer Simpson.

As the thought balloon wobbles, others in the group take turns speaking. The leather-pants guy talks about "finding a new family" in the group. The guy who patted me on the back says, for the first time in his life, he knows "the meaning of 'surrender.'"

Half a million dollars! I think as I smile a watery smile at the blonde. *Half a million dollars!* Then, I notice something odd. There is silence. Everyone is looking at me. People have been speaking in round-robin fashion, and it's my turn.

"Um," I say, "I want to deepen my spiritual life, and I heard about this group. A spiritual life has always been very important to me." I look deeply into the blonde's eyes as I say this. Then I pause, and flutter the fingers of my right hand lightly on my chest, to signify deep sincerity. "Very important!"

A guy across the circle from me coughs, and I suspect for an instant that he is covering up a laugh. But what kind of asshole would come to a meeting designed for spiritual development only to laugh at one of its participants? I find out when it's his turn.

"I can't tell you how much your story touched me," the guy says. He stares at the blonde even more ferociously than I had. He is wearing jeans with holes in the knees and Doc Martens and a tight T-shirt that shows off his biceps and his toned torso. He has big white teeth and blue eyes, bluer than mine

"I know what's it like to have it all—the money and the sex and the fame—and to still feel empty," my newest archenemy says. "I know because I had it too. And now all I have is love." Then he leans forward, and his chin trembles. I wonder how long it took him to learn that trick. I vow to myself that one day I will learn the fake chin tremble.

To my horror, the group is leaning toward the guy. No one leans farther than the blonde.

The guy does the chin tremble some more; then he flutters his fingers on his chest. I can't *believe* this guy. "Now all I have is love to offer. I just need to find someone who will accept it."

Much applause, and then it's time for the meeting to break up. We all hold hands and close our eyes and say a prayer about love, and then the group leader recites a passage about how the next time anyone feels compelled to overeat or act out sexually or gamble, she or he should "hold yourself gently like a kitten." I open my eyes to peek, and I see the chin trembler has his eyes open too. We look at each other, and then he looks at the blonde and back at me and waggles his eyebrows and grins. I think of the snow fox from Animal Planet, a cunning and resourceful predator.

"Smokin', huh?" the chin-trembling eye waggler asks me after the meeting as I'm working over a chocolate doughnut in a Starbucks across the street from the Y.

"Huh?"

"The blonde," the chin trembler says. "The half-a-million-dollar babe."

"Oh yeah, she was pretty. But I'm more interested in trying to find some spiritual grounding."

"Yeah, right," he says. "Me too. I'll tell you, I'd like to hold her gently like a kitten, if you know what I mean."

He's an unemployed actor who was born in Belgium. His name is Frank, and he's been going to meetings for a little over a year. He does occasional voice-over work and works as a waiter at a steak house. He's dating a married bisexual who has a large snake tattoo on her back, "but I wanted to see what else was available, so I decided to check out some meetings."

"You go to meetings to pick up women?"

"Not *primarily* to pick up women. I'm about as fucked up as anyone in there. I'm more fucked up than most, less fucked up than others. But I promise, if I had made half a million dollars a year for even one year, I wouldn't be squatting in a YMCA basement. Someone who looks like her, with that kind of money, bitching and moaning to people like us in a basement on Christmas, now *that's* fucked up!"

"Oh," I say. I don't know what else to say. He seems really angry.

"What are you doing tonight?" he says.

"I don't know," I say. "Watching some TV, holding myself gently like a kitten?"

"Nah, you're not. We're going to another meeting."

Frank and I attend meetings on the East Side of Manhattan, where members tend to wear suits and dresses and complain about the vagaries of the stock market and the considerable difficulties of maintaining a second home. We attend meetings on the West Side, our neighborhood, where members less well-dressed and less well-groomed are more likely to talk about their mothers and their shrinks and to use the phrase "inner child." We attend meetings downtown, where actors and models lament the impossibility of ever finding true love and artists with nose rings and tattoos make me feel very Midwestern. Many of the meetings occur in basements—of YMCAs[1] as well as churches—and others take place in hospitals and conference rooms and high-ceilinged chambers with stained glass windows and tables thick as dictionaries. We sit in circles, in crooked rows, around the thick tables. Sometimes a single speaker shares her (or his) story of spiritual emptiness and salvation. Sometimes people take turns speaking. There are dozens of us at some meetings, hundreds at others. We sit in cold metal chairs, on overstuffed couches, in cheap plastic things that squeak when we squirm. The best meetings, I think, serve cookies, and the Angry Belgian and I tend to arrive early at those. When an hour passes and whatever meeting we're at concludes, we retreat to our favorite neighborhood diner, where we eat blueberry pancakes and bacon and drink coffee and talk about how

---

[1] The group that meets in the YMCA basement is a single part of a loose-knit international organization dedicated to, among other things, helping anxious, angry, sad, and generally lost people find themselves and some sort of connection to others. When referring to the basement meeting—and other similar meetings in New York City—I do so without naming the international organization. This is because I fear the wrath of the meeting attendees I know, certainly. It's also because I respect—in my own admittedly dubious fashion—the organization's long tradition of anonymity.

screwed up the people in the meetings are and which women we'd like to hold gently like kittens.

I ask Frank to teach me the chin tremble; he starts sprinkling the "my spiritual life" line in his shares. Then the bisexual tattooed woman dumps him, and one of women in the rooms he's sleeping with tells him she might be pregnant, and he tells me one night at my place, as we're watching *The Great Escape*, eating Chubby Hubby (I've bought two pints: I'm working on being more generous), that his life is over, that he's in debt, that he's a failure, that now that someone's going to make him pay child support, he'll end up flipping burgers somewhere, forever.

"No, you won't," I say. "Things are going to be okay."

"No, they won't. They haven't ever been okay."

"Look, you aren't even sure she's pregnant."

"I'm fucked. I'm totally, completely fucked."

"Shut up and hold yourself gently like a kitten," I say, which is a little heartless, but I don't know what else to say. "This is the part where Steve McQueen rides into the barbed wire."

But Frank doesn't say anything. He makes some weird noises. I look over at him. His chin is trembling, but more spastically than his fake-chin tremble.

"Really, man," I say as I can't believe I'm saying it. "Things are going to be okay. Maybe we should start trying to work that program they always talk about in meetings. Maybe that would help."

Frank says something, but I can't understand what, through his crying. I feel a little sorry for him. Truth is, I feel sorry for myself too. He's going to be a father to a child whose mother fell for the fake-chin tremble. That's bad. I'm going to be an uncle to a child whose father worries how parenthood is going to affect his rock climbing. That's bad too. It's not a good day. This, too, is *not* going to pass. Pregnancies last awhile, and after that comes birth and then many, many, many years of life. That's really bad. I haven't had a drink or used drugs in sixteen years. I am so lonely that I attend basement meetings for companionship. I am a whore whose disembodied voice and unspoken desires are recognized immediately by the Pakistani guy at the deli across the street. I need help.

"We really do need help," I say. "We really should start working the program."

"Right," the Angry Belgian says. "Then what? We'll start wearing leather pants and crying a lot?"

Of course, we don't do that. Wearing leather pants, crying in public, or working the program. Going to meetings and hitting on newcomers is one thing. But actually doing the kitten holding and praying and helping others, that's something that neither the Angry Belgian nor I are quite ready for.

It turns out that the Angry Belgian's girlfriend isn't pregnant, and relieved, he immediately dumps her. We continue to go to meetings, to hit on women there, to make fun of the others in the room, to watch movies together, and to eat ice cream. He reminds me a little of Denny, but not as sinister or psychotic.

I complain to Frank about my idiot editors and my idiot girlfriends, and he complains about his idiot girlfriends and his greedy producers and tip-hoarding steak house managers. Frank decides to enroll at Hunter College, to get the bachelor's degree he never got around to. That makes me think I should do something big too, something life changing. But what? I apply for some editor jobs, but no one's hiring. Apparently my *GQ* experience isn't impressing anyone anymore. And it appears the rumors Robbie mentioned about my being a hothead are true—none of the places I'm pitching story ideas to is getting back to me.

I spend much of my time, when not watching porn or eating ice cream or hanging out in meetings and diners with the Angry Belgian, honing my letter to my no-good presumably future brother-in-law.

I write.

I don't blame you, Matt. The things that move you—adolescent crushes, sex in exotic locales, the increasingly potent magic of the wilderness and open road, especially when the alternatives are diapers and a job and filing your taxes and numbing responsibility—I can understand. Actually, I can understand them too well. I have been charmed by pretty faces before, seduced by wild places and mild winters. I have called in sick, snuck out early, made jokes about the "old ball and chain," cheated, weaseled, waffled—actions I gather that you're entirely comfortable with. I have hummed "Don't Fence Me In" as I left relationships, "I Gotta Be Me" as I changed jobs, "My Way" as I drove cross-country. Bankers and lawyers and other tax-paying members of the country I have dismissed as hapless and hopeless "wage slaves."

That's not bad, I think. It's manly. Verges on meatiness too. Why can't I bring this kind of manly meatiness to my whore work?

Psychic Rose tells me I should stop using that phrase.

"Why?" I ask at our regular Thursday afternoon session. "You're always telling me to be honest. I'm being honest. It's whore work."

She says nothing. Is she giving me the Stare? No, Rose might be psychic, and she might be fed up with me sometimes, but she's not so evil that she'd give me the Stare. I had misjudged her before. Or had I? I try to send her a telepathic question: "Are you giving me the Stare?"

Rose sighs.

"Steve, by calling your writing whore work, you're devaluing it and yourself."

"But it's honest." Suddenly, I'm obsessed with honesty.

"Plus," Psychic Rose adds, "calling it whore work—even if you think it's honest—is not going to help any of your working relationships."

She has a point there. I promise her I won't call my whore work whore work anymore.

I write, when I settle on the couch that night.

> Matt, as your future brother-in-law, I must tell you that lying about felony convictions, to INS officials, to employers, especially to fathers-in-law with pregnant daughters, is not a good idea. By now I have learned that it was a stolen sleeping bag when you were a rock climbing teenager, and that's why you've been stuck in Scotland all this time. I understand the impulse. I sympathize with your position. I have lied myself. But, Matt, you are almost a father now, and it's time to start coming clean. Coming clean does not mean telling my father, when he says to you, "It's time to grow up now," "Well, your daughter hasn't grown up yet."

That paragraph exhausts me. Time for a reward. I grab the remote and the phone. Ice cream and porn. I wonder when I'll grow up.

Isaac is born on August 6, while his father is still stuck in Scotland. I send Ann a baby-sized T-shirt I buy in Times Square that says "Someone in New York Loves Me." I tell the spiritual development group that I'm an uncle and people pat me on the back. My savings account continues to hemorrhage, and my waistline balloons, and except for the Angry Belgian, who is more and more busy with class work, I have no friends. All I have is my letter to Matt, and I polish it almost every day. I think it's my way of improving the world. If I can't change myself, maybe I can change his. Maybe I can help him.

I write.

I feel a kinship with you. It is not a good feeling.

Honest, but warm, I think.

But I am also confident that you will change. Because I'm confident that *I'll* change. I've long known that one day I would grow up or settle down, stop running, go straight. This portentous day, I was sure, would come when I met someone special, someone sweet and vulnerable and soft. My moment of reckoning, I figured, would come when I fathered a child.

That makes me cry for a few minutes. It's the most heartfelt thing I've written in a long time, the most honest. I should do writing like this more often, I think, as I reach for the remote and the phone. Then I stop reaching. A thought occurs to me. It's the kind of thought they talk about in the YMCA basement. I think it's an epiphany. I close the file, start another.

I write to the editor at *Outside* magazine.

Dear Sir,

My little sister was recently impregnated by a rock climbing, patchouli-scented, carabiner-toting rock climber and extreme skier. I have some mixed feelings about this and have written him a letter. I wonder if you might be interested in taking a look and possibly buying and publishing it?

When I go to sleep that night, I repeat my usual affirmations about it being a pleasant day and all things passing. And then I add a new one.

"I'm not a whore," I whisper to myself and to my chilly bedroom and to the vast blinking, writhing metropolis that I have tried and failed to conquer, that has in fact cowed me into months and months of sugary Chubby Hubbiefied isolation. "I am *not* a whore."

Outside buys the piece, and except for the editor inserting a passage where I entertain "*my recurring daydream in which your Capilene-clad body gracefully executes an unaided free-solo, airborne descent into some bottomless gorge,*" it runs pretty much the way I wrote it.

I push back a little on the death daydream—after all, he is the father of my nephew—but the editor insists, and I, the man who hasn't quite ascertained the exact limits of his whoriness, I go along.

I long ago stopped going to the gym. Kim's backgammon visits become more infrequent, and then stop altogether. I stop going to meetings too—what have they done for me? But I needed to do something. I knew that. But what?

The blubbering kitten lovers in the basements (it seemed like there was at least one at every meeting) had swapped stories of packing up and moving on, of fresh starts and doomed endings, and they had smiled with condescension and contempt at their former selves and their misguided hopes. They had spoken with pity of "the geographic cure" and promised that traveling to a different place in the world would not help anyone escape his demons. But what did they know? They wore leather pants. They blew half-million-dollar salaries. They weren't like me.

I call my sister. I call the airlines. I pack my cold-weather clothes.

Chapter 11

Oy, Wilderness

"Come here in July, and Silverton will play you for a sucker," I type on my laptop as a ragged howling wind rattles the little shack in which I sit. I am wearing long underwear, sweatpants, a sweatshirt, a down coat, a stocking cap, and gloves with the fingertips cut off. Beneath a naked lightbulb, perched on a peeling plastic chair the color of urine, I shiver and huff out moist white cloudlets of condensation.

"It will play you for a sucker as I sometimes fear it has played me," I continue.

"Yeah!" I try to say, but what comes out is "yeh-yeh-yeh-YEH!" I shiver some more, puff out some more clouds.

The shack is eighteen feet by eighteen feet, with windows that don't open and a door that has no lock and a faucet that froze and cracked a year ago and still lies in the sink. In the moonlight it gleams, the long cold neck of a wounded bird. A dented black stove hunkers in the middle of the splintered plank floor, and two long steps from the stove is the peeling chair and a scratched-up card table I pretend is a desk. Up a ladder on another plank floor is a lamp and a mattress.

I push back from the computer, throw two logs into the stove, which sputters and crackles cheerfully. "Eat up, Little Man," I say. I have taken to calling the stove Little Man.

I tell the very few East Coast editors to whom I speak on the telephone that I'm here, in Colorado's southern San Juan Mountains, to visit my sister and her toddler, who live across town. I don't tell them that leaving my shack after dark requires more manliness than I can summon. I don't tell them that fifteen feet of snow, on average, fall on the shack every year, often closing the two mountain passes that provide the only ways into or out of this godforsaken snow-choked village of four hundred, or that even on clear days, it's one and a half hours over the most avalanche-prone stretch of highway in North America to things like fresh vegetables and bookstores and fluoridated water. I don't tell them that every few years the hardy and possibly deranged townsfolk vote down the state's offers to fluoridate the water, and that at a recent meeting, when a dentist had suggested fluoridation might cut down on the town's alarming incidence of dental decay, some of the townsfolk had shouted him down and called him a Nazi. I don't mention that the townsfolk terrify me or that I've taken to thinking of them as townsfolk—that I purposefully don't tell anyone here I live in New York City or that my last name is Friedman. Why take chances?

The shack squats on a mound of gravel across a dirt road from an icy meadow that slopes down to the Rio de Las Animas Perdidas, the River of Lost Souls, which seems fitting. Two hundred feet the other side of the river is Kendall Mountain, its forested slopes scarred by long white avalanche chutes. In February, the shack stays in the shadow of the mountain until 10:00 AM, and the temperature sometimes drops to thirty below zero. One night I lumber down the steps and into the bathroom, and as I'm urinating, I hear a strange sound. The water in the toilet bowl has frozen.

"What's your fucking problem?" I say to Little Man as I struggle up the ladder. "Can't you work a little harder?"

I spend much of my first few weeks on the mattress up the ladder under two sleeping bags, reading. I read *The Great Gatsby*, *The Odyssey*, *Endurance*, the journals of John Muir. I tell myself that I am like a fallow field, like a battery that is recharging. I tell myself I am like a once-thriving bamboo plant, and I just need some more water or sunlight or loamier soil—or whatever bamboo plants need. I wonder if it might have been a mistake coming to this possibly anti-Semitic, certainly dentist-hating, disproportionately toothless mountain town in order to find spiritual nourishment. Maybe I should have stayed in New York and just stepped up my meeting attendance. No, I can't allow myself to be negative. I am just in need of recharging. Or loamier soil. I'm pretty sure that thinking of myself in metaphorical terms and reading admirable authors will help me regain my bearings.

Two months as a bamboo plant with admirable authors and Little Man make me grouchy. By Valentine's Day, I'm deep into a book about the Ebola virus and a two-volume biography of Hitler.

I only venture out of the shack at midday, to walk ten minutes across town. There, my sister makes me lunch and tells me to play with my nephew.

Isaac is a serious child, placid and bemused most of the time. He cries very little, but when he is displeased with something, he wrinkles his forehead.

"Live it up, I-Dog," I tell him one day while he bounces on my knee and burbles peacefully. "Because when you're older, things are going to get bleak and lonely and cold. No one's going to bounce you on his knee, and no one's going to give you assignments, and the only people who will know you will be deli guys." I hear a sound. It's my sister, coming out of the kitchen. Ann gently puts down the knife in her hand—she has been cutting tomatoes to make me a salad, to help me lose weight—and even more gently takes her son into her arms, then fixes me with a look, and tells me I need to snap out of it.

"What?" I protest. "Snap out of what?"

"The Nazi·stuff. The Ebola nonsense. Whore work. Talking to the wood-burning stove."

"How did you know about that?"

"Because I've been listening to you playing with Isaac. Complaining to him how Little Man is lazy. How Goebbels was a public relations genius. How editors don't understand you. How when blood is coming out of your orifices, it's probably too late for medical attention."

"Well, isn't it good for children's language development if an adult tal—"

"Godammit, Steve, he's eleven months old!"

I say nothing. Isaac says nothing but wrinkles his forehead, first at me, and then at his mother.

I try the Stare on my sister, but it doesn't work.

"Why don't you write something?" Ann asks.

"Like what?"

"Why don't you write about Silverton? There are certainly enough oddballs here. What do you call it? Quirky."

"But who would want to buy . . . ?"

"Who cares who would want to buy it? You're always complaining about your whore work. So write a story for something other than money. And here, take your nephew back while I do the dishes. For some reason, he seems to love you."

I spend the next month getting to know Silverton. I spend much of that time at the Avalanche Coffee Shop, frequented primarily by Silvertonians younger than forty, men and women more likely to own climbing rope and laptops than snowmobiles and guns. "Trust fund babies," according to those who hang out at the Miner's Tavern, whose clientele is mostly former miners, descendants of miners, and people who wished the mines never would have closed. The Miner's Tavern crowd tends to distrust the federal government and to believe deeply in homeschooling and the right to bear arms and ride snowmobiles. "Toothless old rednecks," according to one of the regulars at the Avalanche.

I make friends with both groups. I shoot pool at the Miner's Tavern and discuss hemorrhagic fever with a county employee who believes the federal government uses black helicopters to spy on its citizens and that it has discovered the cure for AIDS (but is withholding it to protect pharmaceutical profits). The town librarian knows my name, and she always asks if I'm having a good time. The forest ranger cuts my hair while I sit in her kitchen, and we chat about Yeti sightings and road conditions and annual snowfall and rhubarb pie recipes (Silverton is the rhubarb capital of the world) and the secret to happiness and whether a particular developer is a visionary or a lying profiteer. I kick a soccer ball in the twilight with a teenaged snowmobiling thug. Wednesday and Friday afternoons I visit the town dump and its administrator, a ropy, bearded guy named Fred, who also works at a massage therapist and musician and who tells me to "stay in the right side of the brain." He gestures at the mountains encircling us and then adds, "It's safe behind the walls of Kong here, dude, so whatever you need to do to stay here, do it." I spend many hours on the Avalanche's sunny porch, bitching and moaning about rapacious flatlanders, snickering at the well-coifed, skim-latte-sipping poseurs adjusting their reflector shades before they climb into their BMWs with out-of-state license plates, doing my best to forget—my Missouri roots and my temporary life in the shack notwithstanding—that, basically, I'm a New York Jew with a laptop.

I confess to Isaac after lunch one day that I'm not sure where I should live and I wonder if I'll ever marry and whether Mrs. Friedman might even live in Silverton, and he wrinkles his forehead.

"Whatever becomes of Uncle Stevie, no whore work for you, dude," I whisper to him when I'm sure Ann is out of earshot. "Whore work is for whores." "Nor nerk!" Isaac proclaims, laughing. "Nor nerk!"

All the Silvertonians will come fully, vividly alive in my piece. It will be a clear-eyed and bemused take on an isolated mountain town, a lucid anthropological study propelled by the personal journey of its narrator, a journey that will take him—and the reader—from self-loathing and obsessive, exhausting, blinding self-centeredness to sad, rueful wisdom. It will be my salvation. I will imbue even the most ignorant, judgmental, rude, and toothless old embittered ex-miners with grace and nobility. I will explore the dark and painful secrets of the Silvertonians I love most, like the chain-smoking twenty-six-year-old waitress at the Avalanche who drives a Volvo and reads Hegel and whose cashmere sweaters have prompted talk. I'll get inside Fred the Garbage Dump Man's head. Maybe I'll write a dream sequence from his point of view.

I struggle with the piece for six weeks, in between babysitting and keeping company at night with the Hegel lover, which prompts more talk. I spend lunchtime talking to Isaac about man's search for meaning, and afternoons at the dump, philosophizing with Fred. Winter turns to spring. Would-be Silvertonians relax when the fragrant blue skies of April arrive. Then comes another snowstorm and mud and more snow and more mud. Spring is the season when men and women with just enough grit to have made it through a winter in the mountains realize they can't do it again. Spring is when would-be Silvertonians turn into ex-Silvertonians.

The skies are blue now, but I don't trust them. It's morning, and I'm in the shack, sitting on my urine-colored plastic chair watching the snow fall and listening to my paunchy, plucky stove and wishing I knew what it felt like to have grit.

CHAPTER 12

THE BLONDES IN THE BASEMENT

"Out of towners drive over the mountain passes and into town during the soft summer months." I write, though I haven't really spent much time in Silverton during the soft summer months. But I imagine they're softer than where I am now, which is back in Manhattan. It's May, and I have been here for a week, polishing my anthropological tour de force.

While the children gorge on funnel cakes and cotton candy and fudge they've bought at a store on the town's only paved road [I write], their parents drive up and down the dirt roads and gaze out their car windows at the turn-of-the-century church, the FOR SALE signs, the overgrown yards where rusted-out cars nestle in plush, messy beds of Indian paintbrush and yarrow and daisies and fireweed and yellow toadflax.

I'm not sure what a toadflax looks like, other than being yellow, but it sounds beautiful. Mournful too. "Toadflax" sounds soft and summery.

I write the following because I have consulted the Chamber of Commerce brochures.

> Every summer Sunday evening at 6:00 PM, the brass band plays on a corner of the paved road—polkas and rousing marches—and in the thin air and chilly sunlight, the sounds drift toward the peaks that ring the town, and the music is tinny and fragile and hopeful.

I spend a few pages on the stove, which I think about often. In my anthropological masterpiece, which I have titled *Trouble in Paradise*, the stove is doughty and indomitable.

I write.

> Against the harsh and uncaring cold, the doughty and indomitable engine feeds and warms, feeds and warms, feeds and warms again.

"Don't you think two feeding and warming sessions are enough?" the Angry Belgian asks me one early summer afternoon. We are back at the diner, eating blueberry pancakes and bacon and drinking coffee. I have asked him to read *Trouble in Paradise*, to let me know what he thinks before I send it to *The New Yorker* and to *Harper's*. In hindsight, perhaps a mistake.

"The repetition is intentional," I say. "I'm going for incantatory power. It's a writer thing. You wouldn't understand."

"All I understand is that I'm reading your story and it's feed and warm, feed and warm, feed and wa—"

"Can't you get how the stove is a metaphor for the human spirit?" I say. "Do you know *anything* about the human spirit?" Maybe I scream, because the waitress cuts me a dirty look, and the family of four at the table next to ours edges away.

"I didn't see anything in your story about you calling your stove Little Man," the Angry Belgian says. "I didn't read anything about you *talking* to your stove. That would be a good way to show the human spirit. A kind of deranged, pathetic human spirit. A kind of delusional, fragile human spirit. A sort of weak, girlish human spirit. A human spirit that is so lonely and screwed up that—"

"Will you shut the fuck up."

"I'm going for incantatory power."

I put my coffee cup down. I give Frank the Stare.

"You can give me the Stare all you want," he says, stuffing more pancakes and bacon into his mouth, "I still think that Little Man feeding and warming twice is plenty."

The New Yorker passes. *Harper's* passes. That's the verb I use when I tell anyone the fate of *Trouble in Paradise,* because it sounds better than "rejected," which, of course, is how it feels. It's how it is. It's how it is with everyone. Everyone passes.

My sister tells me on the telephone that whether anyone buys, or publishes the work, doesn't reflect its value. "You wrote this for you, right?" she asks one Wednesday night, early June. I call her every night, to ask about Silverton, where snow is still falling, and the shack and Little Man and my nephew.

"Yeah, I guess," I say.

"Here," she says, "someone wants to talk to you."

"Weebly!" Isaac says on the phone. That's what he has taken to calling me. It means "Stevie!"

"Hi, I-Dog, are you having fun with Mommy?"

"Weebly!"

"I miss you, I-Dog. I hope I can visit this summer, and maybe we can pick some toadflax and go see the train. The choo-choo."

"Choo-choo. Weebly!"

I hear pots banging. Ann must be making supper. I miss mealtimes with my sister and my nephew. I miss Little Man. I haven't watched porn since my return or called the deli guy. I'm trying to live the lesson I learned during my winter in the mountains—namely, that isolation and Hitler books might appear inviting, but they are nowhere near as nourishing as companionship, as proximity to other humans, as connection. I miss the Hegel lover. I think about human connection a lot. But how am I going to get it? I spend my mornings on *Trouble in Paradise*, afternoons with the Angry Belgian at the diner. I swim laps at the gym's pool in the evenings, because I'm trying to keep off the weight I lost in the mountains. Late at night I watch *Law & Order* reruns.

"You know, I-Dog," I say into the phone, "Weebly has been having some trouble adjusting to New York City. He misses you and Mommy. Sometimes he wishes he were back playing with you instead of wasting afternoons in the diner with his stupid friend. Weebly needs to find someone who will love him and cook nice food for him like Mommy cooks for you and will love him whether he does whore work or not."

"Weebly! Choo-choo!"

"Right, I'm Weebly. Weebly here. I just wanted to tell you how much I love you, I-Dog. Do you love me? Do you love your uncle Weebly?"

"Nor nerk!" Isaac screams. "Nor nerk!"

When we hang up, I reach for the remote control and the phone. I punch in some numbers. The porn channel is still there. The deli guy hasn't forgotten me.

I take some nor nerk, but only because I'm running out of money. I'm in my second year of freelancing, and the money I saved from my *GQ* days is nearly gone. I fly to Los Angeles for *Glamour* magazine, to do a cover story on Catherine Zeta Jones, who seems as wary of reporters as I am wary of famous actresses. "What work are you most proud of?" I ask, not caring; sure she'll lie—hating myself. "I'm proud of all my work," she says as if she's reading from a teleprompter. We pick at our respective salads, say desultory good-byes.

That night, I have dinner with an old friend from St. Louis, now a hair and makeup person, and a group of her friends, who are all comedians. I complain about Catherine Zeta Jones. I mention my life as a nor nerker.

"You don't know what whore work is!" one of the comedians says. "You want whore work, talk to Jim. He wrote the book on whore work!"

Jim, as it turns out, makes his living as a cruise ship comedian. "Yeah," he says, "most of 'em are named Shecky, and they're one hundred years old, and they tell jokes that are two hundred years old, and they think, 'Oh man, if I can just work a little harder, *The Tonight Show*'s gonna call me.'"

"What about you?"

"I'm the youngest guy on the ships," he says. "And I really do think *The Tonight Show*'s gonna call."

"You do?"

"I might be hopeful," he says. "But I'm not delusional. If I'm doing this in five years, I'll be Shecky."

I fly to Paris to meet Carla Bruni, who at the time is known mostly for sleeping with famous men like Eric Clapton, Mick Jagger, and Donald Trump. She cooks me a plate of spaghetti and tells me I seem "very French," which shows that she's very dishonest. Back in New York, I walk downtown, to the West Village, to take notes while Christy Turlington tells me how yoga is good for everyone.

I write the stories, I get paid, I continue my nightly dialogue with the deli guy, I rack up chilling porn bills. Basically, I am Shecky, but better dressed.

"Yeah, you kind of are," Frank says, in June, at the diner.

"What?"

"Shecky."

"Thanks for the vote of confidence."

"I'm just saying."

"We have to do something."

"We?"

"Yeah, we. You spend your nights playing snowboard video games, I'm pissing away my life writing dumb stuff about movie stars. We're not kids anymore. And here we are, another afternoon with pancakes and bacon and coffee. And we're wearing hoodies, for fuck's sake."

"I like hoodies," the Angry Belgian says.

"Seriously, Frank, I need to change my life."

"You need to meet a woman is what you need."

"Yeah, fine, okay, I need to meet a woman. Any advice, Casanova?"

"Yeah, come with me to a meeting."

A meeting? I haven't been to a meeting since before I fled to Silverton, since right after I met Frank and studied his fake-chin quiver. He wasn't still going to those, was he?

"I stopped for a while, because I couldn't take all the bullshit. But then I heard about another meeting."

"Another meeting?"

"Yeah, another meeting. Near ABC. It's where all the soap opera actresses go. Talk about souls in need of spiritual salvation!"

"You're going to meetings dedicated to spiritual salvation, where people who are feeling empty and who are searching for some kind of meaning gather, and you're going to stalk soap opera actresses? You haven't changed since the day I met you."

"Why are you so judgmental? The program says we should accept others as they are. You need to work on that."

"How can you live with yourself?"

"Hey, Shecky, I'm not the one who pisses Chubby Hubby. Besides, women seeking spiritual salvation tend to really get into sex."

I shake my head. I give the Angry Belgian the Stare.

"You in?" he asks.

I do the fake chin tremble. I flutter my hand across the chest of my hoodie.

"I have a lot of love to give," I say. "I just need someone who will accept it."

Frank lifts his coffee mug, and I lift mine, and we clink them.

"You're a sad man," Frank says.

"Yep," I say.

"To Shecky," the Angry Belgian says.

"To Shecky," I agree.

Another basement. We sit in the back row. It's the location that old-timers in the spiritual development game call the "Aisle of Denial," because people who sit there supposedly are more likely to be in denial about their inner emptiness. It's also called "Inventory Alley," because people sitting there, so blind to their existential loneliness, so apart from the group, are more apt to judge others or, in the argot of the leather pants wearers, to "take another's inventory."

"Fuck them for naming the back row anything," I whisper to the Angry Belgian, who is seated next to me. "And you're right, there are a fair number of hot women here."

"Shhhh," the Angry Belgian says. "They're starting."

Except for the preponderance of well-groomed slim females, who (like most attractive women) remind me of Susan, and the relative absence of fat people and men in leather pants, this meeting is much like the others I have attended. People brag about all the material success they have achieved; then they whine about how miserable they are, and then—sometimes—they start weeping and proclaim that once they found the meetings, their lives turned around.

"I'd like to turn her around," the Angry Belgian mutters to me as a short chesty redhead finishes a monologue about the crushing terror of life as a six-figure accountant.

"So would Shecky," I say.

"Shhh!" says a middle-aged woman in the row in front of us.

Over the next two months, I flutter my hand on my chest many times. I do the fake-chin quiver. I tell various women—alone, after the meetings—that their stories "resonated deeply with me" or "touched me in a place I hadn't known existed." I ask them if they'd like to get coffee, to talk about spiritual work.

I talk about spiritual work with Nancy the dancer and Irish Mary the nurse and Swedish Anna and unemployed Nicole who doesn't trust men but who is deeply touched by my chin wobble. I avoid the most beautiful women with the healthiest-looking skin and the perkiest ponytails—the most obvious soap opera actresses—the same way that the stealthy and cunning Bengal tiger avoids the swiftest and sharpest-hooved water buffalo. (I'm still watching Animal Planet a lot).

I suggest sharing spiritual work with June the paralegal and Jessica the recovering orthodox Jew and Janie the kooky Catholic who sees saints faces coming out of walls whenever she is around children.

"What you said about the visions of saints resonates with me," I say, "I have visions myself."

Some of the group members who notice all my attempts at spiritual work give me the frowny mouth. Sleeping with members still struggling to understand the program is disapproved of by many of the old-timers. "Don't fuck the newcomers!" is the way one old lady phrases it to me as she grabs my arm after a meeting. I am rushing to catch up with a former dancer named Cassie who had just admitted to the group that, for a time, she was giving blow jobs to strange men in bathrooms "just so I could feel accepted."

"What are you talking about?" I say to the crone, wrenching my arm free. I've never seen Cassie before. Who knows if, or when, she'll be back? I'm in a hurry. I can empathize with the tiger's frustration when an old water buffalo blocks him from a more vulnerable young breakfast.

"I'm talking about you. You're not here to heal, are you?"

"I thought we weren't supposed to make judgments in this group. Why are you taking my inventory?"

The old lady grabs my arm again. She's strong for her age.

"I hope for your sake you get it someday."

"Thanks for your concern," I say, pulling my arm back again and rushing out the door and up the steps. But Cassie is gone.

Vulnerable women that I treat like crippled water buffalo aren't the only acquaintances I make at the meetings dedicated to spiritual development. I make friends with a ruddy, mustachioed blond man named Hank, whom I think of as Fisherman Hank because he spends his weekends in Long Island Sound and often talks about albacore and flounder.

He likes doughnuts, and sometimes we eat them together at a diner after meetings.

Because no one uses full names and because almost everyone shares the oddest, most personal details of their lives and because I might be an utter asshole, I bestow nicknames on almost all my fellow serenity seekers. The scowling former felon (I hear whispers of murder and bank robbery, but who knows?) is Angry Black Hank, because he is the color of eggplant and because he announces to the group one day that "when stupid people upset me, I choke them, and then they're not so stupid."

Some nicknames are purely descriptive, like Pale William, who is pale, and Pale Black William and Psychiatrist William (who rumor has it had his license yanked) and Middle-Aged Black Hank (who's fairly mellow, especially compared to Angry Black Hank) and Tight Clothes Connie. Sometimes I worry that the names work at cross purposes to the deepening emotional life I'm supposed to be gaining. On the other hand, they make postmeeting conversation with the Angry Belgian easier. There's no confusion when we're discussing Cool Glasses Stacy, as opposed to Sobbing Stacy, Bad Feet Stacy (pretty, but limps due to bunion surgery gone horribly awry), or Soft-Talking Stacy, whom Frank and I suspect might be a lesbian, taking into account her short hair, the way she scowls at us when she sees us chatting up female newcomers, and how she snorts when either of us does the chin tremble or finger waggle. But it's just a theory.

Some members (Angry Black Hank, for example) scare me. On others, like the Williamses and Sobbing Stacy, I'm agnostic, emotional-reaction-wise. I revere Jesus John, a sixty-year-old truck driver who invariably has a kind word for everyone, who always helps put away chairs at the conclusion of meetings, and who is the only person who can make Angry Black James smile. Frank and I agree: there is something holy about him. (We revere sweat suit–wearing, gray-haired Jesus Juliet too. Same behavior, no relation.)

Most of the members, I'm still trying to figure out. Firestarter, for example, whose real name is Helen, and who accidentally set her summerhouse ablaze one night and still complains about it, five years later. Word in the meetings is, Firestarter is sleeping with Fisherman Hank. I share coffee with many of them, exchange family secrets and secret pain, but learn only a few of their occupations. (Perfect Little Annie is an exception: she teaches third grade, which I get out of her one day after a meeting. She's too polite to ignore my direct question as to "What do you do for a living?") But comparing our jobs isn't the point of the group. Neither is swapping annual salaries or measuring ourselves against the summerhouses or car models of our fellow sufferers (though I do this, and always come up short, lacking either). Helping one another to some kind of deeper spiritual life is the point. Recognizing in others our own weaknesses, reaching out to each other—that is the point.

The Angry Belgian reaches out to Slutty Sadie, who had announced at a meeting that she likes sex with strangers and until recently used it "to escape myself, to escape my life." (Who hasn't?) She doesn't reach back. At an evening meeting at a synagogue lounge, Frank and I park ourselves in the back row and listen to a curly-haired twentysomething woman recount tales of public nudity, broken furniture, and arrest warrants in two states. When the meeting is over, Frank reaches out to Clinically Insane but Smoking Hot Melissa. She also declines.

I reach out to a woman who, word in the room has it, had years earlier been kindly disposed to other reachers. She is almost six feet tall, with inky black hair and even blacker eyes and thighs (she wears short dresses) as magisterial as the Amazons who harvested the wood of Art's desk. Samantha has such a regal carriage, that I think of her with the same hormonal admiration that I think of the incomparable Egyptian queen. Cleopatra, as Frank and I call her, tells me I should concentrate on spiritual growth for now, not romance. So I reach out to Cleo's friend, Natasha, who is almost as tall as Cleopatra and just about as beautiful, but blond and Russian and often dripping in jewels. Natasha sits in the front row at most meetings and tells long, sad stories in heavily accented English, of which I understand only a few words. She tells me her real name is Oksana. When I invite her for doughnuts and coffee, she tells me she's married.

Why can't I connect?

"Connecting!" I say with great enthusiasm one Saturday morning, in another church basement, in midtown. "That's the point. That's why I come

206

here." I say this to a newcomer named Kelly. I invite her to have coffee after the meeting, and she smiles brightly and agrees and then asks me to wait for her outside while she uses the bathroom. While I'm waiting, Cleopatra approaches.

"Steve?"

"Oh, hi, Cleo . . . I mean, hey, Samantha."

"You're playing a dangerous game," she says.

"What? Huh?" I do my best to feign ignorance, but Samantha's black queen-of-the-Nile eyes bore into me. "I don't know what you mean."

"Have any of your newcomer dalliances worked out? I'd suggest you think about that."

I think about how I have only *attempted* to have newcomer dalliances. I think about how I need to disguise my approach, to be less obvious to others and more persuasive to the newcomers in question. Something like the nearly invisible but extremely deadly sand diver lizard fish. I think about this while Kelly and I have coffee. I think about it while, the next day, we ride bicycles around Central Park. I think about it that evening when Kelly chortles at my stories of Isaac and the nor nerk.

Kelly is not nearly as tall or as regal as Cleopatra, not as exotic as Natasha, but she falls asleep smiling and wakes up laughing. She speaks perfectly comprehensible English. The first Sunday morning she wakes at my apartment, she insists we go to the grocery store "so we can stock your fridge, and I can get some things to cook for you." When I'm taking a shower, she sits on the closed toilet seat "so," she says, "we can be close to each other and learn about each other."

I'm used to more space. In fact, after sex, I like to spend some time by myself in the bathroom, thinking things over. My internist thinks this is a stellar idea (because I use the time to urinate, which mitigates against all sorts of infections), but Psychic Rose thinks it might express fear of intimacy. Previous girlfriends have complained about the practice. Kelly simply knocks on the door till I open it and then joins me in the bathroom. She is seventeen years younger than I am and sells advertising, and if I occasionally still skulk the earth's shadowy canyons as the Qualifier, then Kelly's comic book superhero alter ego is the Plunger. She plunges into things. Pillow-breasted, cheerful, and without immediately recognizable neuroses, Kelly entertains no doubt. She is instinctive, ferociously binary: something is good, or bad. Hamburgers? She loves hamburgers! Woody Allen? She hates Woody Allen. He's so fucking gay! (That's what she says when she dislikes, doesn't understand, or disapproves of something.) Travel to a place she's never been? Definitely! But not on the bus, that's so fucking gay!

The Qualifier realizes the Plunger is the perfect sidekick for him, but also that with her atomic energy and hair-trigger appetites and volcanic instincts, she will mean the final, no-more-resurrections-this-time death of the Qualifier. Which is fine. Because Kelly looks like Mary Tyler Moore, except shorter and blond and younger. She has blue eyes and a big smile, and she shows lots of gum. She could make a decent living as a gum model. She regards sexual activity the same way she does hamburgers. We go to movies. We hold hands. We even attend meetings together, and she nibbles on my ear, and we smile with pity and condescension at the people who tell horror stories about what happens when newcomers date. "They're so gay," Kelly says. "And they're jealous."

I tell her that Cleopatra told me I was playing a dangerous game, and Kelly says, "What does that slutty beanpole know? She's so fucking gay." But she laughs when she says it. She also flies into sputtering rages a few times—once when someone brings cookies to a meeting at which Kelly was supposed to be the designated cookie bringer. "That fucking bitch!" Kelly hisses to me, staring at the oatmeal raisin cookies on the table.

"I don't think she did it on purpose," I say and take Kelly's hand, which she yanks away.

"Why are you always taking other people's sides?" she says and then stands up. "I can't stay here. I hate these people!"

That's a danger sign. I know that, and the Qualifier knows that. There are other signs too. We drive to a bed-and-breakfast in the Catskills, and one night we agree to a Ping-Pong game with two women whom we have met at dinner. Kelly insists that she and I play together as a team, and when, in the middle of the first game, one of the women says, "C'mon, can't you stand to be away from your boyfriend for just a few minutes?" Kelly quits midgame. That night, sex is more ferocious than usual, and Kelly screams, loud and long. That's new. Afterward, she smiles, looks at the wall, which separates our room from our Ping-Pong opponents. "That'll give those bitches something to think about," she says.

I chalk up Kelly's emotionality to the high spirits that, word has it, mark early female membership in the program and to the high spirits of Kelly. I've lived life on a low, sputtering flame. I'm ready for high spirits.

We will have a good life together. She'll be a funny aunt to the I-Dog. She won't worry about whether to take him to *X-Men* as his uncle did, won't spend twenty minutes in the car outside the theater debating the pros and cons of exposing a one-year-old to flesh-wrecking mutants, won't pose questions to a toddler along the lines of "Do you understand what a mutant is, Isaac?" to which he'll answer, "Nor nerk, nor nerk, Weebly!" She'll just take him to the damned movie, and if anyone complains, they'll be so gay.

She cooks me dinner. She stores her running shoes and bicycle at my apartment. Then she dumps me. It's after I tell her that not everything that displeases her is gay, and besides, I know she doesn't mean it, and I love her deeply and want to spend my life with her, but really, it's kind of coarse and homophobic to say everything is always so gay. She nods. She frowns. She tells me I'm "high maintenance" and not to call her anymore. I lose fifteen pounds in two and a half weeks and stop going to meetings. I sit at home, staring out the window. My sister calls and asks if I want to talk to my nephew, and I decline. I beg Kelly to take me back, and she says no too and hangs up, so I call her to tell her she was never serious about the program, that in point of fact her soul is a dusty, musty pile of coal, and then I call her back to apologize and to beg her to take me back. In one of those rare coincidences that people from the program swear is a sign from God and which the Angry Belgian says is "a fucking coincidence," I get a letter from the guy who had solicited my essay for *The Bastard on the Couch*, and he says he's been put in charge of a new column for *The New York Times* called Modern Love. Did I have any ideas?

Perhaps if I can get some of my feelings down about my lost love, I might be able to better understand it, and her. Perhaps a story about my breakup and my hopes to undo it, in *The New York Times*, will advance my career. Perhaps Kelly will read the story and realize how rare and precious was what we once shared.

"Bad idea," the Angry Belgian says at our usual diner one Tuesday. It's a chilly autumn afternoon. "Really bad idea."

"It's a writer thing," I say. "You wouldn't understand."

"Didn't you promise her that you would never ever write about her?"

"This is more about me. This is more about my truth."

"I kind of don't think she's going to see it that way."

"She dumped me," I write.

Direct. Honest. To the point. More about me than Kelly. She could never blame me for that. It's a perfect beginning to a sober but sad, rueful but wise meditation on the transient nature of love, the doomed core of romance, the fragility of the male ego.

I continue to write.

What's important here are not the details but the pronoun placement. There is no villain here. My therapist suggests I repeat this mantra to myself. So I do. *There is no villain here!*

Psychic Rose really had suggested that, and it makes for some nice, rueful humor. This was going to be a great piece. When people talked of me in the future, they wouldn't say "neurotic" or "high maintenance" or "weird rashes" or "decontracted at *GQ*." They would say, "Friedman is one rueful motherfucker."

I continue.

There is no blue-eyed, wasp-waisted, pillow-breasted, big-toothed, healthy-gummed, trilling-like-a-perfidious-nightingale, fragrant-as-a-windswept-beach-before-the-toxic-algae-sweeps-in-and-kills-all-the-tiny-and-defenseless-clams-who-worked-so-hard-and-sacrificed-all-their-love-to-make-it-their-home, sneering-queen-of-the-damned villain who dumped me so swiftly and with such imperious, frigid beauty that I experienced chest pains and shortness of breath that led to something called a Cardiolite stress test, which I just discovered my insurance company might not pay for and which is leaving me not just miserable and lonely and having difficulty sleeping and occasionally sobbing in public bathrooms but about $6,000 in debt. But no one is to blame here. My therapist suggests I repeat this phrase too. *No one is to blame here!*

The editors take out the stuff about the defenseless clams and the perfidious nightingale and the toxic algae, which disappoints me. Kelly doesn't take me back, which disappoints me more.

"Are you okay, dude?" Middle-Aged Black Hank asks me after a meeting.

"Yeah, I'm fine," I say. "The piece was a kind of rueful meditation on—"

He puts one hand on my shoulder, squeezes it. "We love you, you know."

Rock-and-Roll Chris asks if I what I had written was true, if I had really sent post–breakup, "that insane e-mail" to Kelly begging her to take me back.

"Well, yes, but it wasn't really insane. It was heartfelt, certainly, but it was supposed to convey a kind of sad, rue—"

Rock-and-Roll Chris puts a hand on my shoulder too.

"You know, Steve, this is a great place for you to be."

I attend meetings daily. I talk about Kelly. I cry. Jesus John and Jesus Juliet smile at me, which makes me cry even more. As much as I attend meetings, though—once in the morning, once at night, sometimes a nooner—I still don't fully participate. I don't attach myself to a mentor, someone who has been in the group longer than me, who is supposed to walk me through the program of the group. I avoid this because everyone in the group seems kind of fucked up. Fisherman Hank has disappeared, and there are rumors that the police took him away when they found him standing outside Firestarter's apartment, screaming that she had ruined his life. Slutty Sadie is supposedly sleeping with some skuzzy-even-by-her-standards bartenders. Even Cleopatra, who has been in the program for thirteen years, is in the hospital, in the last few months of pregnancy, by a father who no one seems to know. I'm trying not to be judgmental, but is that a spiritually sound behavior? I also continue going it alone because if I do seek a mentor, and he agrees (the program suggests same-sex mentor-mentee relationships in order to avoid, I presume, the kind of trouble I got in with Kelly), and I don't find peace or happiness or at least an escape from my rash-ridden, nightmare-plagued, Mrs. Friedman–less life, then what? I had already tried work and exercise and a fitness plan and ice cream and the porn channel, and those weren't working. It's one thing to sit in the aisle of denial, to take everyone's inventory while occasionally moving into the front row and sobbing about my ex and getting some pats on the back and shoulder squeezes, but it's something else entirely to actually *surrender* to this program, which is what everyone in the program who has surrendered is always suggesting. Because if surrendering didn't work, I would be totally screwed. If the Qualifier stopped qualifying and embraced something with all his meager might, and it turned out to be vaporous, that would not be good. It would not be a good day. That would not pass.

The Angry Belgian doesn't have a mentor either, and he doesn't work the program. But he keeps up his attendance. "Just in case Slutty Sadie comes back," he says. "I think I have a shot at that."

The meetings are distracting, and it's encouraging to hear others who feel more miserable than I, especially when their problems seem so trivial. Fisherman Hank is (reputedly) heartsick over Firestarter? It's just a breakup! Get over it, dude! Don't be so gay! That's what I think, and it cheers me. Clinically Insane but Smoking Hot Melissa can't sleep because her cat, Fluffy, is throwing up? It's a fucking cat! One day, I realize with a start that as all out of proportion my fellow sufferers' interior pain is to their external challenges, so too is my discomfort outsized compared to my life. I'm relatively healthy. I can afford the porn channel and my ice cream habit because of the Modern Love piece, some whore work I don't call whore work, and especially some long profile assignments I've recently landed from a group of sports magazines. I have at least one friend, even if he tends toward dyspepsia and is slightly obsessed with the return of Slutty Sadie. One of the small blessings in my life that I begin to appreciate more—the program teaches us to appreciate life—is the postmeeting meetings that Frank and I share, when we discuss the others in the group and catalogue what is wrong with them.

And then, one day, even that pleasure is taken from us.

It is the morning meeting, a circle. The day's leader (we all get a chance to lead, on a rotating basis) reads a passage from program-approved literature, and today the topic is gossip. "Gossip hurts us in three ways," Handsome Eli reads. (Handsome Eli once had a thing with Clinically Insane but Smoking Hot Melissa; it nearly broke the guy.) "It hurts the person we are gossiping about, because if that person ever learned of what was being said, it could devastate him or her. It hurts the gossiper, because to gossip takes us away from our best, true selves. And it hurts the program, because where there is gossip, people don't feel free to share honestly."

After the reading, everyone in the circle gets a chance to share. The idea is, we're supposed to say something related to the topic, and even though Clinically Insane but Smoking Hot Melissa can usually be counted on to mention poor Fluffy the cat, and Slutty Sadie—before she left—would always connect the reading somehow to a sordid and debased encounter from the previous evening and even though Bad Feet Stacy still whines about her feet and the incompetent butchers who had dispatched her to a living hell of eternal foot torment (even if the topic was connection to God, or charity, or the perils of pride), Handsome Eli seems to have struck a chord today.

"This reading resonates so much with me," Firestarter says. "Because I know I have been the subject of gossip, and it hurts me. It hurts me a lot."

I stare at the floor. Fuck. Was Firestarter giving me the Stare?

Jesus Juliet is up next.

"This topic couldn't be more appropriate," she says. "The temptation to gossip is powerful, and it's with us all the time. But this program gives us an opportunity to resist temptation, to allow ourselves to love one another."

I stare at the floor some more.

"This reading makes me ashamed," I say, when it's my turn, "because I have definitely been guilty of this. Not only have I gossiped, but I've also gossiped about people in this room. And today I want to say that I now see how not only is that unfair to them—to you—but that it's also unfair to me. So thank you, Handom—I mean, Eli, for that reading. It's changed how I think, and I hope it's changed how I'm going to act."

Others confess their past sins too, admit how they have gossiped, and how now they're going to stop. Clinically Insane but Smoking Hot Melissa works Fluffy the cat in ("I know people gossip about how I must seem obsessed with Fluffy"), and Hal the gay cellist talks about the time he saw someone raising his eyebrow at someone else once after Hal shared "and every day after that I didn't feel *safe*."

It's cathartic. For the most part, we all agree that, yes, we have sinned and, *yes*, we shall sin no more.

I say for the most part, because with just a couple minutes left before meeting's end, it is Soft-Talking Probably a Lesbian Stacy's turn to talk.

"I believe that narrative is one of the most powerful tools we as humans possess," Soft-Talking Probably a Lesbian Stacy soft talks. Everyone leans forward. The Angry Belgian has told me this is a trick that actors use, to make everyone pay more attention. Why can't she speak in a normal voice like everyone else does? Does everyone else hate her as much as I do? They should.

"And if I think that my repeating a story I hear in the meetings is going to help someone outside the meetings get closer to a spiritual solution, then I'm going to repeat that story," she says.

Everyone is practically horizontal, so soft is her voice, so wise her words.

She pauses. Why can't I speak as masterfully as Soft-Talking Probably a Lesbian Stacy? I make a note to myself to whisper more.

"As long as my intent is not to gossip," she says, "but to help someone's spiritual development, then I'll tell whatever story I want."

We all nod and pay homage to Soft-Talking Probably a Lesbian Stacy, and I grit my teeth with envy a little (I wish people paid more attention to me) as we hold hands and say a prayer together, and then the meeting is over.

Later that day, at the diner, the Belgian and I regard each other over pancakes, from underneath hoodies.

"Not to gossip but to help your spiritual development," Frank says.

"Yeah? Uh-huh?"

"But did you see what Clinically Insane but Smoking Hot Melissa was wearing today? Can you believe those tits? They're perfect."

"Not to gossip but to help your spiritual development," I say, "but I hate Soft-Talking Probably a Lesbian Stacy. She's definitely a lesbian. Not that I'm taking her inventory or anything."

"Not to gossip but to help your spiritual development," the Angry Belgian says, "but I think she's hot for Slutty Sadie."

We drink our coffee. We run down everyone in the group. Not to gossip, but to help our spiritual development.

Chapter 13

My Cold Wars

My writing career improves. The profile assignments increase. Editors who liked my takedown of the pro bowler call to offer stories about other troubled athletes. A Tour de France champion who died of a drug overdose. A running prodigy who left his wife and kids. Another cyclist, bipolar *and* suicidal. "Sure," I chirp. "Can do." Editors who appreciated the familial rage of my "Dear Dirtbag" piece call to see if I want to wax apoplectic about other personal matters. (One editor is particularly fond of the way I imagined my brother-in-law plunging to death in the gorge. "Oh, yeah," I lie, "I think hyperbolic visions are a great source of humor and narrative tension.")

Editors at women's magazines are impressed at the sensitivity with which I embraced grooming as foreplay, so they ask me to embrace other notions they wish men would embrace. As long as they pay me enough, I'll embrace anything.

My father tells me on the phone every week that he's proud of me for getting so much work.

I follow Psychic Rose's advice and avoid saying the phrase "whore work" aloud. And I have my afternoon sessions with the Angry Belgian and my daily meetings with those who seek spiritual development. But no Mrs. F, though not for lack of trying.

I date another much younger woman, even younger than Kelly, and except for her not allowing me to visit her apartment or to meet her friends, and except for her general reluctance to make plans more than a few days in advance, things are okay. I date a woman who, when I tease her about her Southern accent, threatens to smash a lamp on my skull. I date a few other women who don't work out either. I complain about them to Frank, and Frank complains about his failed romances—he's still a little obsessed with the married snake-tattooed bisexual—to me.

I still entertain hopes that someday I might find Mrs. F, but my hopes are dwindling. I complain about this at the meetings, almost as much as Clinically Insane but Smoking Hot Melissa moans about Fluffy. We both get the same advice.

"Do service," Jesus John and Jesus Juliet and Soft-Talking Probably a Lesbian Stacy and Hal the gay cellist say, until I want to smack them. "Help others, and that will allow you to forget yourself."

Service, huh? There are lots of ways to do service. I could take a fat, sweaty, sobbing male newcomer for coffee and tell him to keep coming back, to open his eyes to the mercy that connects us all. I could offer words of solace to Fisherman Hank, to tell him that no woman, especially one who's a little clumsy with matches, is worth a jail sentence. Instead, I ride my bicycle across Central Park, to the East Side, to New York Presbyterian Hospital, where Cleopatra has been confined to bed to wait out the last two months of her pregnancy. Even bedridden and with a swollen belly, even slightly disapproving, Cleopatra is pleasant to be around. Maybe it's because I think of her—quite delusionally—as a possible Mrs. F, what with our friendship and the coming baby.

To my surprise, the Russian is visiting too. Oksana is easier to understand in a small room, when there are just three people, rather than in a circle of twenty or thirty in a basement with iffy acoustics. Also, Oksana, in addition to being tall and blond and pretty, is quite long legged and plump lipped. Also, her eyes are the green of an old 7Up bottle. Cleopatra falls asleep, and Oksana tells me that she moved here from Russia six years ago. She tells me she is twice married, soon-to-be twice divorced, possessed of a college-aged daughter, grateful that she's "done weeth the marriage thing," and possessed by a fierce desire to "hof fun." I invite her for coffee.

In the hospital cafeteria, she declares that living things are not meant to be together for life, that after mating, the male of the species intuitively and quite naturally seeks other mates. "Thees ees the way it ees," she says, "so why do we pretend it ees not?"

Psychic Rose tells me to be careful. The Angry Belgian tells me to have sex with Oksana, but not to get emotionally involved. "It's just a limbic response," he says. "Nothing more, nothing less."

I think it's much more. Still, I don't pursue her. I congratulate myself on my restraint. I do so publicly. At the time, I am finishing another Modern Love column—this one a speculative essay about spiritual transformation, and she fits nicely.

I write, with wisdom and quiet pride.

I decide to abandon my plans to woo the Russian émigré. I'm not sure, but I think this represents progress.

The next week, I invite her to dinner.

I notice that when she crosses her leg, her right foot curls all the way around her left calf and hugs it and that she has the most graceful slender ankles I have ever seen. I notice that she smells very, very good.

I ask about her work, and she tells me that she volunteers at a charity that helps Ukrainian orphans—raising money, facilitating adoptions, persuading American social workers to train their counterparts in Moscow, linking people who might not know how desperately they need one another.

I imagine CEOs and venture capitalists writing checks and booking transatlantic flights and hospital administrators scheduling symposiums in lecture halls, their hands scrawling zeros and punching telephones and blocking out days on office calendars, all moved by limbic impulses as mysterious and as ineluctable as the tidal pull.

I am being swept away myself. I decide she is wonderful, smart, sensitive, *and* kind. I can't get over the way she strides into rooms, shoulders back, laughing. And such graceful slender ankles propelling such a magnificent stride. What a wonderful contradiction! And the way she makes such melodious sounds of delight when she devours a plate of pasta! Would I care about such things if it was just limbic? Walking down the street alone, I whistle corny love songs and notice people looking at me. I don't care.

When we first hold hands, she says, "Wow!" But she doesn't say it so much as she blows it out her pillowy lips. How could such a small unassuming word carry such emotional freight? A simple one-syllable palindrome with origins I'd never stopped to think about has suddenly taken on layers of meaning and promise that make my chest hurt. It has taken an émigré who only learned English when she arrived on these shores six years ago to reveal the sacred mysteries of my native language. She is Nabokov, and I am her adoring reading public. (It occurs to me that while it's been a long time since I've whistled love songs to myself, I have *never* thought of a beautiful woman the way I think of Nabokov. This should alarm me, but I don't care.)

When we kiss, and I caress the small of her back, she quivers and says "wow" again. It has been a day since we held hands, and by now, the word—as long as she says it—has become my Kabbalah, my Talmud, my Dead Sea Scrolls, concentrated in two letters, one ingeniously repeated twice. Every time it comes from her lips, I learn something new, something important and moving and eternal. (Speaking of the sacred texts, there is the matter of religion. As Frank warns me when I tell him about Oksana, "You know, her great-great-grandfathers probably raped your great-great-grandmothers." But are not humans capable of forgiveness, and is it not sad and nihilistic to revel in historical animosity and centuries-old blood feuds? Besides, I don't care.)

"When a Russian woman likes a man," she says, "she will, how you say, paint the sky for him."

"I think you mean hang the moon," I say and notice with unease that her plump lips flatten a bit. I swear to myself that I will never correct her English again. Ever.

"I know it is weird," she says, "but the day after I saw you at the hospital, I told my therapist, 'I don't know this man well, but I think I just met someone who would be the perfect father for my children.'"

I want her to be pregnant. I want her to be pregnant more than I want to impregnate her, and I want to impregnate her with every single impulse that has ever coursed through my limbic system. I want to walk down the street with her, to whisper, "He will be sturdy and proud, like a mighty oak tree," in Russian, while I hold her hand and kiss her fat lips and pat her swelling belly. Her college-age daughter and I will become pals, drinking coffee late at night while the Russian sleeps. The daughter will tell me some of the Russian folktales she was raised on, and I will explain the nuanced phrasing of Frank Sinatra, and we will chat about J. D. Salinger and Rick Moody and whatever college kids are reading these days, and I will ask the daughter to teach me to say, "You put the 'wow' in Tchaikovsky," in Russian, and the daughter and I will laugh and refill our coffee mugs, and we will be united in the love and care of this sensitive, beautiful émigré and the baby she is carrying. I want to bring her juice in the morning, to read poetry to her, want to gaze into her green eyes, and to gently kiss those lips and to say, "I never imagined I could be so happy," in Russian.

I want all this, but when she tells me about seeing me as a perfect father, all I can say is, "Wow."

I believe the search for Mrs. F has concluded. I believe that I have discovered balance in the meetings, and that balance led me to Oksana.

There are problems. The marriage, for starters. And the Mercedes and the Channel and the Prada and the summerhouse and the trips to Paris and Florence and Athens, and the way she says, when she sees my apartment and listens to me share my difficulties about still trying to publish *Trouble in Paradise*, "You have a very relaxed life," which makes me feel not so relaxed.

I e-mail her from Las Vegas, where I am working on a story, a profile of a crime novelist. I tell her that I have been thinking about her, that it will be good to see her, that it is 105 degrees in Nevada.

"One hundred and five degrees," she writes back. "wow!"

Which makes me think I've been an idiot. "Wow" means nothing to her. I mean nothing to her. I have constructed another elaborate fantasy, guaranteed to let me spin out visions of togetherness and intimacy while the object of my fantasy remains ever unavailable, ever inaccessible, ever lost to me in a deep Siberian lake while I fumble about on the choppy surface.

When I get back from my trip, we go to dinner. She says her therapist has warned her that *she* is trying to live a fantasy. "She told me my vision of you as the perfect father was a delusion. She said that it was the manifestation of my longing for my father, that it was dangerous, and I should be careful." (She says this in her heavily accented English, but now I understand all too clearly.)

"Some psychiatrists are fucking idiots," I say. I have never cursed in front of her before. What am I doing? "We all want idealized versions of our parents, but that doesn't mean all our instincts and attractions are delus—" She cuts me off.

"I want to be with you every minute," she says.

I have trouble breathing.

"But I must be careful. I don't want to jump into something that will consume me, where I will drown. I can love like you can't imagine, but I need to learn how to take care of myself. For the first time in my life, I need to learn to take care of myself."

"I want to be with you every minute too," I say. "And I want you to take care of yourself. I also want to take care of you, but not in a way that's intrusive or unhealthy, in a respectful way. I think this is something special, and I think we should nurture it, and maybe there is a chance we are meant to be together and have children and—"

I have never babbled so in front of her. I can't help it.

"Passion is wonderful," she says. "It is crazy and wild, and it can make you dizzy and sick, and it feels wonderful. But it has nothing to do with marriage."

"No," I say, "that's so wrong. What—"

"Marriage is old sleepers," she says.

"Yes!" We are not so far apart, after all. She can teach me about wild love, and I can be a perfect father and husband. We can heal each other, but in a healthy, boundary-appropriate, decidedly non-codependent, psychiatrically sanctioned manner.

"Marriage *is* old sleepers," I nearly shout, "growing old with someone, comforting them, being comforted, sleeping together as you age, but it's with someone you share a passion with, even if that passion dims and flares up and dims again over time and—"

"No," she says. "Old sleepers. Old *sleepers*. Like on your feet."

Still, I want to marry her. I want to make her Mrs. Friedman. She has been unlucky twice, but I will be her third time, her charm. Marriage can be life affirming, an institution both astonishing and magnificent, and I must show her this. The Big Blue Cell, the Qualifier, et al., and I must persuade the Russian émigré that not all men are philandering cads, that there is no cynic as bitter as the failed romantic, that in this wonderful country, this land of the free and home of the brave, love and commitment can coexist, can *frolic*, just like the deer and the antelope, like the mink and the Siberian tiger, that we are two people who can make each other happy (even though we're happy in our own identities, in a psychiatrically appropriate way), that I can offer what she has so long been seeking, what she has wrongly and tragically abandoned. The Man in the Lime Green suit is stoked.

I share my plans at the circle meeting, which Oksana does not attend. Firestarter and Middle-Aged Black Hank smile and nod and a couple of people pat me. But Jesus John wants to have a word with me.

"Love is wonderful, Steve," Jesus John says.

"I know. I *know*! It's so great. It's really transformed me."

"But you know, it can be dangerous to make another person your higher power. Don't forget that we're all connected. Don't lose yourself."

Don't lose myself? But isn't that what love is? I *want* to be lost.

I looked at women before I met the Russian, and I continue to look. They are women who still excite my limbic impulses as they are still beautiful, and I'm still human. And I talk to them and smile at them and ask personal questions and notice their exuberant freckles and charming lisps and their keen cultural intelligence and their delicate earrings, and I make clear that I find them alluring, but I do so without selfish motive or sexual objective. I am more Nelson Mandela, less any of the cheetahs and crocodiles and sand lizards upon which I had wasted so much time the past decade. Just as the

Qualifier took some almost-mortal hits with Kelly, the Single Guy and his rapscallion ways are withering underneath Oksana's Red Star beauty.

I flirt because it's pleasant and because I don't need other women to make me feel good, but I can certainly do my part to spread cheer and joy, to try and make *them* feel good. I wish for them the happiness that has descended upon me, that I sense as a lifetime possibility. Some women indicate that they're available, one with a freckled neck who quotes entire pages of dialogue from Shakespeare and invites me to travel to another city with her for the weekend, but I decline.

I'm not interested. Because even though there is her husband and her expensive tastes and her dour, despicable, reductionist, and possibly dangerous psychiatrist whom someone should really report to the state licensing board, I can't help it. It's Oksana I want. I don't know if it's destiny or true love or delusion or purely limbic or some devilishly, heavenly combination. I don't care.

There are new problems. When I take her to my favorite neighborhood restaurant, an Italian joint where everyone knows me, and the waiter begins reciting the specials, she snaps her menu shut, waves her hand in front of her face as if she's detected a faint but repulsive odor, and snaps, "No no no. Seemple feesh, Greeled. Plis!"

So, she's a little imperious, a little picky. Who am I to judge an immigrant's woes and the forces that shaped her? This is manageable. Single Guy always looked for something better. The Qualifier let something like possible-but-not-proven homophobia, and a nasty temper cut short his previous dreams of connubial bliss. The Big Blue Cell clutched his belly and fled to the nearest bathroom. I will accept Oksana's imperfections. That's what love is, acceptance.

She refuses to sleep at my apartment. First, she says she's worried that her daughter will get the wrong idea. I tell her that her daughter likes me and attends an Ivy League school and is smart enough to know that her mother has a sex life. Then she says it's because she's worried that her husband will call. I point out that her husband lives in another state, and so what if he calls? Finally, the truth: "I spend all day taking care of other people. Late at night, I just want to sit on my couch at home, alone, and watch reruns of *Friends*."

Not good. This is not good. Even the Qualifier sees this. Worse comes.

The imminent filing for divorce becomes not so imminent. When we meet in June, she says she's planning to file in August. By July, she's going to file in October. By August, the filing date is the end of the year—maybe.

After dinner at a restaurant downtown—they serve simple fish, grilled—I take her hand, and she pulls it away. "The owner is a friend of Wolfgang," she says, "and this was our place."

Wolfgang?

"We dated. We traveled together for two years, and I don't want him to hear about my holding hands with someone else, from a third party."

She's lived in the United States for six years. She's been married for about the same time. This is a New York City restaurant. So, she was dating Wolfgang while she was married?

"Why are you such a child?" she says. "Why are you so needy? Why can't you love me for who I am?"

I think this over for a couple weeks. I think it over, not the Qualifier. I will not dither. I will be decisive. When, one weeknight, she comes to my apartment, I tell her we should break up until she's available. She says I have issues. Actually she says, "You hof eesues. You vant everything now. Vy can't you be patient?"

I tell her I can be patient, that I want to be with her, but that I need my girlfriend to be able to sleep at my apartment, that I want to be able to plan trips with her, that keeping secrets from a husband is one thing, but secrets from a boyfriend named Wolfgang, along with the secrets from the husband, is something else. I am sad, but strong. I tell her that if and when she files for divorce, I hope she calls me, because I love her.

"But we can still talk, yes, and hang out?" she asks.

"No," I say, "it's better that I don't see you or talk to you. It would be too hard."

"Steef," she says. This is how she pronounces my name. "Can we break up without talking?"

"Huh?"

"In the other room," she says. The other room is the bedroom.

Three days later, I call. She asks how I'm doing.

"Horrible," I say. "Bereft, miserable. I miss you."

There is silence on the other end.

"Sweetie," I say. "Are you okay?"

"Vot does mean, 'bereft'?" she asks.

The Belgian wants to tell me what was wrong with Brooke, the younger woman who wouldn't let me see her apartment.

"Why?" I ask. "I haven't dated Brooke in months."

"It'll help you forget Oksana," Frank says.

"I've already forgotten Oksana," I lie.

"Look, you want to hear what I'm going to say," Frank says.

"No, Frank. Really, I don't."

"It'll help you see the truth."

"The truth is, you hate all my girlfriends."

"I do not."

"Frank, you called the one between Brooke and Oksana the Antichrist. The Antichrist! She wasn't that bad."

"I did not call her the Antichrist."

"How can you refer to someone as the Antichrist and then deny it? What is wrong with you? Why are you such a crackpot?"

"You're always calling me a crackpot. I'm not a crackpot. You make stuff up. It's like that time we went hiking, and you got us lost, and then you said—"

"I got us lost? *I* got us lost?" I am shouting.

We are facing off at our neighborhood diner, of course, dissecting the career arcs and talents of Lindsay Lohan and the Olsen twins, the oeuvre of Sylvester Stallone and why we don't at the moment have girlfriends. Frank has thinning hair. I consider myself balding, notwithstanding Frank's insistence that "just because you stick 'ing' on a word doesn't mean you can alter reality." I'm a decade older than Frank, but we're both firmly within the demographic referred to by many of our family members as "Why are you still single?"

Lately, Frank has been wiling away evening hours on his fifteen-year-old green plastic futon, munching popcorn, playing snowboard video games. I've switched from porn to *48 Hours Mystery* reruns and my brown leather couch. Also I've given up Chubby Hubby for Peanut Butter Cup ice cream. This confused the Pakistani deli guy at first; he actually asked if everything was all right with me.

I close my eyes. I take a breath. I need to stay on topic. With Frank, when it comes to girlfriends, this is not an easy thing.

"Okay," I say, "then do you deny saying, when I was headed over to Laurel's for dinner, 'Don't look into its eyes.' 'It'! You said 'it'! Do you deny that?" (Laurel was the Antichrist).

"That's beside the point," Frank says, with maddening calm. "We're not talking about Laurel; we're talking about Brooke, who was about twelve years old, who never really liked you."

"That's a little harsh—"

"You know, Brooke, the one who didn't invite you to her office party because 'you wouldn't feel comfortable,' and who wouldn't let you see where she lives 'because it's a mess,' and who wouldn't make a weekend date with you more than five hours in advance because her 'life is so complicated' and who whenever an old boyfriend was coming to town, she wanted to 'play things by ear.'"

I hate it when Frank quotes me quoting former girlfriends. I hate his Manichean take on women, how just because Laurel once threatened to smash a lamp on my skull, she's suddenly an "it," how Brooke, a woman with a complicated life and a messy apartment and concerns for my comfort level automatically qualifies for Jezebel-hood.

"You hate all my girlfriends," I repeat, again too loudly. I say this because I prefer to remember Laurel as feisty rather than deranged, and my play-it-by-ear sweetheart Brooke as frightened and conflicted rather than manipulative and evil incarnate. Also, because I fear Frank might be right. So, for good measure, I repeat part of it again.

"All of them."

"Do not," Frank says.

It has recently occurred to me that Frank and I are happiest together when we are single and bemoaning our romantic fates. Luckily for our friendship, this has been a fairly common phenomenon.

Over second cups of coffee, I tell Frank that while I pity his stunted and hostile world view and his repellent lack of trust in people and his sad inclination toward corrosive rage when it comes to females, I want him to be happy. Consequently, I wish he would stop finding fault with the women who love him and avoid the women who treat him like topsoil.

"I say that not to gossip," I add, "but to help with your spiritual development."

"You don't know what you're talking about," Frank says.

"Do too."

"Do not."

Why is it, I wonder, that when it comes to women, our conversational rhythms quickly and ineluctably devolve into the cadence of the elementary school yard.

"Oh yeah?" I'm yelling again. "What about Julia? Julia loved you. Julia was great. She was pretty. She was funny. Do you remember why you broke up with Julia?"

"You're a bitter man," Frank says. "Don't take it out on me."

"You broke up with her because you didn't like the way her nose crinkled when she laughed."

"You really think Brooke was worried about your comfort level? You don't think she's finding her own comfort level with her old boyfriend right now?"

"And Carmen," I shout. "What about Carmen? Remember Carmen? Remember Ms. I-Think-She's-the-One, Ms. I-Think-I'm-in-Love? Remember why you dumped the woman who was going to save you from your crackpot self?"

"Do you put sunscreen on your head?" Frank says. "Because you really need to."

"You dumped Carmen because she used the word 'banal' too often. You broke up with the woman of your dreams because she said 'banal'!"

"She pronounced it wrong," says Frank.

"Oh, that makes it reasonable? You give up happiness because the woman who would provide it didn't pronounce a word to your liking?"

"There were other problems," Frank says.

"Were not."

"How about you?" Frank says. "Let's not forget your Australian girlfriend Carolyn. Carolyn was the best. Carolyn was really smart. And hot. I loved Carolyn. I can't believe you let Carolyn get away."

At the moment, I am actually empathizing with Laurel, the lamp-smash threatener.

"Dude," I hiss. I have never uttered the word with such venom. It feels good, so I repeat it. "Dude. You loved Carolyn *after* I dumped her! Do you remember what you said when I told you about my first date with her? Do you remember? You said, 'You should have sprinted down the street, away from her, as fast as you could.'"

"But that's because she was making out with you at her neighborhood bar. No woman does that on a first date. And she said, 'If I give you my heart, will you take care of it?' And she was drunk. You told me all that. I'm just quoting you."

"She wasn't drunk. She was drinking. There's a difference. And I thought she was being open and vulnerable."

"Or a psychotic slut," Frank says.

We stare at each other. Patrons at other tables stare too.

Pigeons fly through ice and sleet and treacherous storms and always find their way home. Pigs (at least some pigs) let not the loamiest, smelliest dirt in the world stand between their snuffling snouts and a fragrant truffle. Frank and I—we, too, know instinctively when we've found the happy spot.

"And what exactly," I demand, "is wrong with a psychotic slut? Psychotic sluts have needs. Who are you to say a psychotic slut is incapable of love?"

Frank can't help himself. He snickers. This is a big deal. Frank doesn't give up laughs easily, like some of the giggly girlfriends we've both had. "Cheap chuckle whores" is what he called them once. Harsh, but funny. That's Frank. When Frank laughs, it makes me feel good.

"Is your heart so shriveled that now you're judging psychotic sluts?" I demand. "Are you not man enough to embrace a psychotic slut?"

Frank stops laughing long enough to frown, then wrinkles his forehead, and strokes his chin. It's his fake thoughtful look. He knows how it amuses me.

"I so need a psychotic slut," he says. "A psychotic slut who will cook me pancakes and who is good at snowboard video games."

Now we're both cracking up. There is a loud scraping. The couple at the next table is trying to move as far away from us as possible. Now the waitress's sighs are no longer silent. She has learned to live with us. But she doesn't like losing customers.

We look at them. We look at each other. We can't stop laughing.

"We need girlfriends in a bad way," Frank says.

"Some sweet and generous psychotic sluts," I say, "who don't say, 'BAHnel.'"

"And who'll invite us to their office parties."

"And whose noses don't crinkle when they laugh."

We can't stop laughing. Then, after a while, we can stop.

"We're so screwed," Frank says.

"So screwed," I agree.

We suck on our fourth cups of coffee, until it's just us and the sighing waitress, who also happens at the moment to be scowling.

"We need to change our lives," I say to my friend, though the truth is, at the moment, in this warm diner on a chilly autumn afternoon, together, I'm perfectly content.

"Aye, aye, Yoda," Frank says.

"No one in *Star Wars* ever said, 'Aye aye,' you crackpot," I say.

"Did so."

"Did not."

"Whatever," Frank says. "Anyway, how are we going to change our lives? What are we going to do, *find love?*"

"I hope so," I say. "But in the meantime, I'm going to get in shape. I'm going to get back to the gym. I'm going to switch from Peanut Butter Cup ice cream to low-fat frozen yogurt. I'm really going to."

"Right," Frank says, "and I'm going to buy a new futon."

CHAPTER 14

THE FAT MAN MAKES ME CRY

We don't work the program, the Angry Belgian and I, but we don't give up on the meetings. Others do.

Bad Feet Stacy moves to California. Cool Glasses Stacy marries an Italian guy she met on a business trip and, according to Emergency Room Ellen (she's a physician), joins an urban Buddhist chanting club and starts drinking too much. "That's what happens when one puts a person, or a practice, in front of our spiritual development," Soft-Talking Probably a Lesbian Stacy whispers at a morning meeting. "And I say that not to gossip, but to help us all with our spiritual development."

Kelly stops coming to meetings. Fisherman Hank stops coming to meetings, and there are rumors that he is in jail for stalking, but no one mentions his name because once when someone does, Firestarter blanches, and it looks like she's going to faint. Angry Black Hank has a stroke, and Jesus John and Jesus Juliet visit him at a Harlem hospice, and then Angry Black Hank dies, and we all say a nondenominational prayer for him. I regret not reaching out to him more, but I'm silently grateful he never choked me for being stupid.

"Are we going to be sitting in this circle for the rest of our lives?" the Angry Belgian again asks me one late autumn morning at the Y. Rather than buying new futons or eating frozen yogurt, we have increased our attendance at spiritual development meetings.

"Maybe we should start working the program," I say. "Maybe we should find mentors."

"Do you *listen* to the insanity coming out of their mouths?" Frank asks. "Do you want to be jabbering about love and connection when you're sixty, like Mystic River Timmy [who is from Boston and had once served time for robbing a homeless shelter] while you're hitting on twenty-three-year-olds at juice stands, pretending you're a movie director 'scouting locations'?"

"I thought that was just something people said about him. He doesn't really do that, does he?"

"Yeah, he does it. I saw him once."

"Did it work?"

"That's not the point. It's wrong!"

"We're not supposed to judge."

"Yeah," the Angry Belgian says, "and that allows people here to be fucked up, with no consequences! Do you understand how fucked up that is?"

The literature of the program discourages us from comparing ourselves to others, but it always cheers me to behold the magnificent rage of the Angry Belgian. It allows me to think I'm mellow and even-tempered. It makes me feel better about myself. It helps me keep hope alive. I tell him so.

"Gee, thanks, Yoda," he says.

Slutty Sadie reappears early one morning, wearing sweat clothes and no makeup, apparently chastened. "I want to bring the principles of the program to my sex life," she tells the group. "I want to value myself and to value others."

"Interesting," the Angry Belgian mutters from the side of his mouth. "I'd value her. I'd really value her."

Fisherman Hank reappears too and tells the group he is on antidepressants, which causes Soft-Talking Probably a Lesbian Stacy to softly cluck in disapproval, which prompts Jesus John to deliver a short but forceful sermon on how we in the group judge no one and aim to love and support all group members, even if medication might seem like the easy, lazy, weak way out of the spiritual morass in which we all are thrashing.

And thrash we do. Fisherman Hank tells us he has lately been hearing mellifluous, melodious voices, that he has been receiving important messages, and though we all smile and pretend they're the good voices and messages to which we aspire—the instructions and directives of a power greater than ourselves the group literature promises, the voices that flow from the program and into our souls as surely as the humble mountain stream flows into the mighty, fathomless sea—the ruddy Long Islander's voices have been telling him to wash his hands twenty times an hour and to eat only baby carrots and, worst of all, to compose and tender to Firestarter a hand-lettered poem each and every day. Hank's voices, it seems, have more to do with side effects from medication or possibly organic mental illness than they do with any spiritual morass.

"Bummer for the Fisherman," I tell Frank at the diner.

"I blame Firestarter," he says.

Slutty Sadie gets pregnant, which surprises no one, and then marries the father of the baby, who turns out to be Mystic River Timmy, who enrolls in night law school, which shocks everyone. Maybe spiritual transformation *is* possible.

Perfect Little Annie has a baby, and I invite the young mother and child for coffee one afternoon and coo over the kid, and then afterward, alone, lament the fact that Perfect Little Annie is not with me, that no one is with me except for the Angry Belgian, that my weekly phone calls with my father, when I tell him how great things are, leave me feeling like a liar. A Mrs. Friedman–less liar.

I'm not the only one with problems, of course. People in the group lose jobs, divorce. Fisherman Hank disappears again. Clinically Insane but Smoking Hot Melissa continues to whine about Fluffy, and Soft-Talking Probably a Lesbian Stacy keeps soft talking.

"We have no lives," Frank says at our diner, the week before Christmas. I think of it as our diner now. "And I swear to God if I hear one more word about that fucking cat Fluffy, I will strangle Clinically Insane but Smoking Hot Melissa. I don't care how smoking hot she is."

"It's good entertainment," I say. "Don't take it so seriously."

"Entertainment? Is that what we're spending five to fifteen hours of our pathetic existence on every week?"

"Well, it's cheaper than porn. And we get to meet interesting people."

"You mean like Kelly?"

"She was high-spirited."

"Yeah, that's one way to describe her."

We peer into our coffee cups.

"Have you thought any more about getting a mentor?" I ask. "You know, working the program."

"So I can be like Mystic River Timmy and marry a nymphomaniac nutjob and be miserable?"

"A lot of people seem kind of happy. The gay cellist got a boyfriend. And Middle-Aged Black Hank got a promotion at work. And Mystic River Timmy and Slutty Sadie just bought a house in Jersey."

"Those are externals," the Belgian reminds me. "Those are just the 'cash and prizes' everyone in the group says *seem* important, but aren't. We're supposed to be concerned with our inner lives."

"But our inner lives kind of suck."

"Good point," says the Angry Belgian.

Neither Frank nor I share too much with the group. Our withholding behavior is not in accordance with the spiritual suggestions of the program, but it barely qualifies as a misdemeanor; physically attacking a fellow meaning seeker is felonious by group standards; sleeping with a newcomer is slightly less odious, but not much. Keeping your mouth shut and hanging out in the aisle of denial, as Frank and I do, is looked on mostly with raised eyebrows and the frowny mouth. Sometimes I wonder what would happen if I were honest with the group—if I told them how lonely I was, how prone to fits of murderous rage when people accidentally bumped me walking down the street; that I spent a month typing revenge scenarios against Bridget and Denny into my computer and only neglected to act upon them because I couldn't devise a way to escape the legal consequences I was sure would befall me if I happened to be caught; that I was moderately certain that I would eke out the rest of my thin gray days as an angry, sad, lonely blob who chronically lied to his father about his emotional state; and that the main reasons I came to the group were, first, that it provided me distraction from my life and, second, that a winter with Hitler and lots of snow had persuaded me that as a mammal, I needed to spend time in proximate contact to other mammals, no matter how much they whined about their sick cats and soft talked, no matter how nonexistent were the chances they would ever understand me.

"If you said all that," the Angry Belgian assures me, "you can be sure of two things. First, you would scare away any newcomer whom you might have had a chance of sleeping with. Second, Soft-Talking Probably a Lesbian Stacy would tell the group that you were loathsome. But softly."

So I keep quiet. I'm writing the sports profiles still and the whore work I dare not call whore work. I keep quiet as I listen to stories of abortion and birth, of birthday parties and suicide, of deathbed reconciliations and middle-aged reinventions. I keep quiet as people share tales of bankruptcies and windfalls, of homelessness and promotions. I keep quiet as, every night, I reach for the telephone, as I clutch the remote control. New York City, capacious and sprawling childhood repository of my watery and hopeful Midwestern dreams, is the size of my one-bedroom apartment now. It's so small. I keep quiet, because who would understand my woes except for Mrs. Friedman, whom I will never find? I keep quiet in the morning circles and in the evening aisles of denial. I keep quiet, until the day the Fat Man speaks.

He wears black leather pants and a black leather vest, and seeing him makes me think of what the Ascot would say about fashion choices. I haven't thought about the Ascot or Kiki or the Queen of Mean in a long time. It's been three years since I left *GQ* and sought peace in the frigid and Third Reich–rich hell of Colorado's San Juan Mountains. But as I regard the Fat Man and consider his world-class fashion sins, I remember my days in worsted wool and Egyptian cotton. I was looking good then. I am at the moment wearing sweat pants and a Hawaiian shirt.

The Fat Man coughs, tugs on his vest. It's noon, and I have just plunked myself down at in my usual spot in Inventory Alley, so I take the Fat Man's inventory. He is enormously fat, cartoonishly fat, more wild boar than human. Underneath his leather vest are waves and rolls of hairy flesh, unburdened by a shirt. Around his porcine neck dangle four gold chains. Crosses hang at the end of two, skulls at the end of the others. More death's head bracelets encircle each wrist. Soiled, tissue-thin jeans the color of dirty snow are tucked into calf-high brown motorcycle boots. I assume that he is a criminal or gay, or a gay criminal.

"A guy bumped into me on the street last year," the Fat Man says. He doesn't mention anything about a spiritual morass or redemption through the program or being connected to a higher power, and I'm grateful for that.

I hate the sanctimonious sharers and their treacly little tales. (I hate them even more than the soft talkers and the my-poor-cat whiners.)

"And he didn't say, 'Excuse me,' or, 'I'm sorry,' or anything like that."

He was probably scared, I think.

"And I thought," the Fat Man tells the group, "that I want to go home and get an Uzi, and I want to kill that motherfucker! And then I want to kill the dozen or so motherfuckers who saw that motherfucker bump me and not apologize, and then I want to blow my own motherfucking head off."

Silence in the room. The Fat Man's neck is empurpled, his meaty fists squeezing the table at which he sits. The Fat Man appears to be, at least in his deranged gay criminal mind, back on the street. He doesn't have an Uzi, but he sure looks like he wants one. No one moves.

"And then I called my mentor," the Fat Man says, "and I told him what I wanted to do. And my mentor said, 'Why don't you have a cheeseburger and take a nap?'"

Everyone laughs, including Frank. Everyone chortles and chuckles and guffaws except for two people. One is me. I at that moment comprehend that the one person in New York City who might understand me even better than the Angry Belgian is a leather-garbed monster in chains. In his grotesque, infantile hypersensitivity and in his inclination toward terrible, unreasonable anger, he is just like me. In his revenge fantasies and in his weakness for food and sleep, he is just like me. The other nonlaugher in the room is the Fat Man, who at the moment is staring at me. I'm sure of it. He is staring at me in a way that no one has ever stared at me. He is staring at me with his gay criminal eyes in a way that would make even the Man-Thing quake in . . . I don't know what it would make the Man-Thing quake in. Not terror, because the Fat Man's stare is not manipulative or cruel. Not confusion, because the Fat man's stare is filled with grace and understanding. The Fat Man's stare is not predatory and ravenous, like the African spotted dog stare when he sees the protein-packed but always dangerous warthog grunting next to the water hole, which I watched on a really excellent Animal Planet special the night before, because the Fat Man doesn't want to chase me down and disembowel me before feasting on my entrails. (That's how the African spotted dog gets by.) The Fat Man is staring at me with compassion.

"So I had a cheeseburger," the Fat Man says, still staring at me. A couple of people in the front row turn around to see what the Fat Man is staring at. They see a puffy-faced idiot in a Hawaiian shirt who is doing nothing to hide his weeping. "And I calmed down. And then I took a nap, and when I woke up, I felt even calmer. And that was the day I realized that beneath all my rage was fear. And that beneath the fear was a certainty that I was alone, and would always be alone."

Now the human in the mutant pig's body is smiling. But why? What could be more woeful to the Fat Man—what could be more woeful to *anyone*—than to grasp with such pitiless clarity his fundamental, eternal aloneness. I am weeping even harder now. I am blubbering. A few others in the room are snuffling and crying too. But the Fat Man keeps smiling, which makes me blubber even more.

And then I feel something warm inside. Like a fever, but not a fever. I understand something that I have never understood before. The Fat Man is staring at me with compassion because the Fat Men *feels* compassion for me. And he feels compassion for me because he knows who I am. And the other people crying in the room, and laughing, and crying some more—he knows who they are too. We are all the same. The rest of the people in the room are just like me. They aren't just like me in the thrashing-around-in-the-spiritual-morass kind of way only. They are just like me in the oversensitive, prone-to-temper-tantrums, easily-mollified-by-a-cheeseburger-and-a-nap-loser-who-felt-disconnected-from-humanity-before-he-realized-that-in-our-feelings-of-disconnectedness-we're-all-connected way. And—oh, blinding, sight-restoring epiphany—that is the way *out of* the spiritual morass.

"That was the day I started asking for help," the Fat Man says. "That was the day I found out that I need never be alone again."

The warmth inside has spread. My hands and feet are tingling. Everything is brighter, as if someone had supercharged the fluorescent lights in the basement room. I think I'm having what my fellow morass thrashers call a "white light" epiphany. It's this: not only are we all scrabbling together, not only can we all take solace in our mutual and mutually understood torment, but there's also a way out! And the way out is not to scrabble and thrash, but to reach out to the other scrabblers and thrashers. The way out is to realize that we are *all* scrabbling, thrashing cheeseburger whores and to help all the cheeseburger whores less fortunate than us. Or is it less fortunate than we?

"Don't you see?" I say, clutching the lapels of the Angry Belgian as the meeting breaks up. "We're all lonely cheeseburger whores."

"Do not touch my shirt," the Angry Belgian says. "You know how I hate to be touched."

I tell the Angry Belgian I'll meet him outside. I leave the aisle of denial—for good, I'm certain—make my way to the front of the room, where Soft-Talking Probably a Lesbian Stacy and Clinically Insane but Smoking Hot Melissa and some others I recognize linger to pay their respects to the monster with the message. When it's my turn, I thank the Fat Man, pump his meaty mitt, tell him he really touched me.

"No problem, Kahuna," he says, "keep coming back."

"You really—"

But the Fat Man has given me his fat back. He has placed one of his enormous palms on one of Clinically Insane but Smoking Hot Melissa's delicate Fluffy-petting wrists. He is looking deeply into her clinically insane eyes.

I don't blame the Fat Man. She has that effect on men, even the most noble cheeseburger whores. I once witnessed even Jesus John giggle and blush when Clinically Insane but Smoking Hot Melissa flashed him some thigh. I will not judge the Fat Man, because the Fat Man has saved me. I will not judge anyone anymore. I will not gossip about anyone. I will reach my hand out to my fellow cheeseburger whores.

"I need help," I say at a meeting the next day. "I've been sitting in the aisle of denial for years, and most nights I've been eating ice cream and watching porn. I'm looking for love and connection, and I feel like I'll never find it."

(I don't mention my afternoons at the diner with the Angry Belgian, because he has asked me not to.

"Bleat all you want about your cheeseburgers and your whores," he had told me. "But leave me out of it."

"Not cheeseburgers *and* whores. Cheeseburger whores. We're all cheeseburger whores!"

"Yeah, whatever, just don't mention my name. I think it could queer my deal with the Firestarter. I think she's starting to like me.")

"Make your bed every morning," Clinically Insane but Smoking Hot Melissa says, in response to my plea for help. "That's what my mentor tells me. To start your day out with a made bed, because otherwise you can't expect to have an orderly day."

"When someone asks for help, never say no," Middle-Aged Black Hank says.

"Keep being honest," Jesus Juliet says.

"Pray," Firestarter tells me.

"We all love you," Jesus John says.

I pray. I try to be honest. I offer help when help is requested (which, speaking of honesty, is rare; the women who listen to my porn and Peanut

Butter Cup ice cream soliloquies seem hesitant to inquire after my assistance). But I don't blame them. I blame no one.

I expand my meeting schedule. I start attending more meetings on the East Side, where the cheeseburger whores complain about their undependable housekeepers and the searing agony of trying to get their toddlers into the very best kindergartens. I don't judge them, though. I judge no one, not even the undeservedly wealthy East Side morass thrashers who badmouth the "group therapy sessions that pass for meetings" in my neighborhood. "God doesn't live on the West Side," one of the sanctimonious pricks pronounces at one of the East Side meetings, but I don't judge him. I don't judge the spiritual development seekers downtown and their nose studs. I strain mightily not to judge the cheeseburger whores at a semifamous-among-spiritual-development-seekers meeting on Park Avenue where group leaders hire professionals to deliver the inspirational stories and who close every gathering by reciting the Lord's Prayer. Paying the speakers bothers me, because I think it runs counter to the whole notion of anonymous cheeseburger whores banding together in a democratic and nonelitist manner, and the prayer bugs me because it's Christian, and my understanding when I first started going to meetings was, this was supposed to be a loosely knit confederation of like-minded spiritual recovery seekers where worship aimed at Jesus and Allah and others was strictly avoided.

I complain about the East Side cheeseburger whores at my regular West Side morning group not to judge or to gossip, but to help everyone's spiritual development.

"They're fucking Nazis on the East Side," Firestarter says.

"Rich, empty, hateful anti-Semitic swine," adds Clinically Insane but Smoking Hot Melissa, whom I'm trying not to think of as clinically insane so much anymore. It seems impolite. Maybe I *am* becoming more spiritual.

"We should pray for them," says Jesus John, who—after Clinically Insane but Smoking Hot Melissa cuts him a look—adds, "even if they might not seem like they are deserving of our prayers."

So I pray. Not for the East Side Jesus lovers. That would require a higher level of spiritual development than I have achieved. I pray that Clinically Insane but Smoking Melissa will stop whining about Fluffy. I pray that even if Fisherman Hank doesn't return to the group, at least the voices will leave him alone and he'll get over Firestarter. Mostly, I pray that I might feel the tingling induced by the Fat Man, but on a more regular, sustained basis.

That doesn't happen. There are the odd moments of delight, to be sure, but mostly it's others who seem to be doing all the chronic tingling—the lawyer who announces his plans to take up teaching at a notorious Bronx high school, the hedge fund manager who says he's walking away from his bulging portfolio so he can build a telescope and look at the stars. Why can't I be more like them? Why can't I tingle more?

I continue praying. I bitch to Frank at the diner. I chat up potential Mrs. Fs. I long for Perfect Little Annie, and I continue to write stories telling editors at women's magazines what men really feel; then I change the stories when the women's magazine editors tell me that men need to feel a little differently. Still, no regular tingling. So I get a mentor.

"Does he tell you to make your bed every morning?" Frank inquires one afternoon at the diner.

"No, smart-ass. He's just a regular guy."

"If he's so regular, how's he going to help you?"

"When I heard him speak at a meeting, he said he used to wake up sure of two things. First, that he was alone. Second, that things were going to get worse."

"Sounds like a smart guy."

"Ha. But then he said that since he'd been working the program, he wakes up every day sure of two other things. First, that he isn't alone. And second, that things are going to get better."

"That's intense."

"Yeah, that's what I th—"

"Hey, you going to eat that piece of bacon? I'm feeling very alone. Like things are never going to get better. I'm so hungry. Please help me."

I turn on my computer every night, intending to write something no one will ever dare call whore work. Instead, I compose short but vivid e-mails, tender glimpses into the heart of a confident, happy slim fellow who makes lots of money and loves puppies and children and wants to share his life, especially with the women on the Internet dating site to whom he is addressing his missives. Every morning, I vow that I won't spend hours on the Internet that night. Every evening, I promise myself that I will reach out to a male newcomer at a meeting the next day. (My mentor has suggested laying off the female newcomers, as well as cutting back on the Internet dating.) Sometimes, waking from a dog nightmare, I wonder if I imagined the Fat Man, if the magical compassion I felt from him ever really existed anywhere but in my perfervid desires.

"Forget the stupid Fat Man," the Angry Belgian tells me one Saturday morning as we settle into our plastic chairs. "But remember to come to the business meeting after the regular meeting today."

"What for?"

"Because I'm going to try to get a rule passed limiting the number of chairs in the room. I'm sick of people cramming themselves in every corner."

"Oh yeah, you don't like people touching you."

"That's not the point. It's that with so many people, the quality of the message gets diluted and then the people who really need spiritual development can't get it because—"

"Shhhh!" says Oksana, who is sitting on the other side of me. Oksana and I have, miraculously, become friends. We don't sleep together anymore, but occasionally we'll go to a movie or have a cup of coffee or some "seemple feesh, grilled, pliss!" She has taken me to hear a Russian pianist at Carnegie Hall. There, she introduced me to her friend, Svetlana, a Latvian who looks like a villainess from a James Bond movie, all Mongol cheekbones and flashing blue eyes and neck-snapping legs tucked into knee-high dagger-heeled boots. Svetlana makes Oksana look like Shirley Temple. I had tried to fix up Svetlana with the Angry Belgian, but Svetlana had laughed after meeting him and said, "But he ees soch a child!"

Frank's motion at the business meeting prompts a long and angry discussion. Young David, who is applying to law school, proclaims that we as the spiritually developed owe a debt of responsibility to the sick and suffering who might be late for the meeting and have trouble finding a seat. Frank, who watches *Law & Order* reruns almost as much as I do, argues that the rights of the individual must be balanced against the collective good.

"Equitable enforcement of a well-drafted piece of legislation can withstand the most vigorous legal challenges," the Angry Belgian says.

"Who the fuck is going to bring a legal challenge?" asks Big Ted, who is a lawyer in real life.

The Firestarter accuses Frank and the other would-be size limiters of "Stalinist tactics." Oksana scowls at that. A newcomer named Sobbing Sissy sobs and says conflict scares her. The vote is 7–7 until I break the tie and vote to limit the number of chairs after Frank whispers to me that he'll buy me pancakes and bacon for a week if I back him.

Other spiritual development business meetings are just as contentious. There is the should-we-ban-texting-or-not meeting. The should-we-open-the-windows-or-leave-the-air-conditioner-running meeting. There is the should-we-limit-members'-shares-from-the-floors-to-three-minutes-or-not meeting. I'm a big believer in the three-minute limit. Once I hear Young David whisper, as I enter a meeting, "Here comes three-minute Steve." I'm fairly certain he's still bitter about his loss in the group-size-limiting business meeting.

But I keep coming back, to business meetings and to regular meetings. I attend because I'm still lonely and because I need to stay away from the Internet as much as possible and because of the attractive newcomers and because I still believe in the Fat Man, even though I can't find him. The Angry Belgian and I continue our pancake sessions, and we are joined by Young David and Big Ted and Oksana. We eat pancakes together at least once a week.

And then one day, as I'm sitting between Oksana and Frank at a meeting waiting for things to get started, I feel a nudge. It's Frank. Frank, who hates being touched, never nudges. What could possibly have inspired this? I follow his eyes.

There, in a row perpendicular to ours, sits Kelly, in tight jeans and a tight sweater, in all her pillow-breasted glory. I haven't seen her in a year. I grin, wave wildly. Kelly is back for spiritual development? Great! Maybe now she'll see that I meant her no harm, that all I ever *wanted* for her was spiritual development. Kelly notices me and scowls, and as she's scowling, Frank leans across my back and tells Oksana who's scowling at me. The three of us look at Kelly, and she sees us looking and slowly peels off her sweater. Every set of spiritually developing male eyes in the room looks. They look and they look. Kelly sees them look, I'm sure of it. Kelly is peeling very slowly, until the sweater is off and she is wearing just a thin ribbed tank top. Something rises in my throat that tastes like bad hot dogs.

Oksana pats my knee, as a mentor would pat a mentee, as a mother would pat a child whose puppy was just kicked by the neighborhood bully, as a kindly Animal Planet producer would pat a widowed shivering bachelor marmot's lonely fuzzy head.

"Wow," says the Russian, regarding Kelly and her fearsome pillow breasts with respect and wary admiration, the way a once-mighty superpower might assess a breakaway rogue republic, "soch a power moof!"

I hunt the Fat Man. I shuffle down grimy stairs and into church basements filled with plastic chairs, hungry for his simple, shimmering vision of cheeseburgery salvation. When I don't find it, or him, I complain to my mentor. I confess to him my sins of ice cream and porn and Internet lies, and he suggests I look for evidence in the universe of a power greater than myself. When I tell him that I'm lonely, that I worry I'll never find a wife, he suggests that I offer my help to the next male newcomer I see in a meeting. When two weeks later I thank him for his suggestions and admit that I now see with great clarity my role in the toxic relationship I shared with Susan and that I'm ready to call her and to confess that role, in the interest of healing and living a more spiritual life, he suggests that I let Susan be, that I let all my old girlfriends be, that I devote more energy to helping others. And by others he means men.

Things are better, but not better enough. I'm still not tingling on a sufficiently regular basis. My mentor tells me to practice patience. I think I need to stop the astrology columns and the relationship advice and the celebrity profiles. But if I did, what would I write other than the agonized athletes pieces and the pieces for women's magazines telling readers how men really feel, after the women's magazines editors instruct me exactly how we do in fact feel? How would I get by? Overcoming my fear is one thing. Being fiscally irresponsible is another.

"You should write what you want to write," my mentor tells me.

"But who's going to pay me for—"

"Look, Steve, economic shortage is a fact of life. I know about the world we live in. But imagine that everything is going to work out in your life—no matter what you do, no matter if you do what you are supposed to, or what you want to. Now, if everything is going to work out, what would you do? What would you write?"

"But who would buy . . . ?"

"What I'm saying is, if you're walking a spiritual path, if you're working the program, then you needn't make a decision from a place of fear. You should make your decisions from a place of abundance."

What would I write if I didn't have to worry about who might buy it? What would I do if everything was going to work out? How would I conduct myself if I was freed from my low-grade anxiety and less-frequent-but-still-troublesome rashes and my bad dog dreams and the gut-churning, chin-trembling sadness that descends upon me whenever the words "Perfect Little Annie" or "Mrs. Friedman" occur to me, which they do more often than I would like to admit?

I remember a funny, sad joker I had met years earlier. I think of the distance between what I want to be and what I am, of the yawning chasm separating all our dreams from the lives we lead. Or is it just mine? I pick up my telephone. I don't call the deli guy.

CHAPTER 15

VOYAGE OF THE DAMNED

"It's 'Bamboleo' time!" one of the bullfight dancers—or maybe it's a bullfight singer—shouts. Some dancers wearing fruit arrangements skip from stage left.

The crowd gapes. Maybe it's simply nausea or reaction to the medication the cruise ship doctor has passed out.

"Can you feel the heat?" a shimmying banana asks as the cruise ship smoke machine pumps out greasy clouds of diesel-scented smoke.

If a cruise ship chorus girl yelled a question in the middle of the Caribbean and no one answered, would "Bamboleo" time suddenly stop? It seems not. More gaping. Profound, confused gaping.

The cruise ship comedian and I gape together.

"Are you a party crowd?" a pineapple screams (with some hostility and desperation, it seems to me) and gets the same querulous, apparently medicated response. Now, people are worried. Husbands look at wives. Did the brochure say anything about responsive readings with plumpish fruitheads?

"Bamboleo" time comes to an end—I think. Then it's "Riverdance" time, and after that, "Don't Cry for Me, Argentina" time, and after that, it's "Memory" (from *Cats*) time. There are many whiskers. The smoke machine labors on.

The cruise ship comedian, who has been sitting quietly, turns. He sees me watching him. Does he wonder how he ended up here, when—or if—he'll ever get off? Does he know that I know that *he* knows that the menacing wraith known as Shecky and the dancing fruitheads and the cruise ship comedian—the fate of all of them—are tied together in profound and uncomfortable ways?

"Look," he says. "You're human. You have dreams of grandeur. If you're a dancer, you saw *Flashdance*, you saw *Chorus Line*, then . . . you're dressed in a cat costume on a cruise ship, hiding in a garbage can, choking on the smoke machine."

It is my first night at sea. The beginning of the end of my whore work.

"A cruise ship comedian plays the faded, ragged jokers that have been dealt him in his floating, queasy, endless five-card-stud game of life," I write in my notebook, then gaze out the porthole at sick-making whitecaps.

"Yeah," I try to say, but what comes out is "blegh," because I've been feeling a little woozy for the past forty-eight hours, ever since I stepped onto the *Celebrity Galaxy* in Puerto Rico and, feeling the ocean pitching beneath me, swallowed a pill I had cadged from the cruise ship doctor. Since then, I have witnessed disturbing, hallucinatory things (in addition to the dancing fruitheads).

I have seen passengers puke. But those aren't the worst passengers. I have seen passengers so heavily doped with motion sickness pills that they nodded off in the middle of the cruise ship comedian's act. But *those* aren't the worst passengers. "The worst," the cruise ship comedian had told me right after "Bamboleo" time, "is the guy who wants to tell *you* jokes. He'll come up to you, big cigar—especially on the pricier lines, the Holland Americas, the Crystals—and kind of whisper, 'You probably can't use this in your act,' and then start. Something like, 'So there were these two Jews in a concentration camp . . . ' And I go, 'What?!'"

"Hmmm," I say. "I see what you mean." In my notebook I scribble, "Cigars/Jew Jokes/Shecky Suffers!"

I have joined the comedian on the ship because I am done with celebrity profiles and how-to-avoid-ear-dandruff sidebars and columns on Saturn rising and giving your girlfriend pedicures. I am going to study this joker from a place of abundance, and then I am going to channel what I learn into life-affirming, felicitous prose that will expand readers' souls.

"Don't you *see?*" I had inquired long before I flew to Puerto Rico, of the Angry Belgian, and Psychic Rose, and Clinically Insane but Smoking Hot Melissa, and, I'm slightly ashamed to admit, Slutty Sadie, before she hooked up with Mystic River Timmy. "Don't you understand that this guy is living all our lives? That his troubles are our troubles? That what saves him could save all of us?" Except for Psychic Rose, whom I was paying to empathize with me, none of the rest of them saw. But that was okay. As long as I got an assignment and then wrote the life-affirming prose, then they would see. Everyone would see. First, I had to get the assignment, though.

I had written to my former colleague, who had somehow leveraged his vast wisdom about sandals and socks into an executive editor position at *Esquire.*

Dear Eddie,

The comedian isn't quite where he wants to be, stuck in a place he wishes he could escape, but can't. Not to get too metaphysical, but isn't that true of many, many, *many* men? I see this as a story

about how men confront the reality of their lives and what they
do when the reality sinks in.

If that wasn't abundant and life affirming, what was?

Then I had added more to the letter, just to show I was the kind of
writer who, though sensitive enough to explore a man's soul, could go mean
when necessary.

Which would be *way* too heavy, except this guy does it surrounded
by slutty cruise ship chorus girls, moon-faced Midwesterners and
twenty-four-hour lobster buffets.

Editors at men's magazines never tired of the word "slutty."

The Ascot had passed, so I pitched it to an editor at *GQ*, who passed.
As did editors at *Men's Health*, *The New York Times Magazine*, and *Details*.
I double backed and tried another editor at *Esquire*, who said he would
run it at 2,500 words. After I agreed, an editor at *Men's Journal* said he
would run the piece at 5,000 words, which sounded much better. True,
I was breaking an agreement I had made. True, this wouldn't help me in
the future with *Esquire*. And yes, my mentor always advised me to live up
to my commitments. But a story coming from such an abundant place
needed abundant words. Once I had touched readers' hearts with the sad
and inspirational saga of Shecky, no one would remember that I had reneged
on a promise to an *Esquire* editor. I had to look at the big picture. Coming
from a place of abundance wasn't simple.

I have learned in my two wobbly days and nights at sea that bad
things happen to cruise ship comedians. They happen with regularity and
predictability. First-night-at-sea performances are troubles—because of the
seasick and heavily medicated crowd. Last-night-at-sea shows mean too
many people worrying about packing and catching the airport shuttle and

how much to tip the cabin boys, whom the passengers also need to worry about remembering to call stewards. Foreigners bring other problems. Once, the cruise ship comedian spotted a flier on a ship bulletin board describing him—a strictly English-speaking cruise ship comedian—as "Der Komicker." Twenty minutes before he was going to go on, he saw the flier. Six hundred people came to that show. Fifty stayed. That was bad.

Of all the bad, sad things that plague the life of a cruise ship comedian, though, of all the horrors I have heard about since stepping on board, the worst is the chilling vision of the watery destiny that sometimes seems to beckon him, the grim fate that awaits any aging yuckster who sails too far too often. It is the liver-spotted specter that the comedian had told me about when we had first met, two years ago at dinner in Hermosa Beach.

"Yeah, of course, I think about Shecky," he tells me as we sit inches apart on facing twin beds deep in the airless and dim entertainers' quarters of the *Celebrity Galaxy*. The room is basically a portholed closet with beds. Our living quarters are not helping my nausea.

"Shecky's a guy who's had his time, and that time has passed him by, or he's a hack who never got where he wanted to. And most of these guys, they think, 'Just one more rung up and I'll hit the big time.' What they don't realize is the ladder was yanked out from under them about two decades ago."

"That's sad," I say to the comedian as I recline on my skinny bed in my little semiprivate portholed hell. Then I heave myself up and lurch into the bathroom, which is as big as a coffin. There, I gaze at myself in the mirror.

"I don't want to be Shecky," I say. "I really don't want to be Shecky. God, please don't let me be Shecky."

For six nights and seven days I try not to be Shecky while also attempting to understand the nobility of Shecky's struggle and to ignore the private but utterly unignorable tidbits of a cruise ship comedian's life. Will it improve anyone's existence to learn, as I have learned, that jugglers have a bad name among other cruise ship entertainers, but they aren't as bad as ventriloquists? Will it expand anyone's spirit to hear of cruise ship ventriloquists, as I have heard from the cruise ship comedian, that "they'll fuck anything"?

"Heh, heh," I say when the comedian gives me dirt on the other cruise ship entertainers and then I jot in my notebook, "Cruise ship ventriloquists = sexual predators." Later, I type my notes into a computer file titled "Whore Worker, Cruise Ship Comedian, Everyman."

I type, in the portholed closet.

> Every man considers his loftiest dreams from a well-worn office chair or a lumpy couch. Most learn to live with the distant, maddening view. Often they do so quietly, desperately. Maybe they take up golf.

"Sentimental," I type into the "Whore Worker, Cruise Ship Comedian, Everyman" file when I learn that my subject has brought along *Play It Forward* and *Tuesdays with Morrie* to read. "So sad, but so incredibly plucky."

"Shecky succeeds and the human spirit triumphs!" I write in my notebook as I watch the cruise ship comedian kill one night. His timing is really quite extraordinary. I wish I could describe how exquisite it is, how Der Komicker pauses exactly the right amount of time to make laughter swell. "Corny, but effective," I write as he basks in wave after wave of roaring applause and adulation.

On our last night together, I put down my notebook and computer, and we watch television. We watch *Black Dog*, starring Patrick Swayze as an ex-con trucker trying to go straight, being chased by a villain played by Meat Loaf. We're kicking back with our regular late-night cruise ship room service snacks (I eat cake and cookies; the comedian has the fruit plate).

While we watch Swayze's frenzied flight from Meat Loaf, we continue our weeklong conversation about comedy and aspirations.

I ask what in his career has made him happiest. It might be good for the story, and it might even be good for me. He seems like a happy guy. He seems like a guy who probably tingles often.

"One time," he says, "I'm going up to the deck to run laps and a little Jamaican guy comes up to me, a crew guy, and he says, 'Hey, mon, I see your show. I really like your show.' And you know what? Sometimes you feel really self-indulgent. You know, you're not curing cancer or anything. But that little Jamaican guy? I made him feel good. I went, 'Fuck, man, that meant more to me than all the passengers who ever came up to me.' That guy sweeps floors; he works hard for a living."

"That's cool," I say. *The little foreign man touches the funny man's big heart*, I think. I will try to remember that line. It'll be mean, but subtle. Editors love that.

Meanwhile, Meat Loaf is closing on the troubled trucker, who spies a diner off the side of the road and pulls his rig in. As he does, the comedian asks me for some book recommendations, for his next cruise.

I mention a few writers I like, offer a few titles.

He puts his fruit plate down, looks at me.

"Hey, man," he says. "Do you realize you're always describing a writer by how old he was when he first published? My friend, you gotta quit being so hard on yourself."

My friend? My *friend*?

The room tilts. It is not a wave. No, the man who endures puking passengers and cigar-chomping bigots and ever-threatening visions of Shecky is reaching out to me. What makes him *happiest* is helping others. This Willy Loman of the High Seas is trying to *comfort* the guy who has spent the better part of a week scribbling down evidence that he—the cruise ship comedian—is a walking, quipping, amusing yet poignant example of cheerful mediocrity . . . of nine-to-fiveish not getting it. Of failure. Sure, I had planned to write a life-affirming, generous, abundant piece. But the details—the dancing fruitheads, the silly jokes, the corny books—have been too irresistible. I was going to take the cruise ship comedian down. I was going to go mean. He was smart enough to know that. He had to know that. Still, here he was, reaching out.

"Thanks, man," I say, but I feel dizzy. In room 401, during the third act of *Black Dog*, halfway between Barbados and St. Thomas, an arm's length from my bunkmate, subject, and hero, I feel a spiritual awakening. More white light. Another epiphany.

We are *all* cruise ship comedians, hawking our tinny wares, meekly demanding that attention be paid, rowing our little boats toward the green light, against the relentless waves, whatever. I see that. I see that none of us is exactly where he wants to be. Some of us are cynical, snarky, note-taking, and vaguely embittered cruise ship comedians. Others are wise, blessed, loving cruise ship comedians. Fruit eaters of the sea. We have a choice.

I gnaw on my chocolate-chip cookie, eyes brimming. Meanwhile, the Dalai Lama of cruise ship comedians regards Patrick Swayze chatting up the roadside waitress.

"All right!" the cruise ship comedian says. "The truck stop scene! Hey, scramble me up some eggs, Sally, and give Meat Loaf a chance to catch us."

I will not let the cruise ship comedian down. I will not do to him what I did to Tesh. Back in New York, I attend meetings in the mornings, and then I retire to my apartment. I make room in my heart for abundance. I spend a week on headlines; then I take a few days off. Then it's time to craft the perfect lead for the piece.

I write.

No child dreams of one day telling lifeboat jokes. No entertainer ever hoists a beer one evening with friends and says, "Gee, I wish it were early morning, and I were typing gags in a floating library." Very few people on this earth long to spend eternity lying beneath a cold marble slab engraved with a cruise ship comedian's epitaph: "At Least He Wasn't as Bad as the Ventriloquist."

That takes a few days. Then I take a week off, because I'm emotionally exhausted, and because I want to do justice to the cruise ship comedian and to the hopes and dreams he and I share with all humanity. Before I know it, I'm a month late on the piece, and I have nothing but headlines and my paragraph about the tombstone, but I tell my editor that it's going well, that I'm just doing some polishing. Lying like this goes against my mentor's general suggestions about leading an honest life, and it's exhausting too, but I need to keep the editor on the hook for this piece. This is the story that will wash away all my previous Teshian and Barbara Hershian sins. I spend another week sitting on a bench in Central Park, trying to compose gags about lifeboats and cruise ship toilets, because I want to *feel* the existential challenge that my hero feels every time he sits down to write something that will make a medicated rich person chuckle. I return to my apartment, and I turn out the lights and sit on my couch and repeat "Shecky" over and over again, because I hope it might help me get in touch with the Shecky who lives within us all, who haunts us. I try writing the "Bamboleo" time scene, and every time I get to the first dancing fruithead, I start crying, and I can't stop.

Finally, I turn in my fourteen-thousand-word cri de coeur.

The next day, my editor telephones.

"The assignment was five thousand words," he says.

"Yeah, I know, but you know, we're all cruis—"

"I have worse news. Our editor in chief just left, and the new guy says we're going a new direction, that we can't use this."

"But—"

"I'm sorry, but you know, if you weren't three months late, we might have published it."

"But—"

"Sorry about this, Steve, but I know you understand."

I call around. I write other editors. I delete "Slutty" in the pitches I send to women's magazines. I add "beautiful sun-kissed beaches" to the travel magazines. An editor at *The Washington Post* says they'll buy the piece for $1,000.

"But it's fourteen thousand words," I say, "and I know you're a newspaper and all, but I usually get paid $4 a word and—"

"We'll run it at four thousand and pay you $1,000."

"Okay," I say.

The Post takes out my lead. They take out the tombstone bit. They take out my musings about passenger-fucking ventriloquists. But Meat Loaf and the spiritual awakening survive, and I consider this a small victory.

"Which headline are you going with?" I ask the editor. "'Voyage of the Damned'? That's my favorite. Or 'The Night Everyman Killed, Then Died'? That's sort of inside baseball, but you have to admit, it's got universal appeal. Or 'The Unbearable Sadness of Sheck'—"

"We're calling it 'Schtick Man of the Sea,'" the editor says.

On the day the story is published, a Hollywood studio buys an option to make the film, which means I get $2,000, unless, by some miracle, the studio actually *makes* the film. If by some impossible, it'll-never-happen chance that happens, then on the day that filming starts, I'll get $80,000. Which I know won't happen.

But then, miracle of miracles: The studio hires some screenwriters. It hires a big-deal director. It sets a schedule.

"I think I might have some good news soon," I e-mail Susan late one night. "I hope we can celebrate together." I know my mentor told me to leave her alone, but he also told me to operate from a place of abundance. It's a balancing act.

Then the director is diagnosed with leukemia, and there is no movie.

My father calls that night. I tell him I'm doing great.

CHAPTER 16

SHE CAME FROM CYBERSPACE

I'm not a cruise ship comedian. That's something to be grateful for. I don't have leukemia. I'm grateful for that too. When I tell my mentor about the movie director getting sick, and how I'm feeling bad about lying to my father, he suggests I write a nightly gratitude list. "Meetings with other cheeseburger whores," I type. "The Angry Belgian," I type. I throw in my father's weekly telephone calls, which at least afford me the opportunity to practice the honesty I'm embracing on a theoretical basis. An oft-repeated tenet of the program is "Progress, not perfection"; I've got that one nailed. One autumn night, I add "another assignment from *The New York Times*" to the list.

An editor from the newspaper asks if I'd be interested in a Valentine's Day assignment. They want me to prepare three different dinners for three different women, and to see which meal is most effective, seduction-wise. *The Times* will pay for the food and the necessary kitchen equipment. I'm not supposed to let the women in on my scheme, which strikes me as a bad way to start a lifelong relationship based on trust, which I would like to do, because I still am looking for Mrs. Friedman, but I need the money. (Freelancing is paying my bills, but there are things like health insurance and trips to the dentist to consider.) I take the assignment in October but don't buy recipe books (which I charge to *The Times)* until mid-January. Four days before the piece is due, I open *Booty Food* and *Cookin' to Hook Up.* I need to seduce three women with dinners on three consecutive nights.

"Get Spanish cheese, and crackers with saffron," Pale Black William opines. "Then it won't matter what you cook. Women go wild for Spanish cheese and saffron. I mean that literally. Wild!"

"The ladies dig mashed potatoes," declares Mystic River Timmy. "And any lady who claims she doesn't is lying."

I tell the Angry Belgian that I'm considering lobster risotto for one of my meals. He tells me to be careful.

"You cannot ignore risotto, dude," he tells me on the phone. I think I hear video snowboard sounds in the background. "Risotto demands all your attention, and much of your time. In many ways, risotto is like a needy woman."

For the second meal (the first is a forgettable but labor-intensive roast chicken, with a farmer's daughter who wanted to play gin rummy and gave me her cheek when I tried to kiss her following dessert, a cheap trifle called chocolate cheaters cheesecake), I invite a thrice-divorced fur-clad and diamond-bejeweled temptress from the East, whose name is Yevgenia and who I met through Oksana, back when Oksana could lay claim in my delirious mind to Mrs. F front-runner status. I decide I will cook Yevgenia sweet melon with prosciutto, move to steak au poivre with pink peppercorns, accompanied by grilled marinated portobello mushrooms. Then, for dessert, "sumptuous stuffed strawberries with mascarpone cheese and dark chocolate." Yevgenia will be like rendered Russian yak fat in my clever hands. Besides, how difficult can such a meal be?

Seven and a half hours later, I have my answer. Shopping takes two hours. Cleaning the kitchen from the night before takes another hour. Then another hour for more shopping (a broiler is necessary to broil steaks, a copper-bottomed saucepan is necessary for melting chocolate, pink peppercorns are impossible to find, and if one is to marinate giant portobello mushrooms in self-sealing plastic bags, I learn, to my dismay, one must actually possess self-sealing plastic bags). Then there's all the chopping and mincing and pouring and patting. And how was I to know the strawberry was such an egregiously difficult little fruit? To decapitate and hollow out a dozen sticky berries is tough enough. But then, to stuff them with cheese and chocolate mix and to plop their lonely little caps back on their pulpy little bodies, well, it takes time. Still, it looks as if I'll pull it off. Eight minutes to set up a fan and disconnect the screaming smoke alarm. Nineteen and a half minutes to shower, shave, and put on clean clothes. The meat and the mushrooms are done at exactly 6:57 PM, at which time I remove them from the oven and let them stew in their own delectable juices while I flip the place mats over to hide the chicken juice stains from the night before, dim the lights, take another peek at my initially intransigent but now-flirty little strawberries and . . . it's seven o'clock and Yevgenia has not arrived. And now it's 7:05 PM. No Yevgenia. And 7:10 PM. And now it's 7:15 PM.

Is this a game to her? Does she think steak au poivre seasons itself? Does Yevgenia not understand that with freedom comes responsibility, that in this country, when a guy cooks dinner for you, there's this quaint custom called punctuality, that maybe it's time for a certain sexy immigrant to hop on that historic diesel locomotive called capitalism and check her goddamned diamond-encrusted Cartier watch once in while? Or to Yevgenia am I just a pretty American face, a Western pair of brawny arms that happens to be handy with a spatula? Is it possible that to Yevgenia, this evening represents nothing but a few laughs, a good time, a quick bite? Am I merely a *snack?* Does she have any *idea* what I've been doing all day? It's at that moment

the pictures, all edgy grays and hard shadows, looks vaguely familiar. She lists her occupation as "writer." Probably cereal box ads, or marketing copy, I think. Should I write back? I study her profile further. Under "Why you should get to know me," she has written "for my pool game; my down dog; my total lack of cynicism." Hmmm, she knows her way around a semicolon. I read further. "For my Knicks tickets." I like this woman. I read further. "A smart mouth is sexy," she has written. "A smart mouth gone soft and wet is sexier."

What is age but a number? I start typing.

"Thank you," I write. "Smart, funny, *and* pretty? What do you write?"

"At the risk of sounding coy," she replies, "a couple of things of mine are pretty well-known, and I don't want to drag them kicking and screaming into a talk with anyone whose face I don't actually see. That said, what do you write?"

Oh, I write plenty, you semicolon-happy sexpot. I wrote a column called The Single Guy for *GQ*. I wrote an essay on the joys of bachelorhood for an anthology called "The Bastard on the Couch." I had launched Modern Love column in *The New York Times*. ("You will always be the man who introduced 'pillow breasted' into the paper of record," the Angry Belgian had told me. "No one can take that away from you.")

What do I write? This was going to be easy.

I type.

I don't mind secrecy, but fair is fair. At this point I'm thinking you either won the National Book Award or you're a sex columnist. But either way, it doesn't matter. I'm exceedingly nonjudgmental, and I respect successful women. If and when we meet, we can scribble the names of what we've written on scraps of paper and slide them across the table toward each other.

Is there a more suave or self-assured cyber dater in the world? Once the swan-necked little minx gets a load of my stuff, she will be mine.

When she writes back that actually, though she never won the National Book Award, she was a finalist a few years ago, I say, to no one but my empty apartment and myself, as I stare at my computer screen, "Whuh?"

The next day, she calls. We talk about the Knicks and the Dodgers. She tells me she's actually forty-six, not forty-three. *Definitely* too old for me. She mentions that her eighteen-year-old son's girlfriend "looks at him like he's a pork chop," and we both laugh. She has an easy laugh. We talk about honesty and dating, about religion and love. We talk about New York City and adolescence and writing.

She's remarkably easy to talk to. She tells me her name and I say, "As in the Violet who has sold something like eight hundred zillion copies of her first book and was on *The New York Times* best seller list for about five years and who is revered by readers worldwide?" That's when I realize what was familiar about the shadowy photo. I'd seen it in a gigantic window display at a bookstore. Yeah, she says, that's her, but it's no big deal.

I try to believe her. I've dated a working actress and a married Russian and the pillow-breasted ad saleswoman. So she's written a couple popular, staggeringly well-received books, been credited with reinventing the American memoir, and created works of art that have not just been beloved but parsed and analyzed and worshipped by critics from many countries? I'm not a big memoir-reading guy, and besides, she writes mostly about girl-on-the-verge-of-womanhood stuff, and she herself takes her poetry much more seriously than her nonfiction. And she's too old for me. This will be fun.

"This will be fun," I say.

She asks what I'm working on and I tell her and she says, "Oh, I can help you with that. The Lord sent me to you." Someone who has moved the numbers of units this lady author has moved, offering to help me with my work? Violet could tell me King Ahasuerus sent her to me, or Shana, queen of the Zebra People, and I would be all ears.

We keep talking. We talk for more than an hour.

It's the standard verbal pas de deux, which if I do say so myself, I'm pretty good at. I'm skilled at getting people to talk, especially when I can silence my whining mouth. But she's better. I talk about my family. I talk about the pillow-breasted ad saleswoman, but I don't use the phrase "pillow breasted." I talk about how I long for more of a link to God. I can't believe how easy it is to talk to her. "Oh yeah," she says, "I'm a fucking black belt at getting people to open up."

We meet the next evening, at a deli in midtown. She's pretty. Not stunning, but definitely pretty. Small boned. Tight clothes. Low-cut blouse. Maybe just a little too much makeup around the eyes. It's a revelation of sorts. A world-famous (at least among memoir lovers), critically acclaimed literary star still feels like she has to lie about her age and wear slightly too-tight clothes and too much makeup. Even a writing sensation like Violet feels like she has to work it. I find this comforting. Maybe she's a cheeseburger whore too.

When the waiter tells her the kitchen is out of hamburgers, Violet says, "Well, I guess I'll have to get a fucking pastrami sandwich then," and the pasty couple sitting next to us, a couple wearing Oklahoma sweatshirts and fingering their city maps, give her a look.

I spin some stories about my nephew, because I have learned that women with children respond to tales of Isaac. Violet is no exception. She leans in; her eyes stay on mine a little longer than absolutely necessary. I notice that for such a little slip of a thing, she seems to possess some startling curves. Maybe not pillow breasted, but pleasant to behold.

And what about her son, I inquire? What was he like as a little boy? Women, I have learned, like it when a man asks about their family members.

"He's strong," she says. "He stands up for himself. When he was only four, he was sitting at the kitchen table at my mom's house, and he reached for a cookie—the last cookie on the plate—and my mom, his grandma, she said, 'No, that's for me,' but he wouldn't give up that cookie."

"That's sweet," I say. "Sounds like a kid who likes his cookies." Maybe she really is a cheeseburger whore, I think. She seems so spiritual.

But Violet isn't done with the story.

"And my mom told me," Violet says, "'I almost smacked his hand, I wanted that cookie so bad.'

"And I told *her*," Violet says to me, grinning, "'If you had, you'd have pulled a bloody stump back, 'cause I'd have cut your fucking hand off with a fucking meat cleaver.'"

Then she tears off a huge chunk of pastrami sandwich and pops it into her delicate little mouth, her smart mouth, her, I can't help but notice, soft and wet mouth. The tourists next to us stare at their plates.

I have dated a lot of women, and everyone is different, everyone possesses her own special charms. Violet is really different.

After she gulps her meat, Violet suggests I pray to God to tell me what to write. She says she seeks God's guidance all the time. She's slim, she's curvy, she's into God, and as we chat about spirituality and motherhood and friendship and meaning, she says "fuck" and "dick" and "pussy" and "cocksucker" in combinations and permutations I have never imagined possible. No person in my life has ever cussed so much, so gleefully or with such wonderful invention and precision. I think she reads my mind.

"I'm a mouthy little bitch," she says to me, right before she snags another piece of flesh from her plate and gulps it whole.

On the walk home, I ask if all her young male fans fall in love with her.

"I gave a young poet a ride home from a party one night," she says, "because he was too drunk to drive. When I dropped him off, he grabbed for me, said, 'You have an ass like a one-hundred-dollar mule.'

"And I said, 'That doesn't sound like enough money.'

"And when he lunged for me, I said, 'You know, you'd be a much better writer if you weren't such a pussy hound.'"

Now my jaw is slightly unhinged. At her doorstep I tell her I had a great time, I hope I'm not being too forward, but I'd really like to see her again. She tells me sure, we can go out again, but she's going to be honest, "I'm right in the middle of a date-o-rama, I'm planning to go out with lots of guys." She tells me that in any case she won't have sex with me for a long time.

"I made my second ex-fiancé wait eight months before I'd fuck him," she says, after I peck her on the cheek, "because I knew he was such a pussy hound."

Second ex-fiancé? Hmm. That's interesting.

When I call my sister in Silverton that night and tell her who I've just shared a pastrami sandwich with, she shrieks.

"I love her," she says. "She's incredible." My sister apparently has read Violet's books.

Yeah, I allow, she seems pretty interesting. And she's pretty. But boy, does she cuss a lot.

Then my sister lowers her voice. I have heard this tone before. She used it when she talked to me about Isaac and the Nazis.

"Do *not* blow this one," she says.

I google Violet, find one of the poems she has written online, and after I finish reading, it I put my head on my dining room table and sob. It is the darkest, most beautiful thing I have ever read. It's about longing and despair and how longing can survive the most irrefutable evidence of its futility. It's about the never-ending cruelty of the world and how when we aim to move toward salvation and the promise of a better future, we are blind, and stupid and only inching toward death, but we can't help ourselves and keep inching anyway, that much closer to doom. How can someone so filled with such utter woe talk of God? How can a woman with such near carnal knowledge of anguish laugh and speak of the wonders of pussy? If she is a cheeseburger whore, she's the wisest cheeseburger whore I have ever met. She's even wiser than the Fat Man. It is at this moment I start to think that Violet might save me.

When I arrive at her apartment the next night, she says, "I really don't think this is wise dating behavior for someone planning a date-o-rama. Do you think it's wise? I don't."

We shop for Easter presents for her son and her godchildren, then walk together to the UPS shipping plant to mail them. In a room filled with scowling, cell phone–barking men and women, the chunky and beleaguered UPS man is screaming into his phone, bellowing at customers in line not to crowd, looking like a man about to slap someone or to quit or both. When it's Violet's turn, she murmurs a few words to him that I can't hear and his eyes widen and I think he's going to scream at her. Has she said something about pussy hounds? Has she told him to shut his cock-sucking mouth? Then she murmurs a few more words and he gets a faraway look in his eyes.

"She's a good girl," he says. Is he about to cry? Or to laugh? What in the world did she say to him? Who's a good girl?

"She's doing real good."

Huh? I think.

"They're all good kids," Violet says. "They're the greatest kids in the world. We're lucky to have them."

I lean in to eavesdrop. It's his daughter. They're talking about his daughter, and Violet's fan letters from young girls. They're talking about the wonders of parenthood, the gorgeousness of the universe.

As we leave, I tell her she's amazing.

"I have my primitive fucking charms," she says.

At dinner, she tells me she knew I was a writer because on my Internet dating profile I had written I was looking for a woman "who has never killed a man intentionally."

"Anyone else would have put 'intentionally' before 'killed,'" she says, "because that's where it naturally belongs, but you, you put it at the end of the sentence, because that's where it has weight, that's where the humor comes, that's where the punch happens. You're a fucking black belt. You are a *fucking black belt.*" As often happens at dinner with Violet, people at nearby tables cast looks our way.

I don't tell her that I didn't intentionally put "intentionally" at the end of the sentence. I don't tell her it was unintentional. A woman whose talent makes me quake with admiration and envy says I'm a writer? Who am I to judge intent? Maybe God put the word there.

Then she tells me her ex-fiancé, the second one, the *current* one, whom she hasn't seen in seven months, has been calling, and writing and e-mailing and she's been ignoring him. They teach at the same university upstate, and he says he needs to talk to her. She says she sent a short note informing him that anything he has to say to her can wait till she visits the campus, in a few months, at which time he can say what he has to say in front of a third party. She says she wishes he would accept what she has—that they're done. She says she's afraid of him. She says she's glad she met me.

We talk about the mistakes people make in love, how sex can complicate things. She tells me that a lot of young women ask her for advice, and she always tells them to wait on sex.

"But you know what? I can't understand when they tell me guys have sex with them, then stop calling. Every guy who's ever fucked me has liked me *more* afterward."

It was the poem I read on my computer screen that started it. Or maybe it was the tight clothes, or all the God talk, or the stories, or the way she got me to open up. Or it was my encounter with the Fat Man, or my decision to live from a place of abundance. Was it the sacred, or the profane, or the combination? Who can tease out the laws of attraction? I can't. But I know what I'm thinking: This is the last woman I will ever date. That's what I'm thinking, long after the waiters have removed my pad Thai and her salmon with barbecue sauce, long after our water glasses are empty and our tea has cooled and we're the only ones left in the restaurant and I'm the only one there to marvel at how sweetly, and deliciously, she cusses. *This is the last woman I will ever date.* I have found Mrs. F.

I am leaving for Aspen the next day, where I will spend a week reporting a story for *Ski* magazine on "mastering the bumps." But the flight doesn't leave until 5:00 PM, so I call Rose for an emergency session. I tell her I'm having trouble breathing, that I feel light-headed and sick to my stomach. I tell her about Violet's magic with the UPS guy, how I can't seem to shut up around her, about how her knowledge of desolation doesn't keep her from reaching toward the divine.

I tell her I know I'm prone to idealization and to romantic delusion and that I've always wanted someone who will validate my work and that Violet is critically acclaimed and revered and maybe that's an issue. I tell her I know I seem to seek out unavailable women. But isn't this progress? I ask my psychic psychotherapist. She's not a twenty-five-year-old waitress! She's not married, or an active alcoholic! She's almost my age! She's available. She seems to like me. Why am I hyperventilating? Why can't I eat?

Rose tells me that Violet sounds wonderful, but that I don't need her to make me whole.

"When you feel yourself falling in love," she says, "it reminds you of when you were young, and your mother was absent, and you feel like a lost little boy desperate to have a woman restore you to life, terrified that she'll leave you and you'll be alone again."

My mom again, I think. I really don't want to talk about my mom. (Here might be a good place to mention that, psychic Rose's theories notwithstanding, I'm not aware of any dark, festering secret between my mother and me that definitively explains my self-destructive romances or my obsessions with televised wildlife and ice cream, any more than whatever festers between any mopey, sensitive, and self-involved man and his at times temperamentally akin mother definitively explains that man's life.)

"Uh-huh," I say. "But I really want to call her. But I don't want to scare her. But I don't want her to think I'm not crazy about her, because I am. But maybe I should give it some time and . . ."

"It's okay to call her," Rose says. Good old Rose. I've been seeing her for almost a decade now and she remains unflappable in the face of my sometimes-extreme flappability. "But examine your motives. If you're calling looking for reassurance that you're worthy, don't do it. If you're calling just because you want to say hi to her, because you like her, it's okay. But examine your motives."

I examine my motives in the taxi ride to the airport, at the gift shop, and as I stare at my cell phone. I examine my motives as I pull out Violet's first book, in paperback, from my pocket, and read the panting blurbs on the back. I examine my motives as I picture Violet naked.

And while I'm examining my motives, sitting in the airport, Violet calls me. She tells me that she's read one of my stories, and really liked it. She says she hates everything, but that this piece was "heart yanking and gorgeous." I tell her that means a lot to me. More than she can imagine. I tell her how much I like her, how I'm really looking forward to seeing her when I return to the city. "Oh, we'll talk again," she says. "Eventually."

I call her the next day, of course. Casual. Not because I need her to restore me. Not out of desperate, pathological need. Not because that word "eventually" gave me a really bad stomachache. Not because just saying her name aloud to myself in my hotel room makes me smile. Just to say hi. Merely to say hi. Only to say hi.

"Hi," I say when she picks up the phone, "I just called to say hi."

We talk for an hour and a half that evening. About music. About poetry. About journalism. About religion and prayer. I tell her that Moses was actually one of the Old Testament's first great scribes, that he wrote the speeches that his brother Aaron delivered to the Israelites. I'm surprised she doesn't know this, so I tell Old Testament stories for a few minutes. Then I tell her some jokes. She laughs, long and loud. She says I'm a charming rogue. Charming is good. I'm not so sure about rogue.

I call her the next day too just to say hi. Only to say hi.

"Are you calling to tell me you want to cook for me the rest of your life? Are you calling me to tell me you want to give me all your money?"

I do my best to chuckle. The truth, of course, is sure, absolutely.

We talk for another hour and a half. More jokes from me. Some stories from her about life as a best-selling author, about the difference between faking a poem and feeling it. I tell her again I really like talking to her. How many times have I told her this now? She invites me to a Knicks game the following Friday night. She tells me I'm a black belt talker. I mention how much I like detective fiction and she asks me if maybe sometime I will recommend some books to her.

She says she's a little frightened about how fast things seem to be going. Me too, I say, which is the truth. But I'm ready, finally, nearing fifty, to deal with the fear. Finally, I've found a woman who can accept my terror, who knows it herself, who won't let it defeat her. Or me. Even if she's not a cheeseburger whore, she's very cool.

She quotes a John Berryman poem about guilt and I quote F. Scott Fitzgerald about delusion.

"My therapist says," Violet tells me, "when you get back, I should just come over and fuck you and get it over with."

"I think I love your therapist," I say.

She tells me that her ex-fiancé has accelerated the writing and calling and e-mailing and it's been upsetting her and scaring her some. She's asked him repeatedly to stop but he won't.

"Um," I say.

"He can sense I met someone," she says.

"Um."

"Will you get a gun and go up and shoot him?"

"Heh-heh."

"I know now why he didn't want me to move to New York City," she says. "He knew I would meet you."

I haven't even kissed her on the mouth (though I've spent hours imagining how her lips would taste—sour, at first, like lemon drops, then sweet entirely beyond reason, like homemade peppermint ice cream at the midway of Missouri's Boone County Fair in August. Or like memories of the midway). But even a kiss couldn't cause what's happening now. There is a Tasmanian devil in my chest, hammering and hammering on the inside of my rib cage. "He knew I would meet *you.*" It's impossible that the beast has been sleeping for half a century; I *must* have felt such unalloyed joy before—but I can't remember when.

When we hang up, I write a two-thousand-word memo on my favorite detective novelists and e-mail it to her.

In the morning, her e-mail is waiting.

> Thanks for all the pats on my knobby head. You make me wanna
> stay up all night smoking cappuccino & sipping angel food cake
> batter through two straws while discussing the three hundred
> detective books I plan to read by next Friday. Pls. remember that
> despite how much I cuss and how tight my pants are, I am reeling
> and vulnerable . . . rather than go to yoga and channel my chi,

I ate two doughnuts (cake) and bought a pair of slutty shoes. Forget what the pope says about fasting and prayer, it's sugar and footwear for this fiend. Come back & we'll wander around our Wormy Apple and talk loud and touch stuff in stores until all the terror goes hissing back into the ether from whence it came.

When I read the e-mail in the morning, the Tasmanian devil, restless and jumpy most of the night, spins and jumps and jigs a St. Vitus's dance. (And that helps distract me from the sad knowledge that try as I might to ignore the evidence, it's better that I just surrender to what is evident: nevermore will I be the most vivid, or deft, or inventive e-mailer with a woman I love. Not for nothing is she a famous poet/memoirist, critically acclaimed, revered worldwide. The sad knowledge: she writes better than I do.)

I eat at the St. Regis hotel in Aspen that evening. I haven't shaved in four days. I'm wearing jeans and a raggedy sweater. Women in fur and jewels smile at me with lowered eyes and moist lips. They smile with intent. I figure they're hookers, either that or they can hear the sweet, savage song of the love crazy Tasmanian devil from inside my chest. They can hear the passion-addled beast bellowing and it makes them smile. They can smell the scent of ardor coming off me like Tasmanian musk oil and it drives them nuts. It draws out the sweetness inside them like sap from old maple trees that everyone thought were dry.

I write to Violet that night.

> You have made me smile so much that the hookers at the St. Regis bar in Aspen couldn't help but look on me with mink-stoled, fake-breasted, diamond-fingered tenderness. Is my crush on you strong enough to make a whore cry? I think so.

I hit the Send button and then reread what I've written. She might be better, but I'm still in the game. The diamond-fingered tenderness might not be world-class, like her cappuccino smoking and batter sucking, but it's nice. And heartfelt. And true. Might Violet be not just my girlfriend and future wife and companion and teacher, but muse too?

She e-mails back. "The whore crying brings tears to my eyes."

My e-mail makes the woman I love weep. That's what I think to myself. But let's be honest. I also think that my e-mail makes a critically acclaimed poet/memoirist revered and adored by millions worldwide weep. This is how my brain works. Or is it my genitalia? Or my heart? Or soul? Do admiration and envy juice up the electrical impulses shooting through my Violet-frayed ganglia, from God-soaked synapse to God-soaked synapse? Is this what makes the Tasmanian devil dance and writhe in exquisite agony? Does it matter?

I don't know. But let's be honest. Here's what I think: I'm talking for more than an hour a night to a critically acclaimed poet/memoirist revered and adored by millions worldwide. I'm telling Bible stories to a critically acclaimed poet/memoirist revered and adored by millions worldwide. I'm understood and appreciated and liked, really, really liked, by a critically acclaimed poet/memoirist revered and adored by millions worldwide.

The working actress I dated—Broken Hand Kitty is how I still think of her—appeared in a Paul Newman movie once. I sent some books to an actress even more famous—Mary-Louise Parker—and she sent me a book of poetry and cried when I told her a story at lunch. The word "star fucker" bristles and drips with ugliness, and I don't think it applies to me, but I'm willing to entertain the possibility. I entertain it; then I dismiss it. Because it's not Violet's fame that attracts me, that enthralls me, that acts like a pair of jumper cables on the balls of the by now certainly bulgy-eyed, dehydrated, and near-death Tasmanian devil beating his curled, exhausted fingers against the inside of my sore, raw rib cage. It's her talent, sure, but it's her nuttiness, her sweetness, what a good mother she is, her laugh, her profanity and prayer. It's her soft brown eyes too and her swan neck and her $100-mule ass and her smoking little body, which even she feels like she has to work. Black belt? Please. *Please. She* is Yoda, not me. She is David Carradine in that television show, but female at her bird-boned core, a wise, doughnut-loving, slutty-shoes-wearing kung fu master in too-tight pants, with a drawl and a way with words. Which makes me Little Grasshopper, of course. Or was Carradine Little Grasshopper? How did Little Grasshopper end up anyway? I can't remember. I don't care.

I call her. Just to say hi. Just to tell her that I like how smart she is, how talented, just to reassure her—or is it myself?—that I'm secure, that I've always been drawn to intelligence, that I find her reinvented-the-memoir status and worldwide popularity and enormous success not at all threatening. On the contrary, I tell her. I find it attractive.

"Yeah," she says, "all men do. "At first." Such a sad voice. Such a weary voice.

I need to bring her back from this desolation, for my sake as well as hers. She likes my humor, so I reach for some. If I write a book that finds a publisher, I ask, will she blurb it? "Would it be okay," I ask, "if the back cover says, 'His e-mails make me weep—Violet Smith'?"

"No," she says, "it should say this: 'His e-mails can make whores weep, this one among them.' (Violet had told me earlier "I can edit like a motherfucker." Apparently, it's an irresistible urge.)

I call her when I return to the city. Just to say hi.

She says she's glad I'm back in the city. Me too, I say. She says the ex won't leave her alone. That must be tough, I say. She says he's begging her to give him another chance. Wow, you're going through a lot, I say. She says she's agreed to let him come to town and to hear him out and consequently she and I will not be going to see the Knicks Friday night or seeing each other all weekend.

I will not break my hand on a solid oak door. I will not accuse her of toying with me, of being addicted to chaos. I will not remind her that her friends and her therapist and her family have all warned her against meeting the ex again, that they have all (according to what she has told me) encouraged her to embrace the advances of the funny, charming, sad-e-mail-typing guy she met on the Internet who adores her. I decline to do these things not because they're beneath me. One of the sad lessons I've learned during my years in New York City is that when it comes to lust and love, precisely and absolutely nothing is beneath me. I decline because I don't think such tactics will work.

I try something else.

"What are you looking for, Violet?" I ask.

She starts sobbing. "To get laid before the world ends," she says.

"Uh, Violet?" I say. "Sweetie?"

"And to be loved, to be taken care of!" she cries.

"But, pumpkin . . . ," I say. (I don't know where I come up with "pumpkin." I have never called a soul "pumpkin." "Pumpkin" is not worthy of her literary chops. It's beneath both of us. But "pumpkin" is what I come up with.)

"All I want is someone who cares about how I feel."

"But, sweetie," I say. "Pumpkin. Buttercup. [Buttercup?!] *I* care about how you feel."

"*No one* cares about how I feel," she burbles.

"Well, I wish you'd give me a chance to prove that I do. Really, I'm volunteering to give you everything you want."

"I need to hear him out," she says. "I know he doesn't love me, that it's something else, but I need to do this."

I tell her of course I understand, that I don't want to interfere in anything she needs to do, that my greatest hope is that she gets what she wants, and what she needs, but that my even greater hope is that this weekend will show her that it's truly, finally over with this creep, that afterwards she will be even more available. I tell her I really, really, *really* want to keep dating her. I don't say "marry" or "move in" or "I'm in love with" because psychic Rose's admonitions ring in my head and because I've read another one of Violet's poems, in which she expresses emotions regarding the betrothed state similar to the feelings that many people express regarding mutilated cadavers, or prisoner of war camps.

"That's my plan," she says. "That's what I fully intend."

He's not coming till the next day, so we have dinner that evening. We meet my older brother, in town for business, and two of his associates. She announces to the table that she's hung out with a lot of professional comedians, then throws her arm around my neck, "and this guy here is the funniest man I've ever met." She whispers to me that I'm special. When one of my brother's associates, a fifty-year-old woman in a sensible blue suit, asks how Violet and I met, I hesitate. Maybe Violet would rather the Internet connection remain our secret.

"Well, you know, Steve here is always trolling for pussy, and he just happened to find me," she says.

Stunned silence, then much hilarity, not just at our table but at the four tables that can't help but overhear.

"Poor baby," she says, and gives my arm a squeeze. "You're blushing."

The next morning, walking back from a dental appointment, I decide Violet is everything I ever wanted. I decide she is the girlfriend I'm finally ready for. I decide she's the wife I long for. Also the teacher, the mother, the father, the muse, the little girl, the collaborator, the best friend. I decide she can see inside me, beyond the bastard, that she recognizes the real me. I decide I want to live with a person whose talent makes me quake with admiration, whose words and music I adore. I decide that next time I'm at dinner with her, I won't hold back, I'll reach under the table and take one of her hands and squeeze, and then I'll lean across and kiss her. I decide she is the person who will make me see past the anguish and the doom to something beyond, who will make me feel like everything's going to be okay if I look deep and do my work and that then I'll feel the tingling every minute for all my remaining minutes on earth.

And in the next instant I decide I'm insane. And in the *next* instant I experience yet another spiritual awakening. (Ever since the Fat Man, I've been having lots of them). I realize that no one can be all the things I want Violet to be. Only God can be that. And then I realize how much I long for God's love. I long to believe that someone or something can restore me . . . to myself, to faith, to love, to serenity and acceptance and truth and out of daily terror. Just knowing that I long for that makes it easier to imagine having it.

I call the Angry Belgian and ask him to meet me at our deli.

Over coffee, I tell him about my life-changing epiphany, my moment of God consciousness.

"Uh-huh," Frank says. "Cool."

I'm not sure he hears me. He is staring at a blonde in yoga pants at the next table.

I shouldn't be surprised that Frank is slightly distracted. He's in the middle of his own romantic drama. He's been trying to break up with his most recent girlfriend, who he met on the Internet, for three months. But every time he tells her that he doesn't love her, she brings a gift to his apartment and has sex with him. In the past weeks he has received a sports jacket, dinnerware, and an air conditioner.

"Did you hear what I just said?"

"Sort of," Frank admits. "And that's really great. But I'm wondering if I have sex with OC again tonight, and break up, whether I can keep the air conditioner. It's not like she needs it or anything, and summer's not that far off, right?"

OC is what he calls his girlfriend, because she believes in past lives. His previous girlfriend was an astrology enthusiast. OC stands for "Other Crazy." It occurs to me that the Angry Belgian might not be the best person to whom I should be confessing my postdental realizations about God.

"Frank," I say, "listen to what I'm telling you. This is important."

I go through the whole epiphany again, ending with my stunning realization about how the Lord might manifest himself through other people, but that it is only through the love of the Lord himself that we can be whole.

"Basically," I confess, "Violet has brought me closer to God."

The Angry Belgian is staring at me and frowning.

"Maybe you should tell Violet that," Frank says. "Maybe if you tell Violet that, she'll finally take off her clothes for you."

That weekend, while I'm waiting for Violet to dispatch her creepy ex back to the land of all creepy exes, I write her but don't send the 1,200-word e-mail I have composed about my spiritual epiphany, and about Frank and OC and Frank's funny crack about God and sex. She'll love that story. After Violet and I have sex, after I cradle her naked, sob-wracked body, which will feel like . . . which will feel like something she'll be able to describe with much more poetic and precise language than I can . . . after that I will show her the 1,200-word e-mail, how crazed I was, how in love, how I likened her to God, and how she led me to a realization about myself and the universe. No one will appreciate such bravery and wisdom and keen awareness of my own delusional capacity like her. We will laugh and cry together. Then we'll have sex again. There is no way I will like her more after sex. There is no way I can love her more than I do at this moment.

I also write her a love poem. I wrote a poem once before, many years ago, in college. It was really, really bad. This time, I write about the magic she did on the UPS man, about the magic she has worked on me. On those rainy afternoons when we lie in bed, nibbling on each other and reading each other's work and discussing Russian literature, reveling in the presence of God and maybe taking some short prayer breaks, we will laugh at my bad but intensely heartfelt poetic fumblings, which she will receive, along with the 1,200-word epiphany e-mail, after I send it, which will be after I talk to her.

Sunday afternoon she calls to tell me she's getting back with her ex.

"You are?" I say.

That's it. No similes. No jokes. No Bible stories. No vernacular, no poems. No lips like lemon drops or weeping whores. A man who gets paid for stringing words together and that's what I come up with. "You are?"

"Honey," she says, "we've got four years together. He's got his hooks in me. I don't know if this is the right thing, but it's something I've got to do . . . Honey? Honey? Are you there?"

I think I'm going to throw up.

"I think I'm going to throw up," I say.

"No, you're not," she says. "You're a tall, sweet, hilarious man and I'm going to miss you, but you don't really know me. I'm not nearly the person you imagine."

Tall? *Tall?*

I will not break anything. I will not remind her of how she characterized her ex just days ago. I will not use words like "crazy" and "dangerous." I will not plead. I will not remind her of what she insisted just days before were her clear intentions. I will not ask her if she tells every tall guy she meets that her therapist suggested she fuck them and I will not wonder whether she dangles promises of cappuccino-smoking, angel-food, batter-slurping dates in front of every dupe who makes her chuckle. Not because such things are beneath me. I would sink to the ninth circle of hell to make her come to me. Or are there ten circles of hell? She would know, of course. She would know the name of every one of the circles, and what parallels they had in Dante's Italy, from whatever fucking century he lived in, which she would also of course know. She would instruct me in these kinds of poetic/musical/classical matters and inspire me to write things true and beautiful during and after and between our sex and prayer, if she would love me, which I now know of course she doesn't. Which I know now of course she never did.

I will not smash my hand on an oak door. I might throw up, but I'll try to wait until after we hang up. I will, for a change, take a few lonely and uncomfortable steps on that frightening and dangerous terrain I've read and heard so much about but have never spent much time exploring. I will take the high road.

"I'm heartbroken," I say. "I'm heartsick."

"No you're not, honey, you're not . . ."

"Let me finish," I say. "I'm heartbroken and heartsick, but I am really grateful I met you. You have no idea how much I was falling for you, but I was. And I really wish you the best. I want you to get everything you want, and everything you need, because you're wonderful and you're a wonder, and I hope in the future you'll remember me fondly, because that's how I'm going to remember you." A little maudlin, perhaps, but no accusations, no threats, no blame. Well, maybe a little implied blame, but nothing too obvious.

She tells me that God is present in all this, and that she hopes we can be friends in the future.

I'm having trouble breathing.

"I feel really sorry for the next woman I date," I say.

Okay, that's not high road. But I've said worse. I want to say worse now. I want to say much, much worse.

"Oh, honey," she says. "You'll be fine."

Sure, I say, okay, and we hang up.

I will not send her my 1,200-word spiritual epiphany document. Do I want her editorial blessing, or her love? Both, of course. I send it.

She e-mails back.

I'm gonna miss you—you're beautiful & noble & wise & hilarious
& deep and kind, but I still contend you've inflated me beyond
human proportions. I feel the nozzle on my neck.

God is in this, I swear.

xoxo,

V

Even as I sit on the floor of my bathroom, clutching my stomach and
rocking, I can't help but admire the nozzle-in-the-neck image. That's good
stuff. That's better stuff than what I could come up with. I bet her creepy
poet/professor boyfriend can toss off nozzle-in-neck worthy riffs in his
sleep.

I will not send the love poem. It would be self-serving, and self-pitying,
and self-destructive. I need to put one foot ahead of the other, on my clear
and straight path. High road. High road. High road. I actually say the words
out loud, to myself. This is a better place. The air is clear up here. I will not
sink. I will not descend. I will not send the poem.

I send the poem.

"You're breaking my heart, honey," she writes.

And that should have been it. That should have been the end. I shouldn't
have called her one more time. It wasn't to plead, or to accuse. Just to have
one more conversation. Actually, I just wanted to hear her voice one more
time, the voice that seemed to touch a part of me that hadn't been touched
before, the voice that turned me from steely-eyed bastard into poetic
blabbermouth.

I dial her number.

"Hello."

"Violet, it's Steve and I . . ."

"Honey," she says. Nothing sweet about this honey. This was sour honey. Angry honey. This was bad honey. Bad, disapproving, disappointed honey.

"Honey, I got to tell you something. I would not at this point go out with you, because your reaction to this has been so out of kilter. You act like we had this grand romance and it did *not* happen."

"Okay," I say. Highly trained professional journalist. The man who introduced "pillow breasted" into the paper of record. Charming rogue, and that's the best I can come up with.

"Okay. Well then, bye. I'm really sorry. I'm really sorry. I'm really, really, really sorry."

More rocking. More stomach clutching. More thoughts of drinking. That afternoon, I tell Rose that I'm done with therapy, that many years with her have accomplished exactly nothing. I tell her I'm an obsessive creep, that I'm stupid, that I'll never find love, that my writing is cheap and mannered, all gimmicks, that I'm delusional, that I'll never succeed at anything.

She asks to hear the whole story, to read all the e-mail.

I tell her. She reads.

"Violet is a sadist," my psychic psychotherapist says.

"A sadist?"

"A sadist! You did nothing wrong here, Steve."

"Actually, I referred to myself in the love poem as a 'pussy.' It was ironic and metaphorical, of course. It served a larger function of illuminating my masculinity. But any woman would be creeped out by . . ."

"You did nothing wrong here!" Now she is yelling. That's a comfort. My psychic and heretofore-unflappable psychotherapist is yelling. I might be a world-class fuckup, a mewling infant and a professional fraud, but I can reduce commercially successful and critically acclaimed poet/memoirists to contempt and psychic psychotherapists (who had their brains studied at Princeton) to rage.

"You were kind and generous! You sent her sweet e-mails. And a love poem! Not a lot of men do that, but . . ."

"Oh, really?" I say. I can't turn my rage on Violet. Rose objects to my turning it on myself. That leaves her.

"Really, Rose, not a lot of men refer to themselves as pussies and . . ."

"But *you* did, Steve. You did so because you cared! And she sent *you* e-mails! She told you she wanted to be with you! Then when *you* say it, you're delusional? How come she's the only one who's allowed to express heartfelt emotion?"

"Yeah, but . . ."

"And the nozzle on her neck? That is hostile, hostile language. This is a damaged woman, Steve, a damaged, damaged woman. You tell her how great she is, how great she makes you feel, and she feels like you're blowing her up and feels the nozzle on her neck? That's damaged, and it's hostile!"

"Yeah, but . . ."

"You have nothing to apologize for, Steve. Do not apologize."

"Yeah, but . . ."

"Do not apologize. Promise me."

"Uh, um, I already sort of apologized."

"Pardon me?"

"Yeah, well, I sort of said I was really sorry. Really, really, really sorry."

"Well, you didn't need to. And don't anymore. Promise me you will not apologize anymore. Okay, Steve? Promise me."

"Yeah, okay. I won't apologize. I really didn't do anything wrong here, did I?"

"No, you didn't."

Then, I have an idea. Maybe it's God's idea.

"I think I should take my apology back."

"I'm not sure that's such a good idea, Steve."

"Yeah, I think I'm going to withdraw my apology. I didn't do anything wrong. How come she gets to ask me to get a gun and go shoot her creepy old boyfriend, and that's okay, but when I call her to say . . ."

"Steve? Steve? You don't need to prove anything to her. As long as *you* know that . . ."

"I didn't do anything wrong here. Nothing. I think I should take my apology back."

"Steve, I don't think that's such a good idea. Steve? Steve?"

My internist had told me during my last physical that I had no cartilage left in my knees, from all my years of playing basketball, and sometimes it's difficult to walk, but I sprint the eight blocks from Rose's office back to my apartment. My e-mail can make whores cry? Well, this next particular e-mail will make one particular whore cry. One very special whore.

I write.

> If you think my being nuts about you means I see you as a plastic
> blow-up doll with a nozzle on your neck, well, honey, as you say,
> that's your issue. Honest to fucking God.
> I wrote you a fucking love poem and some sweet e-mails and told
> you I really wanted to date you.

I sign off—because she throws around some Latin in her poems and takes great pride in her classical education—"Mea fucking maxima fucking culpa."

To which she writes back, "You don't know fuck all!" And, "You don't know me!"

I stare at the exclamation points late at night in my apartment. Never has a simple piece of punctuation, repeated, brought a man such deep and thrilling and, I suspect, utterly toxic joy. Outside, on the broad avenues and twisting streets of the city I once imagined conquering, couples stroll hand in hand, deaf to the terrible honking and polyglot cursing all around them, listening to only the soft and rhythmic thumping of their hearts, the catchy, age-old melody they imagine will provide the soundtrack to their self-satisfied lives together. Good for them. They would wake up soon enough. They would hear the awful noise. As for me, I hear very clearly already. I get my kicks from what's real. I stare at the exclamation marks some more. They provide clear, unambiguous evidence that I have inspired a poet and memoirist famous for her lapidary phrasing and exquisitely burnished sentences to sloppy, common rage. They are proof to me that I have made the brilliant and beautiful Violet stumble and grope for a homely and vulgar exclamation point.

I think I'll put that on my gratitude list.

Chapter 17

Cheeseburger Whores, Unite

The nose stud people are restless. They're giving me the frowny mouth. I have shared with them details of Kelly's pillow breasts, and Oksana's cold comfort, and I am detailing for them my low road/high road peregrinations with Violet. But all I'm getting are dead eyes and the frowny mouth. What's wrong with the nose stud people?

There are at least 150 of them, bathed in sickly fluorescent light, and only about one in ten of them actually wears a nose stud, but as diligently as I have labored to stop judging, categorizing, and otherwise taking the inventory of others, I'm not quite there yet. Progress, not perfection, as the program suggests. To me they're all the nose stud people. It's Sunday morning in the East Village, where the nose stud people live. We are gathered together in a big white room with grimy gray floors, on the second floor of what I think is an abandoned hospital, or a decommissioned psychiatric ward. I'm clutching a microphone, standing behind a pitted plastic table. Kim, the married yoga instructor with whom I used to have sex and argue about Christmas, has joined the spiritual development group and asked me to speak here, at the meeting she leads.

"I was in love with Violet," I tell the group. I'm still on Violet. Violet is such a gripping character. The group should lap up the story of Violet and the hard, sad lessons she taught me. They should be enthralled at how I, betrayed and abused, managed to bravely clamber up to that elevated bluff—the high road—that Rose told me would bring me closer to myself and that Violet promised would bring me closer to God.

But they're not enthralled. More frowny mouths. I clutch the microphone and I picture the nose stud people stampeding into the swollen river on the Namibian plains, where the huge and hungry crocodiles, who have developed an appetite for human flesh, grin and wait.

My mentor has warned me that impressing people isn't the point of spiritual development. He has cautioned me about pursuing fame and glory. He has told me that nursing grudges and calming myself by imagining big crocodiles feasting on my enemies isn't going to help me. He has reminded me where the hunt for bigger bylines and greater recognition leads. Serve others, he has gently suggested. Speak truth. Live humbly. And I have been trying. I've been trying hard! That's what I'm trying to tell the nose stud people, about my mighty efforts to live humbly and spiritually. I'm sharing with them the moving details of my unlikely redemption.

But the nose stud people are fidgeting. They could care less about Violet. What was their *problem*?

I take a breath. I know that many of the nose stud people probably eat too much, and look at Internet porn, and that maybe some of them have suffered through drug and alcohol addiction. I know that a few have probably had sex with married yoga instructors, and that others despair at ever having sex again, and that a miserable two or three might even have assistants who don't always properly fulfill their phone-answering duties, and that this perhaps has driven a handful of the nose stud people to dreadful fantasies of editorial assistant murder. I should be more sympathetic.

A year has passed since Kelly had reappeared at the meetings. She had pulled her sweater back on, refused to talk to me, had drifted away again. I haven't spoken with Violet in months. The days of eyebrow brushes and custom-made shirts might just as well have occurred in another century. The pancake confabs have continued, and I've cut down on ice cream and porn, started writing more, and not just polished e-mails to other cyber daters. I've been spending a few hours a week reaching out to newcomers, talking about the healing properties of cheeseburgers and naps. I have asked people for help, which is what my mentor tells me I'm supposed to do. One man, a landscaper, had told me that he'd gone to sleep angry every night until he stopped worrying about money and love and success. "Now I'm all about quiet service to the plant world," he had told me, and that had seemed profound even though I hadn't quite understood all the ramifications quiet service to the plant world entailed. I'd taken to repeating it, mantralike, in times of stress, even though I owned no plants. Another man, a truck driver, told me that he had been involved in at least two fistfights a month for the past six years, until his mentor told him to follow a simple rule, which was, "No honking."

I haven't come up with any personal credo as elegant or irreducible yet. My big answer is more a bunch of little answers: not saying "whore work" aloud, trying to perform one act of kindness a day, the gratitude list. Also, serving as featured speaker at meetings that have featured speakers, like this one.

"Just tell your story," my mentor had suggested when I had told him I was going to speak at a big meeting. "That's all you need to do, just your story, without dressing it up."

I take another breath.

"Before Violet," I say, "I thought exercise would save me. And at one time I was certain ice cream was the answer. None of them worked. Neither did porn."

The frowny mouths move a little bit. I think the word "porn" stirs them.

"Then I decided that if love wouldn't save me, maybe sex would. And why not sex with some newcomers in the group? The sex would save me and I could help them."

Some laughs.

"That didn't work out too well. Nothing worked out. And that's when I figured out what the real problem was. It wasn't a problem of faith, or spirituality, or a lack of love."

I pause. Der Komicker has taught me the importance of timing. I look over the spiritually bereft nose stud people.

"The problem was New York City."

Bitter, knowing chuckles.

"The problem was this terrible, uncaring city, this writhing metropolis."

More laughs.

"So I left. I flew from LaGuardia to Denver and from Denver to Durango, Colorado. And then I drove from Durango to Silverton, a tiny little town with four hundred people who live there year-round, at 9,300 feet. I drove over two mountain passes, and through a blinding blizzard. I drove over the most avalanche-prone stretch of highway in North America looking for relief.

"So there I was, safe at last. Lying in bed, in a little shack in a town where the temperature dipped to thirty below zero in the morning and the water in my toilet bowl froze solid. There I was, reading the books I was sure would save me. There I was, reading books on the Ebola virus and Hitler."

Hitler gets a big laugh.

"There I was, a lonely, miserable ice-cream-eating porn-watcher guy who had crossed half a continent and a mountain range, who had left nights of Chubby Hubby and Peanut Butter Cup and found frigid days of Hitler and frozen toilet water."

More laughter. Der Komicker would be so proud.

"And I wanted to kill the people who had caused my problems."

A collective recoiling in the first row. The nose stud people look tough, but even East Village nihilists get upset at sincere murder fantasies.

"I imagined those people who had wronged me, in agony. I pictured my former boss, bleeding, on a rack. I saw Bridget, my old drunk girlfriend, with Denny, my former best friend. They were on their knees. Their flesh was suppurating, with terrible sores, and they were begging for forgiveness, but I was granting no mercy. Why should I?"

I let my eyes drift over the crowd. Some obvious newcomers in the front row, wide-eyed. I look around the room. There is Middle-Aged Black Hank, on the right, and Rock-and-Roll Chris, on the left. There is Big Ted, and Irma the immigrant, and Sobbing Sissy. Here and there, some potential Mrs. Fs. There were always some potential Mrs. Fs. I scan some more until I find whom I'm looking for in the back row, slouched, glowering from underneath a baseball cap. I'd seen him before at other meetings around town but never heard him speak. He arrived late. He left early. He always sat in the back row.

"Why should I grant anyone mercy?" I continue, telling my story in the grimy white room. "Who had ever granted me mercy? What I wanted was an Uzi, and some rough justice."

I hadn't really wanted an Uzi in Silverton, but "Uzi" packs such a wallop. I come up with "rough justice" on the spot. I stare at the guy in the back row, the aisle of denial, and he stares back.

"What I wanted was to take that Uzi and blow the fucking heads off of all the motherfuckers who had ever wronged me, and then to blow my own fucking head off."

Silence, but no frowny mouths.

"And then I called my mentor," I say, which isn't completely accurate, because I didn't' have a mentor during my winter in the mountains. I didn't have a mentor until post–Fat Man. But when Soft-Talking Probably a Lesbian Stacy mumbled that morning long ago about the power of narrative, wasn't her point that it didn't really matter if the narrative were technically true? Wasn't what mattered that it *sounded* true?

"And my mentor said maybe I should have a cheeseburger and take a nap," I say and I keep staring at the guy in the back row, who is crying now, while everyone else laughs.

I continue staring at him. It's not the Stare, but it's close.

"I survived that winter, thanks to my sister and her little boy and my mentor," I say. "But it was a bad winter. Those mornings in the shack, I used to wake up certain of two things."

Someone coughs, and I wait. I wait for silence. And silence comes.

"I used to wake up sure that I was alone. That I was all alone. And I used to wake up sure that things were going to get worse, that I would always be alone."

The guy in the back row is blubbering now.

I remember when I used to sit in the back row. I remember the day I looked into the Fat Man's eyes and blubbered myself. I want to reach the guy in the back row. I want to help him. My mentor had told me how. He had told me to tell my story, not to dress it up. But I *had* dressed it up. I'd thrown in the Uzi, and the rough justice. I'd stolen my mentor's riff about waking-up-sure-of-two-things. I look some more at the blubbering newcomer and feel my cheeks flush. He deserves better than I have given him.

But it's not too late to make it right. That's something else my mentor had told me. That it was never too late to make it right. To start telling the truth. To begin serving others.

"And today, I don't feel that way," I say and my chin trembles. I don't do the chin tremble; my chin trembles on its own. Is this what telling the truth does? My right hand goes to my chest and my fingers flutter all by themselves.

"Today, I'm certain of two other things," I say, and I mean it, because it's the truth. Will it always be the truth? I hope so. "I'm certain I'm not alone, and I'm certain that things are going to get better."

Polite applause. I try to speak, but can't. More applause. Rolling applause, waves of it.

I look around the room again. There's Firestarter, and Jesus John and the Angry Belgian and Slutty Sadie and Clinically Insane but Smoking Hot Melissa and Hal the gay cellist and young David and Oksana and Mystic River Timmy and a bunch of other people I know by name. My friends. The Man in the Lime Green Suit has made friends. That's another powerful, strange truth.

I try to say something about friends and loneliness and God, something true and helpful. But I can't speak, because now I'm weeping. The tears probably shouldn't surprise me too much. I have come to accept that I'm something of a weeper.

I take another breath. I make a note to add "friends" to my gratitude list tonight. I make a note to add it to my gratitude list every night of my life.

"Things *are* going to get better," I manage to choke out. Then I pause before launching into my big finale.

"My name is Steve and I . . . I . . ."

I'm not the Man in the Lime Green Suit anymore. I'm not the Big Blue Cell either. I'm not the Single Guy or the Qualifier or the mighty crocodile about to take down an unsuspecting wildebeest into the reptilian death spiral

I have studied for so many hours of my misguided Animal Planet–watching life. What I am is a man who slept with married women, who dumped dozens of kind, decent, generous girlfriends for no reasons other than fear he could barely understand much less articulate and the belief that something better and more beautiful awaited him. What I am is a journalist who savaged people who didn't deserve savaging, a writer who composed gentle odes to flowers he wouldn't recognize if he laid down in a bed of them, an editor who swapped eyedrop stories for the chance to touch some forbidden ponytailed flesh. What I am is a guy who has wallowed in self-pity (much like the Indian forest elephants of Udhagamandalam wallow in the mud pits next to the Obetta swamp), who has devoted weeks and months plumbing the exquisite and singular agony of his precious soul whenever a woman wounded him, but who has devoted approximately zero minutes to thinking about any pain he might have caused to the women he cast aside.

I gaze at the pitted plastic table. I had wanted to impress upon the nose stud people the vastness of my humility. I had *planned* to impress them. I lift my eyes to the guy in the back row. He deserves the truth.

"My name is Steve and I . . . I . . . I . . ."

I'm having a hard time with my big true finale.

"My name is Steve and I am . . ."

Still, nothing. Just a lot of chin trembling and finger fluttering.

"I am . . . I am . . ."

This truth-telling business isn't easy. What I want to say is that I'm a recovering cad who knows he needs to treat women better. What I want to say is that I'm nothing special, that I'm just a slightly neurotic Missouri-born New Yorker predisposed toward corrosive rage and homicidal daydreams; a sometimes feckless lunk who consorts with angry Belgians and Sheckys of the High Seas and melancholy jocks, who lusts after pineapple-headed Bamboleo dancers and eyedrop girls; an occasional liar all too eager to grab and clutch at the most tempting, transient, high butterfat distractions.

What I want to say is that I'm a cheeseburger whore who once bathed and wriggled like a burbling baby in the soft, cleansing light of salvation but who, if he isn't careful, will forget how the light heals, will forget that it even shines, who will slouch and shuffle once again toward Stygian gloom and solitary doom.

I might find Mrs. Friedman and I might not. The guy in the back row might keep coming back, and he might not. It doesn't matter. That's what I want to tell all the nose stud people. That it doesn't matter, because we have each other. That *all* we have is each other. That connection is what's important. That love is what's important. I want to tell them who I *really* am. I want to tell them the truth. I want to tell them that I'm the Fat Man, that the guy in the back row is the Fat Man, that we're all the Fat Man, even the skinny and the female amongst us, and that the Fat Man has been saved. I want to tell them that we can all be saved.

But I don't tell them that. I'm having so much trouble with my big true finale. My chin won't stop trembling. My fingers won't stop fluttering. What would Jesus John do? I'm not looking good (jeans, Hawaiian shirt, hoodie emblazoned on chest with grinning flame-headed demon), but I'm feeling great, and still, I can't say what I want to say about how we're all magnificent cheeseburger whores, how we're all the Fat Man.

"I'm Steve," I say. "I . . . I . . ."

I close my eyes. I don't see the crocodiles. That's a miracle in itself. I see Milo sitting in bed, giggling at *Tom and Jerry*, gnawing on a sparerib. I see I-Dog, furrowing his brow, smiling, bouncing on my lap. I see my father in St. Louis, squeezing a telephone receiver, closing his eyes, asking if I'm happy, laboring to sound like he believes my lies. I see Elaine, my stepmother, clutching a chicken sandwich in one hand, waving a Galaxy Tube in the other, tracing rainbow arcs in the air. There is Candy, peering into an oven, poking a ginormous pot roast with compassion. She is wearing a black cocktail dress and pearls, an apron, and heels, and when she looks over her shoulder, she smiles and her eyes brim with grace. I see the Angry Belgian, mellow. I see serene legions of cheeseburger whores reaching out to each other, holding each other, feeding each other. And I see a really dumb cheeseburger whore, a man who has spent far too many years running away. I watch him stop, and I see him turn around.

"I . . . I . . . I . . ."

I can't speak. Me, wondrous wordsmith in the writhing metropolis. Words fail me.

EPILOGUE

The Queen of Mean married and had a little boy. Candy married and had a boy and a girl. Susan called off her engagement, married a different guy, and had a girl. Broken Hand Kitty married and had a boy, as well as a starring role on an Emmy award–winning television show where she plays a tough cop who does the frowny mouth. Cleopatra/Samantha had her baby, right about the time the lease on her apartment ran out, so I let her and little Lydia stay at my place for a month, while she figured things out. I gave mother and child the bedroom and I slept on the couch, brought spinach pie home from my favorite diner every night; and after Samantha breast-fed her baby, I would hold Lydia and whisper stories about magic cheeseburgers and wise fat men until she fell asleep. Samantha figured things out, and recently finished her PhD in clinical psychology at the University of North Carolina. Lydia is five years old and I'm her godfather.

Kelly never spoke to me again. Denny and I didn't renew our friendship. April the ophthalmologist sent me a birthday card after nearly a decade of silence between us and I sent her a card the following year; then we fell out of touch. Oksana divorced, and we're fiends. Violet got engaged, and we're not.

Allison married, had two girls, divorced, published a critically acclaimed book, and was one of ten Americans to win a $50,000 annual award for emerging writers. My little sister and the rock-climbing father of my nephew married, then divorced, and I-Dog turned into a fifth grader who quit saying "nor nerk," and denies ever having said it. He reads a lot and plays chess and rides his mountain bike. He has a little sister, Iris, who is in first grade and who calls him "big guy." After Elaine died, my father lost weight, then had quadruple bypass surgery, then watched too much television, then danced with a woman named Sharon at a wedding of a friend's granddaughter, and he and Sharon married. I stopped lying to him. I cut back on lying to other people. I continued to see Psychic Rose.

The Ascot was named editor in chief of a magazine that has nothing to do with open-toed sandals. The Angry Belgian, who, like me, is still single, broke up with OC, graduated from Hunter, and somehow managed to get himself into dental school, and he even became a citizen.

The Man-Thing died a few months after Conde Nast executives forced him into retirement from *GQ*, just hours after he suffered a lunchtime stroke in his leather banquette at the Four Seasons. I attended the memorial service at Lincoln Center, and afterwards, I chatted up the Queen of Mean and David, now the editor in chief at *Esquire*. I apologized to Robbie, the *Elle* editor in chief I had offended during my hotheaded days, and I apologized to the *Esquire* editor who had assigned me the story on the cruise ship comedian and whom I had abandoned for a better offer. I pitched an idea to a *Details* editor on living a meaningful life and the nature of true love. I worked the room, and then I felt myself flush with shame as I realized what I was doing—at a memorial service—and then it occurred to me that no one would have approved more of my boldness and decisiveness and lust for life than the Man-Thing, the person who granted me life in New York

City, and then I found a bathroom at Lincoln Center, and I locked myself in a stall, and I wept for Art.

The cruise ship comedian made it on to *The Tonight Show*. Soft-Talking Probably a Lesbian Stacy turned out to be a lesbian. Bridget checked in to rehab, then relapsed, then checked back into rehab, then relapsed again, then, two months ago as I write this, she stopped drinking. She showed me a picture of Milo the other night. He had been living with his father and stepmother for four years, since Bridget's first stint in rehab. He's enrolled in a special program designed for autistic children. He's tall and slim and he loves dinosaurs and basketball. I kept calling my mentor and I picked up a couple mentees myself. I told them things would get better. I told them to eat cheeseburgers and take naps. I told them not to worry so much, to be easier on themselves, that others needed them. (I did not tell them to hold themselves gently, like kittens.)

Fisherman Hank never came back to the meetings, and I don't know what happened to him. I like to think of him in a boat, gently rocking, carefully casting his line into the soft twilight sea. Fluffy died. Melissa wept. I never saw the Fat Man again. I look for him everywhere. I look for him every day.

* * *

As this is a memoir of my usually terrified and at times disastrous writing life in New York City, I reference (and include some passages from) some of the stories that were most terrifying and disastrous.

The stories I reference are as follows:

Chapter 3: "Perfect Pitch," *GQ*, April 1994

Chapter 5: "Losing It," *GQ*, September 1993; "See Me, Feel Me, Touch Me, Heal Me," GQ, January 1994

Chapter 6: "Soul Asylum," *GQ*, February 1996

Chapter 9: "Portrait of a Woman," *GQ*, December 1996; "If God Is the Big Cheese, John Tesh Is Going to Heaven," *GQ*, August 1995

Chapter 10: "Letter to My Future Brother-in-Law," *Outside*, October 1999; "Kingpin," *GQ*, November 1998; "Dead Man Talking," *GQ*, October 1996

Chapter 11: "Why Paradise Is Such a Dangerous Place," *Mountain Gazette* number 87, 2002

Chapter 12: "No? No? No? Let Me Read between the Lines," *The New York Times*, October 31, 2004

Chapter 13: "Boys Don't Cry," *Elle*, July 2007

Chapter 15: "Schtick Man of the Sea," *The Washington Post*, June 3, 2001

Chapter 16: "Cook and Tell Confessions of a Kitchen Romeo," *The New York Times*, February 9, 2005

ACKNOWLEDGEMENTS

Thank you, Jeff Leen, for telling me I should write this book a long time ago. Thank you, Heather Schroder at ICM, for suggesting it again. Thank you, Faye Bender, my agent, for sticking with it for such a long time. Thank you, Jeannette Seaver and the late Richard Seaver, for buying the book. Thank you, Tony Lyons at Skyhorse, for publishing it. Thank you, Jennifer McCartney, for rigorous, imaginative, enormously helpful editing.

Preemptive apologies to everyone in the book, especially to the many former potential Mrs. Friedmans, each one who put up with more than any woman ever should. Special thanks to the Fat Man and all other long-suffering cheeseburger whores. You have helped this particular cheeseburger whore more than you can imagine.

Thank you to readers of early drafts, who generously offered suggestions, criticism, encouragement, and advice. I'm particularly grateful to Don Friedman, Christina Frohock, Ken Fuson, Jeff Leen (again), Jennifer Scruby, Julie Seabaugh, Allison Surcouf and Marji Wilkens.

For wise counsel, great patience, and unflagging support, thank you, Rick M and Ruth R.

Thank you, Jeff C, David E, Jeff L, and Tony M for your friendship in difficult times.

For gently suggesting that I cease making so many lousy choices, and for loving me whether I did or didn't, I thank Barry Friedman, Janet Hupert Friedman, the late Elaine Friedman, Sharon Friedman, Don Friedman, Helen Henry, Ann Friedman, and Steve List.